SET UP & SOl

D0000258

Find Out What Green Really Means

Holly Swanson

Published by
CIN

CIN, P.O. Box 2645,White City, OR. 97503
Copyright © 1995 by Holly Swanson

All rights reserved. No part of this book may be reproduced or
transmitted in any form or by any means, electronic or mechanical,
including photocopying, recording or by any information storage and
retrieval system without written permission from the publisher, except
for the inclusion of brief quotations in a review. Printed in the U.S.A.

Swanson, Holly.
    Set up and sold out : find out what Green really means / Holly
Swanson.
    p. cm.
    Includes bibliographical references and index.
    Preassigned LCCN: 95-70310.
    ISBN 0-9645108-0-4

    1. Green movement--United States--Political aspects. 2.
Environmentalism--United States--Economic aspects.   I. Title.

JA75.8.S93 1995   322.4'4
                                    QBI95-20388

Set Up & Sold Out

Chapter 1

Set Up

Chapter 2

Subvert the Dominant Paradigm

1

SET UP

Every American shares a fundamental concern for and sincere appreciation of the beauty of our natural environment. We can all identify with the special feelings that automatically arise as we experience the wonder of nature; warm summer nights, crisp fall mornings or dark, cloudy, windy days. From creatures in the wild to a box full of puppies, even the scent of a freshly mown lawn stirs our senses. There is no question, Americans care about the environment, animals and nature.

Americans support environmental protection and taking the necessary steps to correct environmental problems. The dilemma we face is different than either of these points. The problem is, the environmental cause is being used to conceal the implementation of a specific political agenda most Americans are not aware of.

Our immediate challenge involves making more and better distinctions about the answers to environmental questions. We need to begin making distinctions between productive steps toward a healthy environment and steps to implement a political agenda under the guise of environmental protection.

Set Up and Sold Out is a revealing look into the secret side of environmental politics. Americans must understand there is a subversive motivation behind the push for drastic change and rigid environmental regulations. We are all involved. This is not a liberal vs. conservative or a Republican vs. Democrat issue. This situation transcends all others. No one is exempt.

Before better distinctions can be made, a general grasp of the situation is required. What does Green really mean? To most Americans, green still means the color. Many people now associate the color green with the environmental cause. Most Americans do not realize the word green is now defined in political terms.

The overall environmental cause is commonly referred to as the Green Movement or simply the Greens. The Green Movement represents a multifaceted political arm. It represents multiple special interest politics, concealed under the political umbrella of environmental protection. The Greens, or Green political party is also part of that group. The problem is, Americans do not understand how their concern for environmental protection is being used by the Greens to advance the Green political agenda, an agenda most Americans would totally disagree with. The Greens use deceptive tactics to advance their goals, such as:

- lying to the American people
- using entertainment to mold public opinion
- taking advantage of children

Why should Green politics concern every American? The American people have been set up to believe Green means, good for the environment and good for the American people. Green politics and environmental protection are two completely different issues. American's support for environmental protection does not equal support for the hidden political agenda of the Green Movement. One does not equal the other.

The Greens are advancing their political plans disguised as progressive solutions to environmental protection. Greens plan to use fear of environmental doom to pass laws that will:

- control individual opportunities and actions
- control business
- end private property rights

This is only the tip of the 'Green iceberg'. Americans need to fully understand the political goals and manipulative tactics of the Green Movement. What appears to be a spontaneous effort to help us find the path to a healthy environmental future is more like being led down the garden path.

The Greens are manipulating environmental issues to force massive social change on unsuspecting Americans. We are not talking about reduce, reuse and recycle. The Green plan calls for a complete social transformation that will erase our culture. The issue is, do we need to change everything about America to protect the environment for future generations?

There is a tremendous amount of good that can result from the universal awareness of environmental issues. Recognizing the oppressive and negative aspects of the Green political agenda will not prevent America from continuing to take positive steps toward our goal of environmental excellence. It will only ensure we make intelligent and informed decisions regarding the future of our country. We do not need to eliminate efforts to protect and clean up the environment. We need to make careful distinctions between ideas that are good for America and the environment and subversive efforts by the Greens to use different issues to advance their political agenda.

We are all willing to do our share. The question is how far do we need to go to achieve our goals? Before we can determine if the Green political plan reflects the kind of future we see for America, we need to look at the kind of America the Greens envision.

Jonathan Porritt is a well-known author, political activist and a leader in the Green Movement. Porritt's book, *Save the Earth* provides a look into the Green future and reveals an insider's perspective of the political goals of the Greens.

Porritt describes the future as a 'Green World Order' that means more than achieving the goal of world government. The Green future includes specific laws to regulate what people can do and how people will live.

Porritt defines this future lifestyle as 'compulsory Green living'. 'Compulsory Green living' means obeying the Green rules is mandatory. Porritt suggests the Green lifestyle will be forced on citizens by their government, from the top down.

The Green rules Porritt described included:

- rationed foods (lentils)
- one washing machine per 20 people
- lights out by 10:00 p.m.
- mandatory tree-hugging every Sunday

Porritt offers us another snapshot of the Green future. Porritt describes a World Order where the Green flag replaces the Red flag and where Green Dictators rule.

'Compulsory Green living' sounds like Green communism. Would transforming America to match Porritt's vision solve our environmental problems? The Greens are not out to save the earth. The Greens are using the environmental cause to advance their hidden political agenda.

The Russian dictator, Nikita Krushchev seemed to share Porritt's dream of seeing his flag fly over America. He predicted on June 19, 1962:

> *"The United States will eventually fly the Communist Red Flag. The American people will hoist it themselves."*

Porritt indicates the Green flag is a replacement for the red flag. One is substituted for the other because they are interchangeable. If Americans accept the Green plan for our future, we will have, in essence, hoisted the Communist flag ourselves.

Green politics and ideology parallel the socialism to communism political process. Socialism is the first step, but communism is the goal. The Greens are using the environmental cause to camouflage their efforts to move Americans toward Socialism, then force us into communism.

Porritt suggests this is just a Green dream and that people would only live this way because they want to save the earth. The alternative to being forced into communism is for citizens to volunteer, as Krushchev predicted.

Excusing this plan as a Green dream is a standard tactic used by Communists. Communists say what they mean, then say, they don't mean what they say. This allows Communists to communicate with comrades by discounting the political importance of what they said by quickly dismissing it as a joke or dream.

The Green slogan, 'Think Globally Act Locally' takes on a whole new meaning when you realize the goal is still world communism.

Mr. Porritt is Green. This does not mean everyone involved with the environmental effort is a Green Communist. It means the political ideas and tactics of the Green Movement mirror communism and Communist strategies. The environmental cause offers Green Communists abundant circumstances to use our emotions and our political system to put themselves in a position to seize power.

This is a calculated political effort based on using the fate of mankind to justify massive changes in our society. It includes justifying more and more government control over American citizens, using fear of pending environmental disaster to gain public support to pass major environmental protection laws. The Green objective is to make control possible by making control legal.

Could we end up in a Green future? We could, if we continue to let the Greens use the environment and other Green causes to dominate American politics. Political leaders and citizens can not continue to let emotions be their guide. From Earth Day to Politically Correct speech, the Green Movement is not what America thinks it is.

Whittaker Chambers was a member of the Communist Party. Chambers defected from the Communist Party for moral reasons and wrote the book, *Witness* in 1952 to warn the American people of the Communist's long term plans to take over America in the 20th century. Chambers states:

> "...the nation, too, wanted peace above all things, and it simply could not grasp or believe that a conspiracy on the scale of Communism was possible or that it had already made so deep a penetration into their lives..."
>
> Whittaker Chambers
> Witness

Information in the following chapters will confirm the political direction the Green Movement is taking fits with the long term plans of the Communists to overthrow our government and take over America.

Throughout this book, all references to the Green Movement or the Greens refer to the Communist faction within the Green Movement that is manipulating our concern for the environment and other issues to advance Communist's goals. Reference to the Greens is used in a general sense to identify those who are Communists and those who may not be Communist, but promote a similar political philosophy.

Communism in America

Communists never stop promoting their political program. It is a lifetime commitment. The language of communism hasn't changed. Communists introduce their ideas as new and progressive but the buzz words and political goals are consistent. The message, the goals and the methods remain the same.

The language among Communists is also consistent. From the early books warning Americans to beware of communism to the most recent environmental publications, the term *fellow traveler* is used. *Fellow travelers* are those involved in the Communist struggle for revolution in America. The only difference between *fellow travelers* and Communists is official membership in the Communist party. Their goals and political philosophies are the same. Comrade is another term the Greens and the Communists use. The Democratic Socialists of America use the term comrade in their Red-Green literature.

The Communists preach the concept of 'true democracy' and use the term *progressive* because it appeals to intellectuals. They seek the political support of intellectuals because intellectuals pride themselves in being on the cutting edge of social thought. This offers Communists fertile ground to cultivate their ideas and get intellectuals to present them as new and creative solutions to existing problems. Communists also con well-known people into promoting their ideas because it encourages others to follow.

Before embracing progressive ideas, those who consider themselves intellectuals ought to take a tip from Hitler on the role they play in political mass movements. They are used like anyone else to enlist the support of others. To illustrate his point, Hitler quotes Hans Sachs:

> *"Despise not your master craftsmen. But the great masses of those who call themselves the 'educated' are the superficial intellectual demimonde, conceited and arrogant incompetents who are not even aware of the ridiculous figures they cut as they dabble."*
>
> *Adolf Hitler*
> Hitler -- Memoirs of a Confidant
> Henry Turner

Communists also target the middle class and the poor to con them into believing their lives will be radically improved if they help do away with capitalism. Once Communists seize power, promises disappear. Force and fear become the tools to control the people. Equality under communism means the masses work as slaves and live under the same conditions. Communism does not end oppression. It makes it universal.

Greens promise equality and social justice. They guarantee people a job, food, shelter and health care. The Green objective is to convince the American masses the only way to achieve these goals and save the environment is to abandon capitalism and let the government take control their lives.

Green Communism

*"the environmental movement promises to bring greater
numbers into our orbit than the peace movement ever did"*
Carl Bloice
McAlvany Intelligence Advisor - March 1995

Carl Bloice is a leading U.S. Communist. Bloice was the
Associate Editor and Moscow correspondent for the People's
Daily World. He is reported to be close to Mikhail Gorbachev.
Bloice's comment makes it easier to understand why
Communists, like Gorbachev have become involved in the
environmental cause. Gorbachev is currently the President of
the international environmental organization, called Green
Cross International, with a chapter in the United States called,
Global Green.

Communists target all radical or popular movements where
they can weave their political ideas into the cause and con the
masses into thinking those ideas are new and progressive.
Communists operate like criminals. They don't plan to get
caught in the act. They plan to get the job done without being
noticed. Green Communists planned to have all their
snowballs in a row before the cat got out of the bag.

The environmental cause was identified in its infancy to serve
as a front for Communists and to be the catalyst to promote
socialism and set us up for communism. Communists
planned to be the organizers and the leaders in the U. S.
environmental movement a long time ago. They identified
fear as the key to convince Americans capitalism threatens
our survival.

Who is Gus Hall? Why should we care?

Americans need to understand this attack on our nation isn't new. It began years ago and it has never stopped. We have been deliberately mislead to believe communism is no longer a threat to our nation so the Greens can carry out their calculated political plan to take over our nation.

> *"**The key factor will be the leadership** of the struggle of the working class...Masses who after all are the power of any revolution...This is true **in the struggle to save the environment. What is new, is that the knowledge of the point of no return gives this struggle an unusual urgency**. Those of us who know that capitalism cannot basically be reformed, must work with and for people who have not yet come to that conclusion. **We must be the organizers, the leaders of these movements.***

> *Gus Hall*
> 1972 - Ecology
> (Bold Emphasis Added)

To understand how dedicated Communists are to achieving their long term political goals, it is important to review a court case involving a group of Communist conspirators. Twelve members of the Communist Party of the United States were indicted by a Federal Grand Jury in July, 1948 and charged with conspiracy. Albert Kahn, author of, *High Treason,* stated:

> *"The indictment accused the Communist leaders of plotting to subvert the Government by:*
>
> *...organizing a political party dedicated to the principles of Marxism-Leninism*
>
> *...Arranging to publish and circulate...books, magazines and newspapers advocating the principles of Marxism-Leninism*

...establishing 'schools and classes for the study of the principles of Marxism-Leninism, in which would be taught and advocated the duty and necessity of overthrowing and destroying the Government of the United States by force and violence."

Two of the men named in the indictment were: Henry Winston and Gus Hall. They were both found guilty and sentenced. Sentences ranged from 30 days to five year prison terms and one of the twelve also received a $10,000 fine.

Gus Hall has been a leader in the CPUSA, the Communist Party of the United States of America, for decades. Hall and others in the U.S. Communist Party convicted of conspiring to overthrow our government in 1948 have continued their efforts. Hall is still at it, 47 years later. Hall wrote the book, *Ecology* in 1972. He outlined strategies and explained how the environmental cause could be used to advance communism in America. Hall is now the National Chairman of the CPUSA.

The CPUSA receives substantial financial support from the Soviet Union. According to an article in *Harper's*, June 1992, the Communist Party of the Soviet Union has been contributing $2 million dollars per year to the Communist Party of the United States. This information surfaced when a letter from Gus Hall was discovered in the personal files of Mikhail Gorbachev.

The letter was sent to Soviet leaders requesting an additional $2 million dollars to cover expenses from election campaigns and increased operating costs. The letter was written to Soviet leaders in January 1987; Hall indicates the Soviets financial investment in America's political campaigns had been successful.

Hall makes the following statement in that letter:

> *"we went all out in the 1986 congressional elections, which, in
> my opinion paid off very well...we were influential, and
> even the deciding factor, in the defeat of some of the extreme
> Reaganite candidates."*

The article also indicates:

> *"Two months after the letter was sent, Hall received $2 million
> from a KGB courier."*

Hall received money from the Soviet Union to finance their
fight against capitalism by influencing our elections, to elect
Communist sympathizers, defeat American candidates and
spread Communist propaganda. Bruce Fellman's article, *What
Secret Soviet Files Reveal* was featured in the *Sacramento Bee*
newspaper. Fellman is the managing editor for the Alumni
magazine for Yale. His article was featured in the May, 1995
issue of that magazine. Fellman explains the book, *The Secret
World of American Communism* is based on new information
from the Soviet archives that relate to the activities of the
Communist Party of the USA. Fellman states the authors:

> ***"demolish what they call 'the predominant view among
> scholars' that the C.P.U.S.A was simply a political
> alternative to the Republicans and Democrats, and not an
> arm of a Soviet government bent on toppling the U.S.
> government."***

> ***"As the documents in this volume show,"*** *the authors note,*
> *the* ***C.P.U.S.A. was in fact a 'conspiracy financed by a
> hostile foreign power that recruited members for
> clandestine work, developed an elaborate underground
> apparatus and used that apparatus to collaborate with
> espionage services..."***
>
> (Bold Emphasis Added)

Gus Hall is a regular contributor to *Political Affairs* magazine. Henry Winston lead the party until his death in the late 1980's. *Political Affairs* is affiliated with the Communist Party. The June 1994 edition of *Political Affairs* featured excerpts from a recent speech Hall made at the Advanced Young Communists League (YCL). Hall's comments included these remarks:

> *"The key to what we have to do in a popular way is what the Communist Manifesto did over a hundred years ago...expose Capitalism, develop class consciousness...and find creative ways to present socialism USA."*

> *"Only our party can provide the organization, the tactics, the strategy and perspective of struggle, change and revolution"*

> *"... only political party capable of leading the working class to revolution and socialism."*

Hall emphasized a goal of the Communist Party and the YCL was to use the anger and militancy of American youth to recruit members and organize acts of rebellion.

> *"the young people...when they meet us on the street or in action, they see the YCL and party as an organization that will help them protest, fight and win"*
> *Gus Hall*
> Political Affairs - June, 1994

Hall indicated Communist clubs would be used to offer a place for young people to go, so they learn, plan and participate in militant actions. This could be a new social life for young people. The Greens are using any opportunity to present socialism as the alternative to capitalism. They are targeting young people, promoting national health care or abusing environmental issues. The plan is to reform our system and con the Americans into believing the only solution is more government control of our lives.

These nine rules were seized in a raid in Dusseldorf Germany in 1919. The files were marked, *'Communist Rules for Revolution.'*

1. Corrupt the young; get them away from religion. Get them interested in sex. Make them superficial; destroy their ruggedness.

2. Get control of all means of publicity. Get peoples' minds off their government by focusing their attention on athletics, sexy books, plays and other trivialities.

3. Divide people into hostile groups by constantly harping on controversial matters of no importance.

4. Destroy the peoples' faith in their natural leaders by holding the latter up to contempt, ridicule and obloquy.

5. Always preach true democracy but seize power as fast and as ruthlessly as possible.

6. By encouraging government extravagance, destroy its credit; produce fear of inflation, rising prices and general discontent.

7. Foment strikes in vital industries; encourage civil disorders and foster a lenient and soft attitude on the part of government toward these disorders.

8. By special argument cause a breakdown of the old moral virtues; honesty, sobriety, continence, faith in the pledged word, ruggedness.

9. Cause the registration of all firearms on some pretext with a view of confiscation of them and leaving the population helpless.

Is there evidence to indicate any of these rules may have been applied to disrupt our society, reform our system of government, or change our constitutional rights? It is important to remember that Communists are dedicated to their political beliefs and spend a lifetime devoted to the advancement of communism. The Soviets paid Hall to sabotage our electoral process. Hall has spent forty seven years working to change America. It is most likely these rules have been followed. Review the list of rules and think about a few of the issues Americans are now dealing with:

- government extravagance
- gun control
- moral decay
- manufactured divisions within society

It is hard to ignore the long range goals of the Communist party when they match the emergence of the Greens in America. At this time, Greens and Communist leaders are calling for mass party building. Recruiting plans include targeting these unsuspecting Americans; the poor, jobless, young people, minorities, the homeless and the illiterate. These Americans are key political targets because they are the most vulnerable to the promise of socialism.

We are in a political fight for our lives. If we ignore this fact, we will probably end up in a Green future. If we plan to avoid, 'compulsory Green living', we must instantly become more committed to preserving our freedom than the Greens are to taking it away from us.

> *"Human society cannot basically stop the destruction of the environment under capitalism. Socialism is the only structure that makes it possible."*
>
> *Gus Hall*
> National Chairman CPUSA
> 1972 - Ecology

Just Like Termites

While most Americans haven't even heard of the Greens, the Greens have been working away for years, just like termites, to weaken the foundation of our nation. Our nation is like our home. Our safety and comfort depend on a strong foundation. Last time we looked, our foundation was in decent shape. We felt safe. We had the time to focus our attention on other things.

Now there is a visible crack in the foundation. If we want to be safe, we need to repair the areas where damage has been done. A house with a weak foundation can collapse. The Green strategy is to change key elements within our society, until piece by piece, the America we know falls apart.

The Greens liken their vision to what appeared to be the overnight collapse of the Soviet Union. The only difference between the collapse of the two superpowers will be the result. The Green goal for a massive transformation in America promises to establish communism.

Hide and Seek

We have seen it. We have felt it. We just haven't been able to put our finger on where all the push, push, push, for change, change, change was coming from.

A great deal of our current social unrest stems from subversive Green activism. What appear to be random, isolated incidents are actually coordinated efforts to challenge long-standing American policies and traditions.

The Greens have set the stage. Each group has a role to play in creating conflict within our society. Green activists are dedicated to the goal of revolution and routinely perform assigned political tasks such as:

- Handing out propaganda
- Stuffing envelopes
- Speaking at different political events
- Supporting different radical causes
- Staging and participating in demonstrations
- Recruiting new members
- Moving as needed to develop or support party ideas

Staged public demonstrations have political value. It's much easier to convince politicians to vote for special interest laws if they are set up to believe citizen unrest is real and political action is necessary. At one Green meeting, the speaker indicated that if they couldn't get the vote, they would import the vote. Whether the Greens stage demonstrations or import the vote, we all lose an incremental piece of our freedom each time the Greens are successful in forcing an end to another American tradition or slaughtering another American value.

The founding fathers knew, from personal experience, too much political power was dangerous. Our government was founded on a system of checks and balances to prevent one political force from dominating government. If one interest group gained too much political power it would eliminate equal representation and put our political system out of balance and at risk.

Americans have responded to the environmental cause by joining environmental groups and offering generous financial contributions. This show of support translates into too much political power. The Greens are pushing for changes in public policies at an unprecedented rate without the scrutiny that is typical of our check and balance system.

Throughout history, revolutionaries have lied to people to gain power. Revolutionaries operate on the 'end justifies the means' plan. Deception is part of the revolutionary process.

> *"I hate deception, even where the imagination only is*
> *concerned."*
> *George Washington*
> Letter to Dr. Cochran, Aug 16, 1779

Is the environmental situation as bad as we have been lead to believe or is our love of nature being used to manipulate us into accepting Green politics?

> *"The great masses of people will more easily fall*
> *victims to a great lie than to a small one."*
> *Adolf Hitler*

Vladimir Lenin, leader of the Russian Revolution, created the Bolshevik party and lied to the Russian people to persuade them to try his political ideas. Hitler created the Nazi party and lied to the German people to persuade them to try his political ideas. Both political movements were based on ideas or ideology. After Hitler and Lenin seized power, they made their ideas law. After they were in power it was too late for people to ask questions or offer suggestions. The time to ask questions is before Green political ideas become law.

The Green Movement is also based on ideas. The Greens are directly and indirectly lying to the American people to convince us socialism is better for the environment. Revolutions are fueled by emotionally charged causes. Trusting people fall prey to political ideas based on feelings, not facts. Emotions are manipulated and ideas become laws.

Can you tell, Hitler or Lenin?

- Public ownership of the Land, Abolish Private Property
- Public ownership of the Healthcare Industry
- Public ownership of the Energy Industry
- Public ownership of the Auto industry
- Public ownership of the Railroad industry
- Public ownership of the Banking industry
- Public ownership of the Insurance industry
- Public ownership of all Natural Resources
- Public control of the Economy and Small Business

Do the above political ideas represent Hitler's political program for Nazi Germany or Lenin's Communist party program? Neither, these are the primary goals of the Greens. Public ownership of all resources includes:

- Land, Water, Mineral, Forest, Plants and Animals
- Electromagnetic, the airwaves, all communication systems including cable and computer networks.

The current push to police the internet, or the information super highway, also fits the Green goal to control everything from the airwaves to the individual.

The Greens are convincing Americans to support Green politics by developing multiple emotional messages that appeal to people in every segment of our society.

It is interesting that in America, we normally refer to a series of political positions or ideas as a *political platform.* Communists refer to their political ideas as a *program.* The Greens use *program* to define their political positions.

More Green Goals on the National Agenda

- 75% Reduction in Military Budget
- National Healthcare
- Biodiversity Treaty
- Forestry Practices
- Gay rights
- Gun control

Even though most Americans haven't heard of Green politics, the Green politics reflect many of the ideas and issues being promoted in America and pushed on the American people.

The Green Party seems like an obscure little band of radicals who are not a threat to this nation. Their ideas appear to receive little or no national attention. Hitler also paraded around, leading his little band of radicals. At first, no one paid much attention. That was a critical error in judgment.

The Greens are successfully incorporating their political ideas into mainstream America. Until we understand the Greens political objectives they will continue to be successful. Recent Green successes include:

- federal control of timber harvest
- 75% reduction in U.S. military
- Gays in the military

Until we recognize when and how the Greens are imposing their political program on America, it will continue. The Green agenda includes working toward crippling and eventually eliminating these industries:

- Cattle industry
- Timber industry
- Agriculture industry

- Fishing industry
- Sport hunting and fishing industries
- Recreationist, off- road vehicles
- Gun and weapons industry

Greens also intend to use our emotions and Animal Rights issues to eliminate these American traditions:

- Rodeos
- Circuses
- Commercial animal breeding
- Animals in entertainment
- Horse racing
- Dog racing
- Zoos
- Aquariums

More Green Goals from the Green Party Program

- Establish a system of nonviolent civilian defense
- Reduce United States border defense
- Abolish arms markets and sales in the United States
- Eliminate the use of all pesticides and herbicides
- Phase out Gasoline and other fossil fuels
- Alternatives to use of Pharmaceuticals
- Work for Global Government
- Transform Food System: from meat to vegetarian
- Cancel Third World Debt, Debt for Nature Swaps
- End government tax benefits for:
    - airline industries.
    - nuclear, energy corporations (utilities)
    - virgin paper
- Support for International Law, World Court and International Treaties such as the U. N. Convention on the Rights of a Child.

This treaty, if passed could result in losing control over how our children are raised to a world panel. The treaty offers no guarantee an American would even serve on the international decision making panel. Congressman Thomas J. Bliley, Jr. warned Americans the U.N. Convention on the Rights of the Child would eliminate the ninth and tenth amendments to the constitution and poses a threat to our government.

Another Green goal:

- Abolish the CIA and covert operations agencies

December, 1993, Jane Fonda spoke at the United Nations as part of the Eminent Citizens Committee and suggested the United States should cut our CIA budget and spend the extra money to help develop Third World countries. Eliminating part of the CIA budget would cut investigations of covert and foreign government activities regarding the national security of the United States. It is not a good idea to hinder the agency that protects our national security when Communists are already in the United States and using the environmental cause to camouflage their activities.

It appears both Jane Fonda and her husband, Ted Turner, support the Green movement. Porritt's book, *Save the Earth*, was published by Turner Publishing, Inc, a subsidiary of Turner Broadcasting System, Inc.

Why was Jane Fonda suggesting to the United Nations what America ought to do with our CIA funding?

The political objectives of the Green movement include; abolishing the CIA and redistributing American's wealth to Third World countries. Do the Turners understand the Green wealth inventory will include their mega-millions?

Like A Thief In The Night, Greens Plan To Steal

> *"The chic upper-class ecologists, with their hot-tubs, their quarter-million-dollar homes, their designer clothes, and their Mercedes Benzes, had best realize that their calls for clean air must be accompanied by meaningful actions that will lead to a redistribution of their own unwarranted economic abundance. If they do no voluntarily begin to make this economic adjustment, then others will make it for them."*
>
> Jeremy Rifkin
Entropy - 1980

Jeremy Rifkin is an active leader in the Green movement. The above statement is from Rifkin's 1980 edition of his book, *Entropy*. It is interesting that in the 1989 reprint of the book the above statement was omitted. Wonder why?

Could it be, now that the environmental cause has been made so popular, Rifkin does not want anyone to notice that part of the Green plan involves redistributing the wealth of 'upper-class ecologists' or the fact that if Americans don't agree to this, 'then others will do it for them'? Was the paragraph left out to cover-up Green plans to steal American's wealth, using force if necessary? That sounds like Porritt's implied idea that we can volunteer for communism or be forced into it.

Would Americans continue to offer their financial support to environmental groups if they realized this was part of the Green plan? Doubtful. Americans would probably stop donating the millions of dollars to finance the Greens and their own demise. The Greens need to keep the money coming in to finance their political efforts to change America.

> *"Foreign policies should further encourage an equitable global distribution of wealth"*
>
> Green Party Program

The Greens call for the redistribution of the wealth earned by all American citizens. This is not just about Americans with abundant wealth. All different kinds of people with all different kinds of income would be subject to converting to 'compulsory Green living'. Rich, poor and in-between, it comes down to limiting every American's ability to choose what they want and the opportunity to pursue their dreams.

Other's have called for the redistribution of citizen's wealth using similar justifications. Hitler convinced people to support Nazi's confiscation of the property and wealth of the Jewish people. Hitler's speeches and writings show the propaganda ideas he used to manipulate the masses.

> *"We see that the primary cause for the existing tensions lies in the unfair distribution of the riches of the earth."*
> *My New Order*

> *"Against the infection of materialism, against the Jewish pestilence we must hold aloft a flaming idea."*
> *The Speeches of Adolf Hitler*

> *"The Jews are a people under whose parasitism the whole of honest humanity is suffering, today more than ever."*
> *Mein Kampf*

> *"Jewish parasites...plundered the nation without pity."*
> *The Speeches of Adolf Hitler*

Hitler played on people's fears. Hitler set people up to actually believe the Jewish people were irresponsible, evil materialist (capitalists) who had raped Germany and stolen wealth from the German people. Hitler convinced normal people to seek revenge against the Jews he decided to hold responsible for Germany's problems.

The Greens have duplicated many of Hitler's emotional ploys. This time the scapegoat is the American people. Americans are portrayed as materialistic capitalists who rape the earth, steal its riches and are to blame for causing environmental problems around the world. Hitler suggested redistributing Jewish wealth to protect the sacred soil.

The Greens imply redistribution of American's wealth will save the earth. The Greens blame Americans, capitalism and materialism for environmental problems. Hitler blamed the Jewish people for Germany's problems. The environment instead of race is the issue this decade. Is there any significant difference in the message?

- problem caused by unfair distribution of wealth
- against infection of materialism
- causing the rest of honest humanity to suffer
- plunder the nation without pity

Hitler was well aware, if you repeat a lie often enough, people will begin to believe it. Hitler blamed the Jews. The Greens blame Americans. If we look at the list of Americans on the Green hate list of environmental crimes, we can see how the Greens have used Hitler's simplistic methods to shape the opinion of the masses.

The Greens shape public opinion by labeling Americans who questions Green politics as anti-environmentalist. Hitler was successful using labels and his tactic appears to be working well the second time around. We all need to understand, the only difference between self-proclaimed environmentalists and anti-environmentalists is the label the Greens put on them. As in Nazi Germany, the only difference between the Jews and other people was the label they were forced to wear.

Hitler used that label to create division and promote intolerance towards the Jews. The Greens are using labels to create intolerance towards certain Americans. Hitler labeled the entire Jewish population as sub-human and people accepted it. The Greens have labeled any American concerned with Green politics as anti-environmentalists and have convinced some Americans to believe it without reason or fact.

Hitler did the same thing. He presented one group as good and another as bad, so the public would pick the pre-designated correct side to be on. This tactic discourages citizens from thinking or asking questions because the politically correct opinion has been provided in advance. Have the Greens been successful using the Hitler approach? Does it work? Read the following list of political issues.

Ranchers	or	Wolves
Dolphins	or	Fishermen
Recreationist	or	Turtles
Delhi Sands Flies	or	Developers
Spotted Owls	or	Loggers
Farmers	or	Wetlands
Animal Rights	or	Citizen Rights

Which is the politically correct side? What is this political opinion based on?

- Knowledge from an in-depth study of the issue
- A ten second sound byte on the evening news
- Newspaper headlines
- Green political messages in movies
- Green propaganda from environmental organizations

We need to remember as we form political opinions that these issues are multifaceted. Real people, just like us, are attached to these issues. Their families and their futures are involved.

"There are people who eagerly accept their own freedom but do not respect the freedom of others...They would do well to look at what has happened in societies without moral foundations. Accepting no laws but the laws of force, these societies have been ruled by totalitarian ideologies like Nazism, fascism, and communism, which do not spring from the general populace, but are imposed on it by intellectual elites."

Margaret Thatcher
Prime Minister of Britain -1979-1990
IMPRIMIS - March 1995

(Reprinted by permission from IMPRIMIS, the monthly journal of Hillsdale College)

Our futures are involved also. It is irresponsible for us to accept unqualified, simplistic information that impacts the lives of our fellow citizens and determines the future of our country.

The key to the Greens successful manipulation of the American people to date, stems from copying the political ideas and tactics of both Adolf Hitler and Vladimir Lenin.

BIG MISTAKE

How did Hitler convince a nation to go along with his ideas? Many Germans jumped on the Nazi bandwagon but others didn't take Hitler seriously or consider the Nazis a threat. Citizens did not believe the Nazis could gain enough political power to force their ideas on the German people. They stopped paying attention to the politics of the Nazi movement and went on with their lives. Big mistake!

Meanwhile, Hitler and his little band of Nazis continued to have parades, sell Nazi trinkets and promote their cause. What started out as a small but solid band of fanatics grew into the Nazi movement. The Nazi parades were similar to the Greens Earth Day events. It wasn't a good idea for big business to help finance the Nazi movement and it isn't a good idea for big business to finance the Green movement.

Hitler convinced thousands upon thousands to join the Nazi movement using emotional ploys, political fanfare, clever propaganda, hate and terrorism. He promised all things to all people. He even persuaded German parents to involve their children in the Nazi movement. Hitler lied all the time and manipulated himself into power, lie by lie. Hitler began his political career by finding people he felt comfortable with and superior to. He surrounded himself with other derelicts, perverts and a few ambitious politicians who felt he was on the right track. Slowly but surely, Hitler built a coalition of militant, intolerant outcasts.

Hitler planned for the future. He knew what he was doing when he involved children in national politics. He formed the famous Hitler Youth groups so he could grow a loyal Nazi army. Germany's children were molded into pledging their allegiance to Hitler and no one else.

Children were taught to believe Hitler was a God. They were loyal to Hitler over friends and family. Germany's children grew into murderers because they were trained to be Nazi terrorists and political activists as young children. We can not blame the children. It was their parents who initially allowed them to participate in national politics as children. Nazi leaders taught them Hitler's ideology. How could the childern know it was wrong? They could not. They were sacrificed to the Nazi movement.

Tolerance from most citizens and aggressive support from others gave Hitler the time he needed to set up the right political opportunity to put himself in the position to attain absolute power over Germany. Hitler made control possible by making control legal.

The American people are making the same mistake about the Green movement the German people made about the Nazi movement. Americans are buying into the Green Movement based on emotional ploys, political fanfare, clever propaganda, hate, lies, terrorism and the promise of all things. American parents are allowing their children to be involved in the national politics of the Green movement.

Many Americans have jumped into the Green movement without fully understanding the scope of the movement. Other Americans are too busy to pay attention or are looking the other way because they don't understand how this affects them. Many Americans do not believe the Greens can gain enough political power to force their ideas on the American people. Big mistake!

There are so many aspects of Green copy-cat politics. Even the color is significant. Anne Frank noted, it was the Green Police who came to arrest her. The Greens also want to establish a Green Police force or the Green Helmet forces to enforce ecological laws. The Green party, like the Nazis, originated in Germany. The symbol of the Green Party is the Sunflower. The Sunflower was a Nazi symbol of honor. Sunflowers were used by the Nazis to pay tribute to fallen soldiers. Sunflowers were planted on soldier's graves. When they bloomed, the cemetery became a field of bright yellow and a striking memorial to the Nazi cause.

Subliminal Green political messages are prominent in numerous television programs, movies and advertisements. The Sunflower emerged a few years ago. It can now be seen on display everywhere. The Sunflower is more than a fashion statement. It's a political symbol that is being promoted for a reason. The plan is to get us to identify with this symbol and get attached to it. The plan is, if we like the symbol we will support the politics that go with it.

S.S.D.D. Same Stuff Different Decade

Green political ideas and propaganda messages mirror the psychological and emotional ploys Hitler used to successfully manipulate a nation.

Nazi Ideology	Green Ideology
Used Nature	Using Nature
Save the Fatherland	Save Mother Earth
Earth is a Living Organism	Earth is a Living Being
Used Animal Rights	Using Animal Rights
Green Police-SS men	Green Police - Eco Cops
Sunflower was Symbol	Sunflower is Symbol
One people, One nation	One people, One planet
Promoted Women	Promote Women
Fascination with Wolves	Fascination with Wolves
Religion - Hitler was God	Religion - Earth is God
Myth, Pagan, Goddess	Myth, Pagan, Goddess
Nazi - High Holy Days	Greens - Earth Day
Nazis - mostly teachers	Greens - mostly Teachers
Children taught Nazis	Children taught to be Green
Stressed Community	Stress Community
Hitler stressed Activism	Greens stress Activism
Jews root of all Evil	Americans root of all Evil
Nazi Party began Germany	Green Party began Germany
Scapegoat - Capitalist	Scapegoat - Capitalist

The Greens are using Hitler's ideas because he successfully convinced thousands of reasonable people to support political insanity. Nazism in Germany seemed to happen spontaneously, but there were certain factors that helped

Hitler. The Greens have recreated some of those same factors by introducing alternative ideas that enticed the German masses to abandon their traditions and morals. The same alternative ideas that prompted the people to become Nazis are prompting Americans to go Green.

> "at the turn of the century, there was a rising tide of materialism in Germany and Austria, with a countervailing reaction that yearned for a more harmonious and spiritual past. Many of Germany's youth became known as 'the birds of passage' with vegetarianism, herbal healing, communal living, nudism, and meditation becoming fashionable...and in every major city, cults devoted to spiritualism, astrology, magic and the occult formed."
>
> Dr. Dennis Cuddy
> Now is the Dawning of the New Age New World Order

Obviously, similar circumstances can produce similar results. That is what we must avoid. There is nothing wrong with herbal healing or vegetarianism. We need to understand it was the combination of all the new, alternative ideas that led to the broader acceptance of Hitler's fanatical blend of spirituality and politics. Once the German people started dabbling in alternative ideas, it was easier to justify changing traditions and accepting the Nazi's political and spiritual ideas. Americans must understand our acceptance of this combination of alternative ideas can lead to a broader acceptance of Green ideas on spirituality and politics.

Talking Points

The Greens even use the same language and arguments Hitler used to justify his actions. Hitler persuaded a nation to support theft and murder in the name of saving the sacred soil of Fatherland, sometimes referred to as the Motherland.

Hitler convinced a nation of intelligent people to try his blend of spiritual politics that included aggressive and intolerant political opinions combined with a fierce commitment to:

- protect the sacred soil
- preserve the German species
- animal rights above human rights
- see the earth as a living organism
- identify with the earth as their Mother

The Greens are convincing intelligent Americans to accept copy-cat spiritual politics. Green politics include aggressive and intolerant political opinions combined with a commitment to:

- protect the sacred soil
- animal rights above human rights
- see the earth as a living organism, or Gaia
- have a spiritual connection with the earth
- identify with the earth as our Mother

Hitler preyed on emotions to create a fanatical political following dedicated to protecting the sacred soil of the Fatherland. The Greens are preying on emotions to create the same type of political loyalty based on the same kind of spiritual relationship with the earth. It wasn't a healthy or normal mentality then and it isn't a healthy or normal mentality now.

The Greens justify their political actions in the name of environmental protection. The Greens are using Hitler's reasons to promote and justify their actions.

- the earth does not belong to us, it is not given as a gift
- earth belongs to those who take control and preserve it
- not wrong to take property in name of cause
- preserve it for future generations

The Greens also use Hitler's method of controlling opposition.

- divert public's attention, attack character of enemy
- avoid public debate of issue and measures to be taken
- blame current political actions on injustices of past

After he achieved power, Hitler operated by the 'comply or die' rule to maintain government control of citizens.

Eliminating the opposition was a key factor in the success of the Nazi movement. Gun control was a priority. Hitler rendered the people defenseless by seizing all the weapons. Then it was easy to eliminate anyone who opposed him. Hitler accomplished this by force and by promoting the idea that Nazi troops would protect citizens so they did not need guns. Americans are supporting parts of the Green movement without realizing the political ramifications.

Consider the politically correct position that gun control will prevent crime in America. Same stuff, different decade. Gun control in Germany did not keep citizens safe. It rendered them helpless and vulnerable to escalating Nazi terrorism and excessive government control. Americans must protect their right to bear arms. Hitler successfully conned the German people into trying his Nazi ideas, but they didn't have the blaring historical example of the Holocaust to refer to. We do.

Germans and others watched as their neighbors lost their freedom and did not realize it was connected to their own. The German people were upset. Their country was in economic ruin. Hitler presented a political alternative and they tried it.

The Greens have set Americans up to make the same error in judgment, to take leave of our senses and try the Green political experiment. We can be guinea pigs or we can learn from the mistakes of others. Had citizens taken Hitler seriously, had the Jewish people not been so accommodating and tolerant of Nazi demands, things could have been different. How different, we'll never know. One thing we can safely assume is those poor people would have had a chance.

> *"Perhaps in a hundred years another genius will take up my ideas and National Socialism, like a Phoenix will arise again from the ashes."*
>> *Adolf Hitler*
>> Psychopathic God

Review the following quotations. Note the same goal to transform public life. Note the same goal to reorganize society around a political cause. Note the same idea to set public policy based around a political cause. Note the same level of commitment to the ideals of the political cause.

> *"the new Green vision places the environment at the center of public life, making it the context for both the formulation of economic policies and political decisions"*
>> *Jeremy Rifkin - Carol Grunewald Rifkin*
>> Voting Green - The Framework for Politics

> *"The task of saving the earth's environment must and will become the central organizing principle of the post-Cold War world"*
>> *Senator Al Gore*
>> Putting People First

> *"No compromise in the name of Mother Earth"*
>> *Earth First*

> *"Our ideology is intolerant ... and peremptorily demands ... the complete transformation of public life to its ideas"*
>> *Adolf Hitler*
>> Psychopathic God

More Copy-Cat Politics

The Greens aren't taking any chances, they not only have borrowed from Adolf Hitler's bag of political tricks, they have borrowed most of the ideas Lenin used to force the Russian revolution and establish communism.

Lenin glorified his utopian vision in the minds of citizens. The world the Bolsheviks described sounded like heaven. Writers helped promote Lenin's ideas to the public and targeted the working class to gain support for the party.

Lenin made it sound wonderful, but it was a lie. Communism and total oppression were not what the Russian people expected to see at the end of Lenin's rainbow. Lenin conned the Russian citizens into trying his ideas, instead of sticking to capitalism. The Greens have updated the terms to make the ideas sound new but the following ideas are basically the ideas Lenin used to get Russian citizens to try communism.

Lenin	Greens	Political Promises
Social	Public	Control of Economy
Societies	Bioregions	Form small communities
Talents	Abilities	People do socially useful work
Trade	Barter	No money needed
Share	Redistribute	Wealth, people will share
Bolshevik	Green	Politics are true democracy
Utopian	Ecological	Society better than rat race
Riches	Wealth	Put people before Profits
Shorter	Shorter	Work week will free the people
Bottom-up	Bottom-up	People will control government

Lenin stressed, before he could take power, he had to build a well-organized alternative political party. Lenin spent 17 years working behind the scenes to develop the Bolshevik party as an alternative to the existing Russian order.

Both Lenin and Hitler's plans for revolution included the need for the people to help eliminate an obstacle before the perfect society could be formed. Lenin set up capitalism and capitalists as the obstacle Russians had to eliminate to establish utopia. Hitler set up the Jewish capitalists as the obstacle that had to be eliminated before he could create his version of paradise. The Greens are offering Americans an alternative to our political system. The Greens are setting us up to believe capitalism must be abandoned and our society transformed to save the earth. This must occur before the Green version of a perfect society can be formed.

Changing all our values, abandoning capitalism, agreeing to socialism or submitting to communism will not create a perfect society nor will it save the environment.

Lack of awareness of the political goals of the Greens is at the root of American's inability to understand what is happening in our country and why it is happening. Americans are not supposed to discover that beyond the headlines of environmental disaster lays a network of radical Green groups whose goal is not just change, it's revolution.

Some Green concepts are reasonable, some are unreasonable but most are extremely, extreme. Americans need to remember the politics and propaganda of Lenin's communism and Hitler's national socialism before falling for Green politics and propaganda. To avoid revolution, we must be able to recognize when and how we are being manipulated.

The Greens political propaganda tactics and ideas look like a combination of both Lenin and Hitler 'politics of persuasion'. How do Green politics match the ideas of the master manipulators?

	LENIN	HITLER	GREENS
Created Crisis-Level Mentality	x	x	x
Promised all things to all people	x	x	x
Used Children as political pawns	x	x	x
Capitalism, Capitalists root of all evil	x	x	x
Goal to Transform Society	x	x	x
Public control Production/Distribution	x	x	x
Promise Bottom-Up not Top-Down Rule	x		x
Vision to create a Perfect Society	x	x	x
Violent beginnings, People Terrorized	x	x	x
Classless Society over hierarchy	x	x	x
Public to Share Wealth equally	x		x
Seized, sequestered Private Property	x	x	x
Intolerant, End Justified the Means	x	x	x
Individuality must submit to cause	x	x	x
Render Public Helpless-Seized Guns	x	x	x
Deplete Financial Assets of Enemy	x	x	x
Dehumanized life and death issues	x	x	x
Keep real agenda out of public eye	x	x	x
Political Ideology form of Religion	x	x	x
Plans to Relocate part of Population	x	x	x
Political Objective, Rule the World	x	x	x

So far, only two out of three revolutions have ended in dictatorship and mass suffering.

The politics of Lenin, Hitler and the Greens are like the story of *Hansel and Gretel*. It's the same concept on a larger scale. The candy on the outside of the witch's house was put there to entice children to come closer. Like a snake in the grass, as soon as the children came close enough, the witch struck. She lied to get the children into the house. Then she lied to get the children to look in the oven so she could shove them inside and slam the door. Like the Greens, the witch knew, it was easier for her if the children came along willingly until she was in a position to take control.

> *"Just because all the rest of the children stick their heads in the oven, does that mean you ought to do the same thing?"*
>
> *Grandma Hacker*
> Teaching Us to Think -- 1960

Lenin, Hitler, the Greens and the witch have something in common. What you see is not what you get. Hitler preached that the Jewish people had to be eliminated. At first, both the Jews and the Germans thought that meant the Jews would be relocated to work farms. It was not originally common knowledge that Hitler meant extermination.

Lenin promised peace, land and bread for all. He promised people would be happier and that the people would share the wealth and governing power. Utopia didn't turn out that way. Lenin abolished private property ownership, took control of the banks, police and the army. Russia quickly became a dictatorship sustained by slave labor.

The Greens are making similar promises and blaming the evils of capitalist and capitalism for environmental damage. Sharing and equality means different things to different people. Russia's social elite benefited and the general public lost it all.

Generous People or Selfish Pigs?

Capitalistic Americans are the most generous people in the world. When there is a crisis, where do the eyes of the world turn? Who helps? If we were selfish, as the Greens imply, we would not be willing to share our resources with those in need. Before we allow ourselves to get conned into accepting socialism or communism is better for the environment, we ought to revisit the value of capitalism.

> *"The moral foundations of a society do not extend only to its political system; they must extend to its economic system as well. America's commitment to capitalism is unquestionably the best example of this principle. Capitalism is not, contrary to what those on the Left have tried to argue, an amoral system based on selfishness, greed and exploitation. It is a moral system based on a Biblical ethic. There is no other comparable system that has raised the standard of living of millions of people, created vast new wealth and resources, or inspired so many beneficial innovations and technologies. The wonderful thing about capitalism is that it does not discriminate against the poor, as has been so often charged; indeed, it is the only economic system that raises the poor out of poverty."*
>
> *Margaret Thatcher*
> IMPRIMIS - March 1995

(Reprinted by permission from IMPRIMIS, the monthly journal of Hillsdale College)

Capitalism and freedom promote generosity, increase business opportunities and offer different choices to people in different situations. This includes the freedom to develop environmentally friendly products. We can change our lives to better protect our environment, but only if we are free to do so.

Recycling isn't new, although you'd think the Greens invented it. The Red Cross, Goodwill Industries, Salvation Army and Church groups prove recycling has been a part of our culture for a long time. Over the years, generous donations to these organizations by thoughtful Americans have helped thousands of individuals and families all over the world.

Americans constantly volunteer to lend their support to charity, telethons and other events intended to help those in need. The January 31, 1994 edition of, *Newsweek*, featured the article, *Here's Some Good News, America*, by Robert Samuelson. Samuelson reported 10 good news items. Number nine on the list was:

> *"We remain remarkable generous with our time and money. About a fifth of adults do volunteer work. Of these, 37 percent work for churches and religious groups, while 15 percent work in schools. In 1991, we gave $125 billion to charities. Most ($103 billion) came from individuals. Americans now give more of their disposable income to charity than in 1970."*

Samuelson also reported that:

> *"Most children still live with both natural parents and the divorce rate may be stabilizing."*

American families are a unique and intricate part of how our system promotes recycling and family fun. Americans love to explore second-hand stores, garage sales and swap meets. One man's trash is another man's treasure! What's the ultimate form of recycling in America? Americans have made the antique business an art form. We collect special pieces of our history and restore them or sell the piece for someone else to enjoy. We know how to save, reuse and recycle. As a nation, we went through a depression. We understand the difference between want and need.

Another old idea being introduced, as if it were the first time, is the idea that Americans need encouragement to *'commit random acts of kindness.'* The concept is a nice reminder, but this is not a new value to the people of this nation. Americans have earned the reputation for 'giving other's the shirt off their back'. It's another tradition we can be proud of.

America is a kind nation, with few exceptions. Americans always drop what we are doing to help someone in need. This attitude has always been a part of being an American. Caring is part of what makes our society work.

The purpose of reinventing some of our time honored traditions is to make Green feel comfortable, something we are familiar with, so it seems friendly and non-threatening. It makes it easier to believe the old ways are outdated if similar concepts are introduced as new and progressive.

Communism may sound enticing to those who would prefer not to take responsibility for their own lives. The grass is always greener on the other side of the fence. In this case, it's really Green. Life under communism would be like slavery or living as indentured servants. The government has total control. Citizens trade work time for products. Communism offers citizens little freedom, few rights and limited opportunities to improve their status in life.

There is a gap between *have's* and *have-not's* in America, but there are many degrees of wealth within our economic structure. Communism operates under a different premise; the *have's* live in luxury and *have-not's* live in poverty. Life in our country spreads the wealth around. Everyone has the opportunity to excel. This is why we have millions of 'rags to riches' stories. From Abraham Lincoln to Elvis, those who start out with little can become millionaires in America.

Americans have set up ways to assist those in need. We share our wealth voluntarily. The dollars to finance assistance programs come out of our paychecks. We have never refused to help others. The Greens condemn capitalism, but it would be wise for them and for us all to remember, capitalism and the generosity of caring Americans helped finance their cause.

Turning Up the Heat

The frog in the pan story is a good example of how the Greens have and are executing their political agenda. If a frog is placed in a pan of warm water and the heat is turned up gradually, the frog doesn't notice the gradual change in temperature. The frog doesn't register the slight changes in temperature as life threatening so it will sit there and gradually expire.

If you placed a frog in a pan of boiling water, the frog would notice the temperature of the water is dangerous to its health and it would jump out of the pan to save itself.

This story parallels Green politics in America. The Greens have been turning up the heat gradually so the American people will not notice slight social changes or connect the shifts in public policies to socialism and indirect steps toward communism.

We are not expected to protest Green calls for social change because we have been set up to believe the Green Movement is good for America. Like the frog, if we don't sense the 'Green heat' is dangerous to our health, we won't jump out of the pan and save ourselves.

The Green plan is to turn-up the political heat and legally force change after change, until life as we know it, gradually expires. Many Americans have not yet sensed danger because the heat of choice is the environmental cause. Exposing the Green political agenda now is like placing the American people in a pot of boiling water. How will the American people respond?

Free Speech or Treason?

People in America have the right to free speech and recruiting support for their ideas. What words and deeds are considered treason? Openly running for office as a Communist or discussing the merits of communism is different than abusing our system by running as an independent with the intent to advance the goals of the Communist party. When does the Communist plan to overthrow our government become an issue of national security?

We have to pay attention to anything that smacks of socialism or communism and vote against it. A democracy operates on the premise, we are free to challenge and change. People must be free to think and speak. How do we define the difference between the political freedom to promote change and at what point that freedom becomes a threat to our national security? Greens call for revolution at meetings and in the alternative press but that does not translate into public awareness.

> *"What's public is propaganda, what's secret is serious."*
> *Charles Bohlen*
> U.S. Ambassador -- to the U.S.S.R 1969

Treason describes citizens who are disloyal to a nation and who are considered untrustworthy. The difference between free speech and treason seems to hinge on whether or not terms like force and violence are used to describe how the traitors are planning to execute their plan.

We have learned that the CPUSA:

- are working with the Soviet Union (like agents do)
- are paid by the Soviet Union (like agents are)
- are 'using our system to break down our system'
- is not just an alternative to the two party system
- lied to Americans about secretly working for the Soviets
- plans to overthrow our government (like agents do)
- planned to use environmental cause to hide behind
- has indicated the takeover may not be peaceful

What is the difference between the activities and objectives of the members of the CPUSA and Soviet paid KGB agents? Aren't Communist agents, bent on destroying our government, still considered a threat to our national security? The CPUSA and the members of that organization are enemies of this nation.

Facts show the CPUSA is an extension of the Communist Party of the Soviet Union. This is no longer an issue of free speech. The activities of the CPUSA, the long range political goals of the Soviet Union and the political objectives of the Green movement are a serious threat to our national security.

Political leaders are supposed to be the first line of defense and guardians of national security. Americans can't trust politicians to ensure our safety. We must be more responsible.

> *"The important point about the Washington apparatuses is that, in the 1930's, the revolutionary mood had become so acute throughout the world that the Communist Party could recruit its agents, not here and there, but by scores within the Government of the United States. And they were precisely among the most literate, intellectually eager and energetic young men in a nation..."*
>
> *Whittaker Chambers*
> Witness

Chambers was working for the Communist party at that time. Unfortunately, some politicians are not in politics to serve the people of this nation. If they are not acting in our best interests, they are there for the wrong reasons.

The political objectives of the Green movement must be reevaluated by the American people. We must demand accountability of our political leaders. We must support those who are dedicated to the principles of the Constitution of the United States. We ought to remove from office those who do not understand the job description.

We do not need to abandon our goal of environmental excellence. We need to recognize how the environmental cause is being used to advance Green Communism in America. We must make more and better distinctions about environmental issues and legislation. We ought to insist that environmental decisions and laws be based on scientific facts and common sense, not Hitler-like Green spiritual politics or pseudo-science.

When making distinctions about environmental issues, we ought to keep in mind, nature is an ever changing, dramatic and unpredictable force. It can be gentle. It can be violent. It can nurture. It can destroy. We can not predict, completely protect, or expect to control nature.

> "Nature has no mercy at all. Nature says, I'm going to snow. If you have on a bikini and no snowshoes, that's tough. I am going to snow anyway."
>
> Maya Angelou
> 1974

Nature controls nature. We ought to be able to use, not abuse our natural resources. We ought to be able to strike a fair and reasonable accord by discouraging extremism and supporting moderation. We need to protect our country and the environment. One doesn't do us much good without the other. The Greens, like the Nazi movement, believe the sacred soil or the environment comes above all else. We need to respond, not react, to Green claims and political demands. The Greens are using most of the exact ideas Hitler used to convince the Germans to join the Nazi movement. The Greens hope Americans will fall victim to the temptations and join the Green movement.

It was too late by the time the world figured out Hitler was insane. The Green idea for us to accept the earth as our Mother, a living organism is not a 'Green original'. It was Hitler's idea to get the German people to abandon their traditional beliefs. Note, Hitler's message:

> *"I address myself to all those, who detached from their mother country...now, with poignant emotion, long for the hour which will permit them to **return to the heart of their faithful mother.**"*
>
> > *Adolf Hitler*
> > Hitler's Ideology - Mein Kampf
> > (Bold Emphasis Added)

Like Lenin and Hitler, the end justifies the means when the goal is political power. Green Communists are working behind our backs to foster revolution. This is indecent, insulting and ought to be considered treason.

We are being 'Set-Up' by Green abuse of environmental issues and 'Sold-Out' one step at a time due to the false perception by our political leaders and others have that the Greens speak for the American people. What other Hitler ideas are on the Greens political agenda hidden under the guise of environmental protection?

Hitler's political program included these points:

- *We demand colonies for settling our surplus population*
- *All citizens shall enjoy equal rights and duties*
- *First duty of a citizen is to work for the common good*
- *We demand that the State take over large businesses*
- *We demand profit sharing in large concerns*
- *We demand land reform*
- *We demand a ruthless struggle against profiteers*
- *We demand our whole system of education be revised*
- *State must provide for the improvement of public health*

Hitler and Nazism
Louis Snyder

Everyone of these demands is included in the Greens political agenda. Like the witch in the forest, if Green promises sound too good to be true, run the other way.

The choice is still ours. We do not have to accept being Sold-Out. We can stand up for reason, use our personal power and work within our political system to push the pendulum back to center.

The Green assault on America has nothing to do with environmental protection. This is about power and control, Green Communist's control of America. Americans are not accustomed to being told what to do or how to raise our children. Are we ready to be told how to live? All these things and more are integrated into the Green political agenda.

The only Americans Green politics won't affect are dead. Americans are famous for an irrepressible independent streak. There may be a few Americans who won't mind the government controlling their lives, then there are the rest of us.

"Forgive your enemies, but never forget their names."
President John F. Kennedy

2

Subvert The Dominant Paradigm

*"In an effort to assess the most significant environmental
events of the year, Earth Journal independently polled 19
environmental and special interest groups, together know as the
Green Group. The CEOs of each group meet roughly once a year
to discuss issues that impact them. The participating groups
believe the Green Group Alliance makes them more effective and
gives them additional lobbying power. Listed below are the
members of the Green Group. "*

- Children's Defense Fund
- Defenders of Wildlife
- Environmental Defense Fund
- Friends of the Earth
- Izaak Walton League of America
- National Audubon Society
- National Parks & Conservation Association
- National Toxins Campaign
- National Wildlife Federation
- Native American Rights Fund
- Planned Parenthood
- Population Crisis Committee
- Sierra Club
- Sierra Club Legal Defense Fund
- Union of Concerned Scientists
- Wilderness Society
- World Wildlife Fund
- Zero Population Growth

1993 Earth Journal

It's A Numbers Game

What matters in Washington is who shows up. Since most of the largest environmental organizations and associated Green groups have headquarters in Washington, D.C., they can show up every day. Americans who live outside the beltway can't physically show up everyday. This is why American's support for any part of the Green movement can be used to show support for other Green political goals. Here's how.

Several different Green groups show up to lobby in favor of the same bill. Each Green group has (x) number of members they represent. Because of the total number of members the Green groups can hold up, it appears to our political leaders, the bill in question has as much voter support as they have members. Big numbers get attention and bills get passed. It doesn't matter if America or the members of those Green groups have a different opinion. If we don't show up or share our opinion with our Congressman or Senator, our opinion doesn't count. This is one reason Green ideas are influencing public policy. The Greens are over $2.5 billion dollars strong with a political lobby that knows how to 'play the game' in Washington D.C. That was Money magazines 1991 estimate, according to the authors of the book, *Trashing the Economy.*

The Greens separate their calls for change so politicians and the public won't see they are part of one political movement. John Rensenbrink, spokesman for the Greens puts it this way:

> *"all the parts of the movement need to be interrelated ...*
> *to have the opportunity to align their strategies with one*
> *another. Alignment of strategies is the creative way forward,*
> *not the integration of strategies. In this way maximum*
> *pressure is applied to the prevailing system dominated by*
> *the oligarchs. It is maximum because it comes from a*
> *variety of sources: the many parts of the movement."*
> (Bold Emphasis Added)

This allows the Greens to promote change in multiple areas. Many little changes are the Green way to quietly force a shift to socialism. It is a step by step process. The Greens are not flamboyant about their victories or associates. It is better for them to work behind the scenes, sneaking their political ideas into legislation here and there. The Greens want to keep America's focus on progressive ideas or environmental doom so we will not recognize Green socialism. This is the Green way to make control possible by making control legal.

Green Quicksand

The Greens pretend the push for social change is coming out-of-the-blue due to America's concern for the environment. When discussing the emergence of Green legislation or Green legislators, Greens create the impression Green politics are just now evolving. They pretend the political goals of the Green Party are not part of the environmental movement. This allows the Greens to use the environmental cause to advance their political goals. John Rensenbrink, national spokesperson for the Greens or Green Committees of Correspondence (GCOC) describes their strategy:

> "Green party organizing committees (and in some cases, full blown party structures) are forming side by side with the movement-centered GCOC. Some say this is a good thing, meaning that party and movement should be strictly separate. **Others argue that the two are essentially one and should be treated that way.**"
>
> (Bold Emphasis Added)

Are most Americans aware of the political goals of the Green party? Do most Americans understand the Green party and the Green movement are one? If not, Americans have been left out on purpose. This way, the Greens can move their political program forward unchallenged. This prevents

Americans from recognizing how, when and who is promoting Green politics. The politics of the Green movement are like quicksand. What seems safe, can be fatal.

> *"Green strategy should include at least three elements; steady alliance-building on the basis of an evolving holistic program that stresses the interconnection of all the issues: grassroots organizing which fosters a Green community in as many locales as possible: **and a working distinction between party and movement.**"*
>
> John Rensenbrink
> (Bold Emphasis Added)

The Greens have built a broad political coalition with a variety of special-interest groups. American's support for environmental protection may inadvertently be showing support for any or all of these parts of the Green movement:

- Environmental Organizations
- Eco-Socialist
- Democratic Socialists of America
- Gay and Lesbian
- Gun Control Groups
- Eco-Terrorist, Monkeywrenchers
- American Indian Rights
- Animal Rights
- Feminist, Eco-Feminist
- Peace Groups
- War Resisters, Amnesty
- Radical Education groups
- Holistic Health and Holistic Education
- Anarchist
- Deep Ecologists, Earth worship, Spiritual Politics
- Mother Earth, Gaia, Goddess spirituality
- Witches, Pagans, Atheist
- Vegetarian Activists
- Population Control

This is a quick study and does not represent all allied groups. The list reveals some of the emotional traps the Greens are using to get political support from different segments of our society. We need to recognize all these interest areas are being targeted to help promote different parts of the Green political program.

> *"The Communists never do anything in their own name that they can do in someone else's."*
>
> John Drakeford
> Red Blueprint for the World

Gil Green is a well-known U.S. Communist who joined the party in 1924. Since that time he's served in a variety of leadership positions for the Communist party. During an interview for the 1993 book, *'New Studies in the Politics and Culture of U.S. Communism'*, Green indicates that several Communist districts split off of the party to:

> *"form **Committees of Correspondence** as a transition form to something new"*

The U. S. Green Party has gone by the name, 'Green Committees of Correspondence' for years. The party just changed its name to the U.S. Greens or Greens.

Green political power is generated by Green propaganda. In addition to lobbying in Washington; the Greens increase local and regional influence using the following methods:

- establish and fund activist groups across the nation
- work together to achieve goals, locally and nationally
- use environmental conferences to brainwash attendees
- use media to spread propaganda
- get Green political messages into entertainment
- sponsor State initiatives

Most of the Green political agenda can be camouflaged as environmental legislation. This allows the Greens to use any subject that can be stretched into an environmental issue and use it to present socialist ideas to protect the environment.

To date, a key factor in the success of Green Communists involves to change America by 'planting ideas' and setting us up to 'think Green' years before they make their move. Specific examples of how the Greens have done this and are doing this are found throughout this book.

The Greens pick a target and then hit it with their combined political power. This is one reason Americans are in trouble. The Greens frame their public image as, 'local environmental group fights industry'. That is what Americans hear on the evening news. What gets deliberately lost in this propaganda is that the big Green groups and their hired guns run the show. What is also conveniently left out is that the Greens are not attacking an entire industry. They are attacking the individual business people that make up the industry. The little guy, the individual American, cannot stand up to the Green onslaught alone.

The Communists targeted the environmental cause years ago and have spent the last 20 plus years developing the best ways to con the American people into accepting socialism. The Greens are using environmental issues to hide a massive land grab. Their goal is control of our land base and control of individual land owners using environmental ruin as the alternative to surrendering control to the federal government.

We do not know to what extent the Communists have infiltrated or established environmental groups. We do not know how many agents are working in key positions within our government. We do not know to what extent environmental issues have been exploited to advance the Communist's objectives.

The Greens have spent time and money (yours) to present their argument on an emotional level. Business and industry organizations attempt to defend themselves from Green accusations by explaining facts. Green Communists do not focus on facts. The Green focus is to 'use our system to bring down our system'. The American people do not understand the way Greens think or that they are being used.

Inner circle slogans, popular among allied Green activists and other progressives within the Green Movement are revealing. Many Americans are not privy to these Green thoughts and feelings. America's support for environmental protection, including financial, may be advancing these political ideas:

- **Die Yuppie Scum**
- Question Authority
- **Go Reds, Smash State**
- **Recycle or Die**
- **Eat the Rich**
- No Compromise in Defense of Mother Earth
- **Sure, I'm a Marxist**
- Stop Treating Our Soil Like Dirt
- No cows
- **Visualize Industrial Collapse**
- Born Again Pagan
- **Ban People for a Safe Future**
- Pregnancy: Just Another Deadly Sexually Transmitted Disease
- Think Globally, Act Locally
- Earth Police, One Planet, One Precinct
- **Alternative: The Greens**
- **Subvert the Dominant Paradigm**

Subvert the Dominant Paradigm? What does that mean? Words that mean the same as, Subvert, Dominant and Paradigm are listed under each word:

Subvert	Dominant	Paradigm
Overthrow	Governing	Model
Destroy	Common	Standard
Ruin	Controlling	Example

Apply the Green slogan, Subvert the Dominant Paradigm to the Green Communist's call for revolution. The political objective remains the same. Overthrow the United States government and destroy the American way of life.

- Overthrow the Governing Model
- Destroy the Common Standard
- Ruin the Controlling Example

Overthrow the Governing Model sounds like a plan, not a suggestion. The Greens present themselves as peace loving but consistently use aggressive language, hint of violence and call for revolution. Peaceful coexistence is not the objective.

Subvert the Dominant Paradigm sounds like the 1948 Communist's attempt to subvert the government of the United States. That subversive effort led to the arrest and imprisonment of Gus Hall and his comrades.

The priorities of Mikhail Gorbachev's environmental organization, Green Cross International include creating a new paradigm for a global civilization.

Too Close For Comfort

Many Americans currently involved in the environmental cause may not know about the Green party or understand the overall objectives of the Green Movement. Other people know exactly what they are doing. There is no excuse for those people, political leaders included, who understand the Green agenda and are using their power to put it in place. Our politicians took an oath. They ought to keep it.

America's national security is threatened because some Greens are positioned within our political system now. Many Greens will run for office as Greens. Most will run as Democrats or Independents with a strong environmental focus. This is dangerous because the American people will not realize they are voting for a Green. It is also dangerous because newly elected Greens would join the existing Green legislators whose political ideas enjoy the political clout of:

- some members of the Clinton Administration
- some Democrats already in office
- some of the largest environmental groups
- some media and entertainment

We need to bring the Greens and the environmental issues out in the open and get the facts to the American people. We need to know who supports what and why.

Green Politicians

Green politicians have been identified by *Voting Green, Your complete environmental guide to making political choices in the 1990's* by Jeremy Rifkin and Carol Grunewald Rifkin. *Voting Green* identifies the following politicians as the: "Green Leadership for the '90s."

SENATE		HOUSE	
Albert Gore	D-TN*	Barbara Boxer	D-CA
John Kerry	D-MA	Ted Weiss	D-NY
Joseph Lieberman	D-CT	Ronald Dellums	D-CA
Claiborne Pell	D-RI	James Scheuer	D-NY
Alan Cranston	D-CA*	Nancy Pelosi	D-CA
Timothy Wirth	D-CO*	Edolphus Towns	D-NY
Patrick Leahy	D-VT	Major Owens	D-NY
Harry Reid	D-NV	Cardiss Collins	D-IL
Brock Adams	D-WA*	John Lewis	D-GA
Daniel Moynihan	D-NY	Peter DeFazio	D-OR
		Wayne Owens	D-UT

THE 'A' LIST (Combined 101st and 102nd Congresses)

Gary Ackerman	D-NY	Edward Markey	D-MA
Chester Atkins	D-MA	Christopher Shays	R-CT
F. (Pete) Stark	D-CA	Barney Frank	D-MA
Peter Kostmayer	D-PA	Robert Mrazek	D-NY
George Brown	D-CA	Thomas Foglietta	D-PA
Howard Wolpe	D-MI	Frank Pallone	D-NJ
Samuel Gejdenson	D-CT	Arthur Ravenel	R-SC
Bernard Dwyer	D-NJ	Gerry Sikorski	D-MN
Charles Bennett	D-FL	Jim McDermott	D-WA
James Jontz	D-IN	Mervyn Dymally	D-CA
Gerry Studds	D-MA	Don Edwards	D-CA
G.Hochbrueckner	D-NY	Andrew Jacobs	D-IN
Mel Levine	D-CA	Norman Mineta	D-CA
Anthony Beilenson	D-CA	Jolene Unsoeld	D-WA

Voting Green - * Retiring

The Clinton administration has filled key positions with well-known members of the Green Team. These individuals stepped away from leadership positions in some of the largest environmental organizations to take a government position. Many Greens have been elected to office. Identifying Green leaders, Green followers and Green ideology is an important part of protecting ourselves and our country.

This book is not about people. It is about people's politics. It is about the duties and responsibilities of those involved in politics and other positions of pubic trust. People who choose a career in politics have a responsibility to let those they represent understand their political position. We cannot decide who to vote for, without these basic facts.

Are these Americans unaware of the Green political agenda and is their personal philosophy clouding fair judgment? Is it political irresponsibility or dereliction of duty? We pay the salaries. We need to know the answers.

The following quotations help us to better understand how the Green political agenda resembles the ideas of some members of the Clinton administration.

> "We believe the concept of national security must be re-examined to include health, education, economics and the health of the natural environment, rather than the present focus on military hardware"
>
> > Greens

> "President Clinton and I are broadening our definition of security in the post-cold war world. Security means having a stable, good-paying job; having clean air to breathe and clean water to drink; raising our families without fear of crime and violence; and preventing conflict in the global community that can result from over population, environmental degradation and famine"

> "we must reinvent environmental protection to protect public health and natural resources"
>
> > Vice President Gore
> > Earth Times, June, 1994

The Greens are promoting the idea that environmental health and public health are the same issues. The reason for linking all environmental issues with public health issues is to give the Greens a universal excuse to completely transform our culture. The point is to mold public opinion to accept that when the Greens insist on rapid changes in the name of public health, Americans will not question the need. Hitler also justified his actions in the name of public health.

It is not wise to give the Greens a blank check. We cannot trust one interest group with the future of our nation. Anything, from the right to smoke or eat beef, to own private property or drive a car could fall into the category of a public health issue. Linking environmental issues to public health issues is a political power play. It is not about environmental health and it is not about public health. It is about making control possible by making control legal.

Greens are also linking equality, national security and having a job to environmental health. Communists believe all citizens ought to be guaranteed the basics: food, job, healthcare and housing. We are starting to see all these issues come to the forefront in American politics. It can be seen in the battle for nationalized healthcare. These ideas are evident in Vice President Gore's statements. This idea is also evident in legislation proposed by Congressman Ron Dellums D-CA. in July, 1995. Congressman Dellums introduced H.R. 1050, *A Living Wage, Jobs for All Act.* The opening sentence of the bill reads:

> *"To establish a living wage, jobs for all policy for the United States in order to reduce poverty, inequality, and the undue concentration of income, wealth, and power in the United States and for other purposes."*

This *'jobs for all policy'* is supposed to reduce poverty and inequality by guaranteeing a job and income for all. Beyond the fact that communism guarantees all citizens a job, healthcare, and set income, how does Dellums propose this could be financed? Congressman Dellums explains:

"this proposal would mandate the transformation of the entire U.S. budget of more than $1.5 trillion into a jobs for all budget."

To change our society into a jobs for all society; Dellums indicates we must change the:

"concentration of income, wealth and power in the United States"

Dellum's bill mandates we transform our entire budget and using over 1.5 trillion to finance his idea. Dellum's requires diffusing the concentration of wealth and power in America. Before the government can redistribute or spread America's wealth around, the government must have access to the citizen's wealth. Unless Americans volunteer to give all their money to the government, the government would have to acquire or seize control of citizen's wealth. The following items are addressed in Dellum's bill.

- distribution of income and wealth
- a wealth inventory
- includes personal wealth
- wages and benefits: urban, suburban and rural

The final statement in the bill reads:

"There are hereby authorized to be appropriated such sums as may be necessary to implement the policies, programs and projects set forth in accordance with this Act."

If our representatives pass this bill, industries and individuals across the nation will have given the government access to their business or personal bank accounts. The last sentence can be interpreted to give the government permission to find and allocate what ever dollars they deem necessary to achieve the objectives listed in this bill. If this bill passed, the result would be the Green goal of economic conversion and more government control of people's lives. The Basic Rights promoted in the bill include the right to:

- earn a living, do a useful job
- adequate income
- adequate medical services
- environmental rights
- quality of life information
- personal security
- shorter work week, work year
- stronger rights for employees to organize
- farmers to produce and sell goods at living wage
- business to trade without unfair competition
- business to trade without domination by monopolies
- every family to have a decent home
- protection from fears of old age, sickness, accidents
- good education

These rights apply to adult Americans who are able and willing to earn a living. Does that mean Americans who are able but not willing to work, are entitled to these rights? Dellums describes the purpose of the act:

> *"One of the basic needs in our lives is a job which will pay us a living wage...It is unrealistic to expect that corporations which are only market oriented will take responsibility for a healthy, national economy"*

Taking a closer look at the idea of socialism, Congressman Dellums is proposing that a job ought to be guaranteed. No one disagrees people need jobs. Communism guarantees jobs. Dellums attacks American corporations for being market oriented and infers if corporations were responsible, his bill would not be necessary. Capitalism is to blame. It is the reason our government needs to pass a law that guarantees everyone a job and a living wage. What Congressman

Dellums seems to be saying is; our society puts profits before people and he wants the government to legally put people before profits. Lenin, the leader of the Russian revolution who established communism successfully used the same idea; 'People not Profit.' The Greens are using the idea, 'People Before Profit'.

> "Today our economy entails nearly total domination by 'for profit' corporate enterprise. The corporate sector has failed to meet human needs and has consistently abused the environment. Therefore, we will work to promote alternative economic structures that put human need ahead of profits and that are accountable to the communities in which they function."
>
> Greens

This bill has all the characteristics of the Green Communism. The May 1995 summary of this bill states:

> "This is a policy measure designed to help nurture an activist movement based on high ideals of democratic human rights and responsibilities."

The movement is the Green movement. It's no wonder the Greens are secretive. Their ideas would be considered un-American by most people in the United States. Green politics are not what Americans imagine or would accept.

Five of the fifteen co-sponsors for Congressman Dellums, 'A Living Wage, Jobs for All Act' were identified by the Rifkins as Green legislators, including Congressman Dellums. The other Green co-sponsors are:

- Nancy Pelosi   D-CA
- Major Owens   D-NY
- Edolphus Towns   D-NY
- Jim McDermott   D-WA

Congressman Dellums also is launching the *'Campaign Against Poverty'* and is working with a coalition of groups to hold hearings across America to draw attention to America's *'Economic Insecurity'* but most of all gain public support for this bill. The coalition includes the Democratic Socialists of America and Americans for Democratic Action.

The focus on helping to end or reduce poverty in America hits anyone in the heart. It can also blind Americans to the magnitude of the ramifications of this bill. Beyond the political objective to access and redistribute citizen's wealth, this bill will serve to help transform our society.

Democratic Socialists

The Democratic Socialists of America (DSA) have been working to build a broad social coalition that includes the Greens. DSA goals include turning America's economy away from capitalism toward a public controlled economy with a focus on environmental issues. DSA's vision is to overturn the existing way America operates. The following quotations are from the DSA brochure:

> *"We're Greens, and we're Socialists too"*

> *"We stand in the traditions of the earliest anti-capitalists rebellions"*

> *"the Green agenda cannot be achieved without a broad social movement that challenges the ideology of profit and free enterprise head-on"*

Lenin challenged profit and free enterprise with 'People Not Profit'. Greens use 'People Before Profit'. Same Stuff, Different Decade. To gain the political power to execute DSA goals, a Green American party would emerge in one of two ways, by:

*"a revived Democratic party, or through the splitting
off of the left-wing Democrats to join a popular mass
movement."*

The Green Party is the left-wing split off. The environmental
movement is the popular mass movement assembled.

*"I think of myself as a hired hit man up against those
right-wing'ers."*

Barbara Ehrenreich
The Progressive -- January 1995

It is hard to understand why those who call for peace have a
violent attitude towards those with different political ideas.
Barbara Ehrenreich is a DSA Honorary Chair, serves on the
DSA Environmental Commission Advisory Board and is a
socialist writer with a regular column in *Time* magazine.

DSA's talking points are like Lenin's and the Greens. DSA's
political goals include:

- economic conversion
- demilitarization
- cooperatives
- community planning
- worker ownership
- decentralization
- shorter work week
- socially useful work
- bottom up, not top down government.

Congressman Dellums 'Living Jobs for All' bill includes most
of the above points and if passed, would achieve the goals of
the Greens, the Democratic Socialists and liberal Democrats.

DSA's political priorities include:

- anti-capitalism
- education
- Earth Day
- industrial conversion
- environmental policy
- post-Communist society
- multi-culturalism
- foreign policy
- eco-spirituality
- national health care
- third party politics
- ecology politics

The following information is from the newsletter of the Democratic Socialists of America. The *EcoSocialist Review* is the newsletter of the environmental commission of DSA. The following articles were featured in the Summer 1990 issue.

- Building EcoSocialism in the 90's
- Prison Notebooks on Earth Day at Wall Street
- Critique of Commodity Consumerism
- Tools for Watermelon Activists

Upcoming events listed in the newsletter included highlights of the upcoming Midwest Academy Retreat sponsored by the Democratic Socialists. Participants and speakers listed for the three day retreat included:

- **Ron Dellums**
- David Dinkins
- **Barbara Mikulski**
- **Pat Schroeder**
- **Jesse Jackson**
- **Al Gore**
- **Edward Kennedy**
- Ruben Zamora
- John Sweeney
- **Jane Fonda**

Ron Dellums	Congressman	D-CA?
Pat Schroeder	Congressman	D-CO?
Al Gore	Senator	D-TN?
Barbara Mikulski	Senator	D-MD?
Edward Kennedy	Senator	D-MA?

Then Senator, now Vice President Gore participated in a Democratic Socialist Retreat? Were our tax dollars used to pay for these representatives to participate? Ron Dellums, D-CA and Major Owens, Congressman D-NY, are members of the Democratic Socialist of America. Congressman Dellums promotes DSA and appears on the DSA brochure. Dellums runs on the Democratic ticket but has referred to himself as a socialist. Congressman Dellums is the Chairman of the Armed Services Committee that oversees America's military establishment. Dellums has a curious reputation. When the military budget comes up for the final vote, he votes against it. The reason given for this Jekel and Hyde performance is he believes in less military funding. It seems that would stagnate our political process and further the Green objective of downsizing our military.

It has been reported that in 1982, Congressman Ron Dellums, Patricia Schroeder and other Congressional representatives were connected to a communist-front organization, the World Peace Council. According to the report, House Intelligence Committee Chairman at the time, Edward Boland, attempted to modify a report to hide this information.

What are Watermelon Activists?

> *"watermelon describes those whose politics are green on the outside and red on the inside, though some add that there are anarchist black seeds scattered throughout."*
> *EcoSocialist Review*
> Summer, 1991

Other events listed included a national health care, radical teacher's conference and the DSA youth conference.

The Spring 1994 edition of the *Eco-Socialist Review* featured a letter from the Sierra Club Legal Defense Fund. The letter attacked private property rights advocates for being concerned about the ramifications of the Endangered Species Act on private property. The Sierra Club called these groups anti-environmentalists and accused them of trying to destroy all environmental laws.

The letter takes the usual approach of blanket condemnation without qualification. It ignores the issue of why citizens are concerned. The Sierra Club Legal Defense Fund letter takes citizen concern and sensationalizes it as an effort to destroy all environmental laws. The allegation is absurd. The exaggeration generates fear or dislike for citizens who are concerned about the language and legal interpretation of some environmental laws. Citizens have good reason to be concerned. The letter from the Sierra Club Legal Defense Fund closes with this statement:

> *"Environmentalists argue that the protection offered by strong, effective environmental law is pro-property rights.* **Restrictions on individual behavior, not only environmental restrictions but also those regarding health, safety, civil rights and consumer affairs ensure that powerful property and business owners may not ignore the rights, including the property rights of others.** *If the so-called property rights or takings movement succeeds, it will be too expensive to implement environmental laws."*
>
> Sierra Club Legal Defense Fund
> (Bold Emphasis Added)

We need to look at the Green goal to gain control of our land base and individual property owners. The Sierra Club Legal Defense Fund is looking for ways to set legal precedents to force government control of private land. That is socialism. The issues outlined by the Sierra Club Legal Defense Fund include; health, safety, civil rights and consumer affairs. These additional issue areas are not about environmental protection. These issues are tossed in to ensure there are more than enough excuses to justify gaining legal control of private property. Make control possible by making control legal.

The political sentiments of the Sierra Club Legal Defense Fund are obvious from the publication their letter appears in. Eco-Socialist are the same as environmental socialist. The Sierra Club Legal Defense Fund, a mainstream environmental group, is working with the Democratic Socialists.

Democratic Socialist, Eco-Socialist

Review the following quotations from the Democratic Socialist brochure.

> "Socialism doesn't mean the government ownership of everything, down to and including the corner store. It does mean social control of such areas of the economy as banking and credit, monopoly industries and natural resources, with decisions being made democratically from the bottom up rather than handed down from on high."

> "We are working to build a new American left that goes beyond traditional liberalism by embracing radical democratic reforms"

> "Through a meaningful social wage, we can collectively guarantee everyone economic survival and dignity ...

> ... traditional liberalism is also inadequate for the task of altering the status quo. It fails to recognize the need to challenge the maldistribution of power and wealth in America and the way key economic decisions are made."

Compare DSA's ideas to these political opinions:

*"I have news for the forces of greed and the defenders
of the status quo: your time has come and gone. It's
time for a change in America."*
> Governor Bill Clinton
> Democratic National Convention -- July, 1992

*"It is time to radically change the way government
operates - to shift from top-down bureaucracy to
entrepreneurial government that empowers citizens
from the bottom up. We must reward the people and
ideas that work and get rid of those that don't."*
> Governor Bill Clinton -- Senator Al Gore
> Revolution in Government - Putting People First

Compare those statements to Green politics:

*"The old politics based on top-down organization and
leaders and followers simply doesn't work... Our strategy
is to build a grassroots democracy from the bottom up... Green
politics calls for a fundamental restructuring of
our political and economic institutions."*
> Greens
> Building a Green Movement in America

Compare all of the above to Lenin's ideas:

"rule from below, not from above"
> The Sealed Train

*"The Bolsheviks were proclaiming the only program that the
masses could support: peace, land, and bread , and all power to
the Soviets"*
> Journey Into Revolution

Lenin's Bolshevik party promised peace bread and land for
all. He promised to transfer ruling power from the capitalists
and give decision making power to the people. Lenin
promised people rule from below not from above. He lied.

Lenin professed the end of capitalism was the only way to solve the people's problems. Lenin, shared these ideas for public control in his *April Theses:*

- public control of production and distribution
- dismantling the army and bureaucracy
- confiscation of all private lands for shared ownership
- rule from below, not from above
- public control of banking
- no support for the existing government

The Greens are using the same ideas to trick the American people into believing our environmental future depends on abandoning our culture, changing our government and overthrowing capitalism.

Is it just a coincidence the language and ideas of, Lenin, the Greens, the Democratic Socialist and some members of the Clinton administration are almost exactly the same? Shouldn't we ask?

The Mexican Bail Out

We need to begin again to take politics personally and pay attention to political issues. From environmental issues to economics, we can't complain, if we don't get involved. Political decisions impact our lives and our pocketbook. If we don't want to spend more money, we have to say so. We can't hold our political leaders accountable if we don't make sure they know exactly what we agree and disagree with.

Consider the recent $20 Billion dollar loan to Mexico.

The February 13, 1995, edition of *Time* magazine carried the headline:

> *"Clinton rescues the Mexican economy - and finds a bold new way to circumvent Congress."*

President Clinton used the power of executive order to guarantee Mexico's $20 Billion dollar loan. Regarding the use of executive order, the authors of the article Bob Cohn and Bill Turque point this out about President Clinton's action:

> *"But as the Mexican bailout suggest, he is looking for a different way to govern, flexing what executive muscle the office provides."*

Executive orders are not new. Presidents use them. If executive orders are Clinton's *'new way to govern'* then we have a problem. The people of the United States sent new representatives to Washington for a reason. They wanted change. If President Clinton did not get agreement from those representatives on this massive financial commitment, then he is ignoring the people of this nation and dictating policy.

Time included another article on the Mexican bail out titled: 'Why the Mexican Crisis Matters'. Author Michael Elliott states:

> *"the Mexican mess is an example of the kind of economic crisis that will increasingly become the focus of U.S. foreign policy in the post-cold-war era."*

If we are expected to pay for bail-outs in the future, we ought to be part of the decision making process. Continued financial extravagance could force this nation into poverty. The *'Communist Rules for Revolution'* include:

'encouraging government extravagance to destroy its credit'

According to a March, 1995 news brief, President Clinton signed an executive order preventing companies from replacing striking workers permanently. This means workers have a right to strike without fear of losing their jobs.

> *"The right to strike must be treated as an inherent right"*
> Communist Party of the United States - 1969

Without regard for the public interest or America's national security, workers 'rights' are to be the first concern. Basically, this executive order treats striking as an inherent right.

> *"We cannot put people first and create jobs and economic growth without a revolution in government."*
> *Governor Bill Clinton - Senator Al Gore*
> A Revolution in Government - Putting People First

There is a difference between using terms like reinvent and revolution and meaning them.

> ***"The line and policies presented in this resolution are a guide to the day-to-day work of our Party. In applying these policies, we should never lose sight of our strategic and ultimate goals.*** *They are intertwined elements, and both are present at all stages* ***as the struggle for social progress moves inevitably on the path toward socialism and communism."***
> *Communist Party of The United States of America*
> (Bold Emphasis Added)

The long term Communist's goal is to carefully and quietly move Americans toward socialism. The first step to communism is socialism. It is critical to understand how the Communists use socialism to achieve communism.

John Drakeford, author of *Red Blueprint for the World*, describes two kinds of socialism. This author summarized Drakeford's explanation to clarify how Communists use socialism to manipulate citizens into a position to force them into communism.

According to Drakeford, Utopian socialism occurs when all private property becomes public property and the profits generated from the property are shared equally among the people. Drakeford defines the next form, the Communist's version, as Scientific socialism. Drakeford indicates Scientific socialism occurs during the shift from one government system to the other.

If the United States shifted from a capitalist system with a democratic government to a socialist system, a temporary, centralized, government would have to be formed to handle government affairs until the transition to the new government system was complete. The transition period is when members of the oppressed masses believe they will start to control their government and their lives.

At this time, when the government would be disorganized, the nation would be weak and the masses would be struggling to adjust, the Communists use force and violence to seize power. Scientific socialism is only a brief, interim stage followed directly by the Communist dictatorship. Communist dictatorships don't have laws to protect people from brutal government actions. Once in power, all actions carried out by the dictatorship; from food rationing to mass murder are justified for the greater good. For the greater good, people are forced to:

- do what the government dictates they do
- live how the government dictates they live
- earn what the government thinks they are worth

Scientific socialism includes the idea that people who produce more, can have more. This makes Scientific socialism sound and feel like capitalism so it will appeal to capitalists. The Green version of Scientific socialism is being promoted in the alternative press. It's called, *ParEcon,* short for *Participatory Economics.* The basic ideas of *ParEcon* are:

> *"...an equitable and viable economy designed to minimize self-advancement that is socially counter productive...*
>
> *...ensure that people who live better than others do so only by having undergone personal sacrifice...*
>
> *...there are participatory councils of workers and consumers at various levels, work is divided among balanced job complexes...*
>
> *...One is paid according to one's effort not according to one's output or one's control of the means of production...*
>
> *...economic justice requires that no one be 'free' to appropriate more goods and services than warranted by their personal sacrifice."*

Peter Crawford
Common Future

Karl Marx, shares a similar idea in the, *Communist Manifesto,* he states:

> ***"In a higher phase of communist society*** *..only then can the narrow horizon of bourgeois right to be fully left behind and society inscribe on its banners: **from each according to his ability, to each according to his needs.**"*
>
> (Bold Emphasis Added)

Bourgeois means capitalists. The Communist's goal is to destroy capitalism and leave it behind. Communism operates on the idea; people work to their best ability and in return receive what has been determined they need. *ParEcon,* promotes the same concept. People would be compensated based on their effort but someone else would determine what their compensation will be. With *ParEcon,* no citizen is free to acquire more than is determined they have earned. *ParEcon* also fits with the Green idea to do socially useful work. *ParEcon* stresses working for the good of the people not for personal profit. Socially useful work is what communist workers do.

How does the Communist promise to empower the people of a nation lead to the Communists taking control of the people and the nation? Communists use the *'bait and switch'* strategy. The Communists *bait* people with promises and *switch* the rules when they are ready to take power. The first phase of a Communist revolution involves mentally preparing the people to believe socialism is the best solution to their problems.

The Set Up...Advance Propaganda

Communists promote socialism by degrading capitalism. To prove to the people that change is necessary, the Communists must devalue capitalism. Communists magnify anything negative about capitalism. They use some of the following tactics to mentally prepare the masses to think socialism is better. Communists attack society from all angles by:

- criticizing traditional values
- creating social conflicts to disrupt society
- helping masses feel sorry for themselves, victims
- directing citizen anger toward system of government
- promising socialism will give the masses a better life
- introducing socialist ideas as only solution

The Bait

After the Communists have deliberately created citizen unrest, they start promoting the following ideas and promises to take care of the frustrated masses:

- public control of economy and government
- equality, no more class distinctions, share wealth
- the basics; food, shelter, job, income and healthcare

Citizens buy into these ideas because the current system seems to be falling apart (due to their deliberate disruptions). The Communists set the masses up to think:

- they want or need to be taken care of
- new government system would be for the greater good
- present government system is to blame for all problems

Communists create discontent and blame the capitalist system to lure the masses into socialism. The Greens plan to keep America uptight and misinformed until they are ready to emerge as our political salvation.

> *"The Greens have built carefully for years. They've been busy laying the foundations of a strong social movement...*
>
> *...They are now in a position to build rapidly for transformation. They can decisively assist a society in search of answers to overwhelming problems of ecology, democracy, and justice."*
>
> *John Rensenbrink*
> Greens National Spokesperson, 1992
> (Bold Emphasis Added)

The Switch

Communists lie to the masses. Communists promise citizens complete equality. What the Communists forget to mention is that freedom gets lost in the translation. Equality under communism means, all slaves are created equal.

The Green Bait

A key obstacle for the Communists was how to approach, justify and promote an economic conversion in the United States. Even with all the attack strategies outlined in the *Communist Rules for Revolution*, the Communists had to find some other compelling reason for Americans to consider socialism. What kind of a scam could work in a country where independence is king? A scam that would:

- not be suspected or recognized as socialism
- direct anger towards fellow Americans
- justify more government control
- hit us in the heart
- appeal to our sense of duty, of right a wrong

Protecting the environment and saving the earth for future generations fits the bill. This is the Green *bait*. It is a compelling reason to consider an economic conversion from capitalism to socialism. The Greens are playing off the fear of environmental ruin to persuade Americans that only drastic change will save the earth.

Many Americans have accepted the idea. This is not because Americans are ignorant. It is because Americans are being manipulated. The emotional hooks the Greens are using are powerful, not factual. We need to make more, better and constant distinctions between environmental protection and efforts to advance Green politics. Multiple calls for drastic change in America can be traced back to Green politics.

The environmental movement offers Green Communists many opportunities to quietly weave socialist ideas into America's public policies. The Greens are using every opportunity to magnify anything negative about capitalism, our way of life, individual freedom and independent thinking to diminish American values. Some basic rights now under attack by the Greens are:

- property rights
- food choices
- right to bear arms

The Greens have created compelling reasons for the American masses to consider major changes. The hook is survival. It is the reason many Americans are going along with Green ideas without qualifying the information. The Greens are tying environmental protection to public health issues and human survival to changing our values. Private property is a key American value. The Greens are tying human survival to environmental protection to change our independent attitude about property ownership. They are using 'fear of extinction' because it is the path of least resistance. The Greens need Americans to 'accept' socialist land-use policies will be better for the environment. They are using *Chicken Little* messages to scare Americans into socialism.

The Green Switch

The Green *switch* will occur if Americans allow the Greens to warp our judgment to believe Socialism is the only way to avoid their alleged environmental disaster. If we allowed that to happen, a transition from our current government and economic system would need to occur. Then, Americans would be at the scientific socialism point and the Communists could make their move to seize power.

The Greens are aggressively working to influence Americans to replace our idea of private property rights with the Green idea of intellectual property rights. The Green excuse to end private property ownership is placing all lands under government control will ensure environmental excellence. That is socialism and a major step toward Green communism. The Greens promote their calls to end private property rights in America using general messages like these:

- Americans can't be trusted to own property, too much risk
- Americans don't care and are destroying the environment
- the public (government) ought to control the land
- survival depends on abolishing private property

Americans are well known for fierce pride of ownership and for placing a high value on private property rights. The above statements are absurd, but they fit *the sky is falling* Green way to mold public opinion. Fear of environmental disaster coupled with promises of a utopian wonderland is the Green way to persuade Americans we must change our values and accept government control of our lands for the greater good. This is what happened with the Spotted Owl issue.

Why are the Greens really attacking private property ownership instead of focusing on pressing environmental issues? If we put our emotions on hold, we see survival is not really the Greens objective. It is the Greens excuse.

> *"The theory of Communists may be summed up in the single sentence: Abolition of private property."*
> *Karl Marx*

The critical difference between capitalism and communism is the right to own private property. Karl Marx is the author of the *Communist Manifesto*, a book likened to the Communist's bible. Marx makes the political motivation behind the Green attack on private property clear.

Keeping our emotions on hold; consider how the Greens are using issues like Endangered Species, Wetlands and Ecosystem Management to set Americans up to accept the end of private property. Americans need to realize this is the top priority for the Greens. We are in serious trouble because the Green movement is also a powerful political lobby. They are pushing hard to increase the power of government (public) control and decrease the rights of individual Americans. We have reached a distress point and we must start protecting each other's property rights.

How are the Greens manipulating environmental issues to abolish private property rights? The Green calls to protect and manage entire ecosystems is a good example. We need to look at the Green term, ecosystem. What does it mean? A rough definition of an ecosystem is, everything that lives within a given geographical area and how each piece of the system interacts with other pieces. An ecosystem means everything, living or dead. It includes all species, insect, animal, vegetation, the air, soil and water.

Author Jeremy Rifkin; a well-known leader in the Green Movement, explains the Green position on ecosystems and land ownership in his book *Bioshpere Politics*. Rifkin states:

"The very idea of private ownership of part or all of an ecosystem is inimical to biospheric political thinking."

Inimical means adverse, hostile or opposite. That means, private property ownership conflicts or is the opposite of biosphere politics. The opposite of private is public.

"Only by placing ecosystems in public trusts will it be possible to reverse the process of rampant short term exploitation of the environment"

Rifkin is using environmental protection as the Green excuse to switch from private to public ownership of land in America. Rifkin's biosphere politics, Green politics and Communist politics all share that political objective. Public ownership is 'inimical' or opposite of our American tradition.

Rifkin uses many interesting terms throughout his book; like *fellow traveler* and *bourgeoisie*. *Fellow traveler* is a phrase used by Communists when referring to comrades who travel the same political path. Rifkin uses *bourgeoisie* to define American capitalists. Karl Marx used *bourgeoisie* to define capitalists in the *Communist Manifesto*.

Ecosystem management is a Green priority because it creates the opportunity to justify government (public) control of large areas of land. To set aside vast habitat areas, private property rights will be an issue. The ecosystem management idea allows the Greens to:

- designate any area, anywhere as critical habitat
- justify 'taking' private property
- play the survival card over and over again
- make control possible by making control legal
- transform our society
- eliminate private property rights

Do Americans need to take Green ideas seriously? Yes.

"We must promote the preservation and extension of wildlife habitat by creating and preserving large continuous tracts of open space (complete ecosystems)"
                                                                Greens

"adopt ecosystem management as a comprehensive,
coordinated approach to protecting the natural environment
rather than have several agencies operating."

Vice President Al Gore
Earth Times - June, 1994

"Remove the U.S. Forest Service from under the Agriculture
Department, place USFS, the Bureau of Land Management,
and the Fish and Wildlife Service under the Environmental
Protection Agency."

Environmental Groups
Earth Island Survey - 1991

The idea of ecosystem management has the support of the Greens, Vice President Gore and environmental groups. Ecosystem management involves basing all our decisions, from political to economic around one view of nature. Beyond ecosystem management is the idea to form one government agency to handle all environmental issues.

Coordinating environmental efforts would actually eliminate the checks and balances that come from the shared power and the different viewpoints of multiple agencies. This is not a good idea. It would create a Green environmental dictatorship with the authority of the federal government. This would be a big mistake. Too much power corrupts.

Private property ownership is the key distinction between communism and capitalism. Independence vs. Dependence, Freedom vs. Slavery and Opportunity vs. Poverty are also key distinctions between the two systems of government.

The Greens are aggressively working to give the government more control over property owners by seeking to increase the power of the Endangered Species Act. This act already offers the Greens multiple ways to erode property rights. Fortifying this act would create unlimited excuses to destroy every American's private property rights, urban and rural. The

Greens advocate no private ownership locally, nationally or internationally. It sounds like global Green Communism.

Are the Greens enjoying any success in eroding private property rights in America. Yes, absolutely, no doubt about it. A recent example is found in the Supreme Court case decision of Babbitt, et.al. v. Sweet Home Chapter of Communities for a Great Oregon. According to the Summary Judgment of July 7, 1995, by William Perry Pendley, President and Chief Legal Officer of the Mountain States Legal Foundation:

> "the Court had decided, by a vote of 6-3, that federal regulations, which interpret the word 'harm' in the Endangered Species Act as prohibiting 'habitat modification' on private property, are 'reasonable' and therefore legal."

Pendley explains the ramifications of this decision:

> "I think what the Supreme Court did was say to the property owners of America who have land on which endangered species might be found, Mr. Babbitt, Secretary of the Interior, is now your landlord."

What does it mean to the American people? According to Pendley, the decision means:

> "The Supreme Court's ruling gives the federal government power over the two-thirds of the country that is privately owned. Now the U.S. Fish and Wildlife Service will move aggressively to enforce regulations that define 'harm' as habitat modification', a definition that includes actions that impair essential biological patterns..." As if this weren't vague enough, **the landowner need only intend to perform the act (plow the field, cut the trees) not intend to harm the species, to be criminally liable."**
>
> (Bold Emphasis Added)

These rulings affect all Americans, in one way or another. We foot the bill. These are the kinds of rulings that make control possible by making control legal. This is not to say we don't need to protect wildlife habitat. The Greens are using the Endangered Species Act to achieve their goal to end private property ownership by ending private property rights.

An article in the February 1995 edition of the *San Joaquin County Citizens Land Alliance* illustrates the impact of the Endangered Species Act or ESA. The article reads:

> *ESA Cost: $413,774 Per Fly*
>
> *The Endangered Species Act (ESA) as applied to the construction of the San Bernadino County Medical Center resulted in an expenditure of $3,310,199 to mitigate for the presence of eight (8) Delhi Sands Flower-Loving Flies. The effort as negotiated with the U.S. Fish and Wildlife Service and California Department of Fish and Game resulted in moving and redesigning the facility to provide 1.92 acres of protected habitat for eight flies **believed to occupy the site**. Cost per fly amounted to $413,774.25 and resulted in a one year construction delay. This cost is equivalent to the average cost of treatment of 494 inpatients or 23,644 outpatients.*
>
> California Forest Today - December 1994
> (Bold Emphasis Added)

The use of the phrase *'believed to occupy the site'* ought to indicate to us that all this was done without absolute proof. Is this stewardship or deliberate sabotage of the project? We need to examine all the pieces of the ESA puzzle. Does this species exist or flourish in other parts of the United States? How many were there? How many are left?

The Greens focus on one species (like the eight flies) at a time because it is costly and disruptive, not because they care about the flies. Imagine the ripple effect of the Supreme Court ruling regarding the meaning of 'harm' in the Endangered

Species Act. Heaven forbid we should swat or even think about swatting a fly before checking to see if it is a Delhi Sands Flower-Loving Fly.

What if the Greens said eight flies were 'believed to occupy' your backyard? What if federal regulations prevented further use of that area. Imagine, no more family barbecues or mowing the lawn because it might disturb the flies. It might be a good excuse to let the yard go for a while but would it be reasonable in the long term? No, it would make life difficult. People and flies have been coexisting for years, but this illustrates no one is exempt. All landowners can be impacted by extreme Green regulations. Pendley made it clear in his summary judgment on the Supreme Court ruling, he stated:

> "...the landowner need only intend to perform the act (plow the field, cut the trees), not intend to harm the species, to be criminally liable."

Everyone who owns property or plans to own property could be in the same position as a farmer who can't plan to plow, let alone, plow their field. We must realize, before it is too late, the Greens intend to end private property ownership. This is not about environmental health. This is about controlling the American people and taking control of the land base. The ESA is just one more way the Greens are making control possible by making control legal. Why are extreme interpretations of the law finding support? One reason is the Greening of the Judges. The Environmental Law Institute began holding law conferences in 1991. An article in *E magazine, 'First, Green the Judges'* outlined the organization's plan to educate judges on:

- Wetlands identification
- Scientific topics
- Retroactive liability
- New laws
- Legal land use issues
- Basic geology
- New Scientific Concepts

This amounts to programming judges to render Green judgments on environmental issues. It is not equal representation if the judges have received their instructions in advance from a biased group. Judgments are supposed to be rendered after evaluating facts and circumstances presented by both sides in the dispute.

The Greens are using our legal system as a political hammer. Teaching judges how to correctly interpret the law to advance Green politics ought to be illegal. Isn't fixing a court case the same as fixing a horse race? If the Greens know how the Judge will rule in advance, isn't that the same as knowing how the race will turn out? The Judge's integrity is not the question. The Greens have set them up and can con them as easily as the next guy.

> *"Lobbying is the art of forcing a specific change in attitude, legislation or government policy. This can be done on the streets and through the media in campaigns aimed at creating the climate where a decision-maker has no choice but to make the decision you're lobbying for. Or it can be done through the courts and no-one does it better than the Natural Resources Defense Council (NRDC), widely considered the most effective lobby and litigating group on US environmental issues."*
> *State of the Ark*

The founding fathers studied other governments before they crafted our government. They designed a check and balance system to give citizens the power to protect their freedom. They understood people who wanted to live free would have to protect their rights and defend the land they love.

> *"You are now the guardians of your own liberties"*
> *Samuel Adams*
> Philadelphia - 1776

Personal freedom offers individuals hope and potential. The right of privacy, the ability to own property and the chance to prosper offers pride, security and creativity. People who are free to speak and think are also free to be innovative.

People who operate by the ethic of working together are more courteous to others. Good people, freedom and our system of government are the reasons America grew into a great nation and a superpower. America still stands as the beacon of hope to people around the globe. If we intend to preserve freedom for our children and keep America intact, we, the people, need to become a stronger voice in Washington, D. C.

Save the Earth, by Jonathon Porritt is a series of worldwide environmental issues and stories. It includes multiple inspirational environmental quotations by influential people such as; Ted Turner (who published the book), Senator Al Gore, Robert Redford, Carl Sagan, Petra Kelly (former Green Party Leader), the Prince of Wales and Jeremy Rifkin. Rifkin's quotation explains the new politics understands the Earth is a living organism. He states:

> **"The new politics envisions the Earth as a living organism and the human species as a partner** and participant, dependent on the proper functioning of the biosphere...**the transition to the biospheric culture will spell the end to the nation state as the dominant political institution and the end of the multi-national corporation as the primary economic institution. The biospheric era will spawn political and economic arrangements** more in keeping with our new ecological understanding of the Earth as a living organism."
>
> (Bold Emphasis Added)

Getting Americans to accept the earth is a living organism or being is critical to the Greens. Relating to the earth as a living being with human like qualities would change the way we view politics. It would advance the Green goal of mixing environmental protection and Green spiritual politics.

Compare Rifkin's political ideas to the following political ideas.

"In place of ...the State ...must be set the living organism ...of the people"

"Economics...is a living process, one of the functions of that body which is the people"

"From a dead mechanism (the state) there must be formed a living organism"

"Our movement alone was capable of creating a national organism"

"The task...was to build up the entire administration...until it became a close organic whole, pulsing with life"

Although they sound Green, all the above statements were made by Adolf Hitler. He used the same ideas to entice the German people to believe, as he did, that Germany was a living organism. He transformed public life and government to reflect his political ideas. The book, *Hitler's Ideology*, by Richard Koenigsberg, outlines these and many other phrases Hitler used. The above statements are from: *The Speeches of Adolf Hitler* and *Mein Kampf.*

Hitler's idea to build a government or administrative system around that living organism or earth is very similar to Vice President Gore's call for the earth to be our political focus:

"The task of saving the earth's environment must and will become the central organizing principle of the post-Cold War world"

Green ideas sound exactly like Nazism. Hitler indicates from the death of the state, a living organism will be formed. Rifkin indicates the end of the nation state will make way for the new politics. The Greens are using the same words and ideas to achieve their goal to gain government control of the American people and our land base. Same stuff, different decade. We need to remember Hitler was a psychopath.

Transform the Values of American Life

The transformation of the values of American life is not about environmental health and well being. Many more specific political goals are outlined in the Green Party Program, like banning CFC producing products. Some products that contain or use CFC's when manufactured are listed below:

- Bronchial-inhalant
- Cameras
- Copy Machines
- Eyeglass lenses
- Freezers
- Radios
- Telephones
- Tobacco - Low tar
- Vending machines
- Calculators
- Contact Lenses
- Dishwashers
- Heat Pumps
- Microwaves
- Smoke alarms
- Televisions
- VCR's
- Washers and Dryers

We are all willing to make sacrifices. Most of us can live without these items. Some Americans can't. Before these products are banned, shouldn't we have some additional information?

Which of these products produce the most CFC's and which ones produce the least? What are the latest findings? How many scientists believe we have an ozone problem and why? How many scientists disagree and why? Before our political leaders take any drastic steps based on Green propaganda, the American people have a right to full disclosure. They deserve the facts and the answers to these basic questions.

More Green goals to transform our society include:

- eliminate private automobiles
- terminate trucking
- **shut down most airports**
- **eliminate the military establishment**
- end chemical production
- **abolish the arms industry**
- reduce meat consumption
- **organize communities around communes**
- **limit production and distribution of goods to local area**
- limit products and services to local areas

Are these the best and only ways to effectively address our environmental problems? The time to ask these questions is now, before we transform our lives and eliminate these businesses. The Greens are pushing the panic button to get people and politicians to support taking steps toward these objectives.

A good example of how Green politics work is the push to impact the trucking industry. Lately, we have been deluged with media reports that present negative images of trucking practices and truck drivers. From running triples to drug abuse and rear trailer design; the trucking industry is another industry that has been put on the Green hot-seat. The question is, are these reports accurate? Is the intent to improve safety or is it a Green con job to destroy interstate commerce?

Three Green goals are advanced by these negative reports. First, generate public concern and support. Second, by presenting this as a public health issue, both safety and environmental issues can be used to cripple the industry. Third, the Greens gain control over the production and distribution of more goods and services. If truckers can't haul, the Greens take control over a key part of our distribution process. If truckers can't deliver goods across this nation, the Greens, have moved closed to their goal of limiting production and distribution to the local area.

The threat of environmental collapse is only one excuse the Greens are using to set Americans up to surrender control of production and distribution. Controlling production and distribution is how Communism works.

Who decides what American businesses are acceptable? The free market used to be the determining factor in which businesses failed and which were successful. Sound science and the opinion of the majority ought to be considered. Here are some other opinions on the subject of free enterprise.

> "The Federal Government is the largest purchaser of goods and services in the world, and we are committed to using that massive purchasing power to spur markets for environmental technologies, save taxpayer's money and lead by example."
>
> Vice President Al Gore
> Earth Times, June, 1994

> "boycotting socially and ecologically destructive businesses."
> Green Party Program

Choosing to buy from one business and not to buy from another has the same effect as boycotting a business. Is our government now deciding what is and is not an acceptable business? Are our tax dollars being used to put Americans out of business?

Using the power of government to boycott business owners is not new. Hitler used government power to separate the Jews from the rest of society by boycotting Jewish businesses. Nazi soldiers were used to prevent patrons from entering Jewish shops. Government boycotts of certain businesses is not a good idea.

Tolerance Or Intolerance?

How did Hitler train his army to assault innocent people? It all started in the name of the Nazi cause. Nasty remarks led to vandalism. Rocks through shop windows led to beatings. Hitler also threatened to kill people. The injustices escalated from there.

Isolated incidents became a regular part of German life until terrorism became the norm. Terrorism is not a good thing to condone. Nazi terrorism grew into control without conscience.

Hitler started out by promoting the idea that Jews were different than other Germans. He kept adding lies to that idea until he successfully labeled the Jews sub-human. Soon, normal people began to treat the Jews like they were sub-human. He separated the Jews from the rest of society, first mentally, then physically. Hitler gave people permission to be aggressive and mean.

The Holocaust is not only the result of Hitler's ideas, it is the result of the people who followed his ideas. If no one followed, he would not have had the power to carry out his ideas. The people of that nation allowed their standards to be eroded. They allowed themselves to ignore senseless acts committed against their fellow citizens. They allowed themselves to become barbaric, uncivilized animals. They followed the politically correct behavior of the day. Normal people became mean-spirited Nazis who justified what they were doing was necessary and right.

Most Americans are familiar with the David Koresh incident and the Randy Weaver episode. What many Americans don't realize is that other Americans are also under siege.

Some individuals who were hired to serve and protect the American people are operating outside of the law. Perhaps they feel what they are doing is right, but it can not continue to go unchecked. We need to pay attention to hostile actions against innocent people.

The following story was featured in the June 1995 issue of the *San Joaquin County Citizens Land Alliance:*

> *"Last May, A Bureau of Alcohol, Tobacco and Firearms (BATF) squad showed up at the home of gun-show promoters Harry and Theresa Lamplugh. When Mr. Lamplugh asked the BATF agent (most of whom did not wear identifying vests) if they had a search warrant, an agent stuck an MP-5 submachine gun in his face and told him, "Shut the f---up, motherf----r. Do you want more trouble than you already have?" During the six-hour search, BATF agents refused to allow the Lamplughs to get dressed. The search squad held a pizza party in the middle of the search, stomped a housecat to death, spilled Mr. Lamplugh's cancer medicine on the floor, and seized 61 guns, along with the Lamplugh's birth certificates, marriage certificate, medical records, business contact lists and personal mail. **To date, the Lamplughs have not been charged with any crime, or even told that they are suspected of any crime, but the Federal Government has refused to return their property.***
>
>
>
> National Review
> March 1995
> (Bold Emphasis Added)
>
>

This doesn't sound like something we expect to hear about in the United States of America. It sounds like illegal use of government force. How many Americans has this happened to? Where do we draw the line? Who is responsible?

According to the article: *Yeltsin's eyes and ears,* featured in the August 7, 1995 edition of *U.S. News & World Report,* Russia's KGB or secret police have regained their authority to:

'arrest and interrogate suspects for days or weeks without bringing a formal charge...the rejuvenation of the secret police occurred in the name of fighting crime and corruption.'

The BATF agents are not alone in stepping over the line. Other government agencies are arming their agents with semi-automatic weapons to question or arrest unarmed, normally law abiding citizens. The justification for this extreme display of force are environmental accusations or disputes. Not all BATF or other government agents are hostile individuals. These agencies need to reevaluate the need for such aggressive actions against innocent people.

The Greens are abusing the environmental cause as an excuse to ruin Americans financially, terrorize people and cause others to lose their way of life and their property. Animal rights issues are another Green excuse to gain control over the private lives of Americans. One poor old gentleman was fined for killing a sewer rat in his back yard. The Humane Society sited him for murdering the rat in an inhumane fashion.

These are the same kind of absurdities people ignored in Germany. Green ideology is not flexible or reasonable. It is to the point of beyond ridiculous. Why are we putting up with this? If we do not bring the Greens under control, it will only continue to get worse.

All legislation; from the crime bill to the Endangered Species Act, that will give the Greens or government agencies more power to control our lives or nullify our rights ought to be brought before the people. We can't afford to allow our political leaders to let Green legislation slide by under the guise of environmental protection. We are at a pivotal point. The Greens, like Hitler, intend to make control possible, by making control legal. We have to get personally involved to stop that from happening. Our government system is not the problem. Human error is to blame for the challenges facing the American people. It is the politics of the people we have allowed to gain positions of power and influence. We, the people, must take responsibility for our future by taking responsibility for the future of this country.

> "We a civilized, humane people, had allowed ourselves to become indifferent to brutality committed by our own government on our own citizens. At best, that seemed to make us cowards, at worst brutes ourselves."
>
> Alfons Heck
> A CHILD OF HITLER

Alfons Heck grew up with the Nazi movement. He was a leader in the Hitler Youth. Alfons describes his life in his book, *A Child of Hitler*. He shares his despair that people did not try and stop Hitler. He blames the people for allowing themselves to be taken in by Hitler's lies. He blames parents for sacrificing their children to the Nazi movement. He blames teachers who worked with Hitler and lied to the children about the Jewish people. He blames the people for not protecting the children.

The Hitler Youth were taught Nazism was their new age. It was Hitler's new order. Greens refer to our future in similar terms; calling for a New World Order and for a New Age in the 21st century. Hitler said, One People, One Nation. The Greens say 'One People, One Planet.' Same stuff, different decade.

Why didn't the people stop Adolf Hitler? History reminds us, the fate of a nation depends on the strength and will of its people. We have enjoyed the benefits of freedom and we share the duty to pass that legacy on to the next generation and they the next. We have nothing to lose by challenging the Green Movement. We have everything to lose by closing our eyes and ignoring the Greens.

There is safety in numbers. At first, there were more regular citizens than there were Nazis. If the majority of the American people stand together, the minority will be forced to listen.

Eco-Terrorism

The Greens have another approach to crippling businesses and affecting the economy of this nation. It's called Eco-terrorism and it's on the rise in America. The Nazis also used terrorism and destroyed Jewish businesses in the name of the cause. It became routine. The Greens profess to be nonviolent, but they don't condemn monkeywrenching or Eco-Terrorism. Both these terms describe actions of sabotage or terrorism executed under the guise of environmental protection.

Recreation is another industry under attack by the Greens. From snowmobilers' to horseback riding, the Greens want to control these industries by controlling the individuals who enjoy the sports and buy the products. The Greens work all the angles, lobbying, limiting access to the recreation areas these Americans go to relax and committing acts of violence.

If the Greens don't want people to use a certain outdoor area, they invent ways to discourage the recreational activity. For instance, one monkeywrenching activity involves stringing piano wire across mountain trails to trip riders on horseback. Recently a horse tripped, sending both horse and rider down a steep hillside. The woman was hurt and her horse had to be destroyed.

This random act of meanness cannot be justified. What if the woman had died? Her death would not have been an accident. What is the difference between this act of eco-terrorism and pre-meditated murder?

Monkeywrenchers go by the book. Dave Foreman, founder of the well known eco-terrorist group Earth First co-authored *Eco-Defense, A Field Guide to Monkeywrenching*. The book details what to do and how to commit terrorists acts. Of course since the disclaimer says the book is a joke, no legal action is taken.

Monkeywrenchers ambush motorcycle riders by spreading nails on roads and placing spiked railroad ties inside tunnels so the riders will crash. Eco-terrorists also hammer spikes into trees so a logger's chainsaw or millsaw will hit it and cause serious damage. These acts of violence are promoted as a real 'high' for those who participate in sabotage activities.

Earth First publicly stated in April 1990, that they would stop spiking trees, but they lied. The March 1991 edition of *Earth First Journal* revealed a different thought. The statement was; *"don't forget the (f-ing) spikes"*.

The Nazi cause gave people this same sense of false glory. Committing violent acts against innocent people was justified in the name of protecting the sacred soil. The Nazis set out to cleanse their German soul and rid the earth of undesirable people. The Nazis were on a power trip too and they went power crazy.

The environmental cause is being used to get people involved in the same kind of power trip. The Greens are encouraging a similar level of intolerance toward the American people. Eco-Terrorists commit acts of violence, terrorism and harassment in the name of saving the sacred soil of Mother Earth. The

Nazis committed acts of violence, terrorism and harassment in the name of saving the sacred soil of the Fatherland. The Green Movement is cultivating hate against our own people in the name of Mother Earth. Same Stuff, Different Decade.

Wrong is wrong, right is right. We can not let this slide. When they came for the Jews, no one came to their aid. The rest is history. What is the difference between these violent attacks on American citizens and the initial Nazi attacks on the Jewish people?

As a society we can not continue to ignore these actions in the name of the Green environmental cause. The Greens official political position is, they do not condemn Eco-terrorism. Creative sabotage is an individual decision. If the Greens were really non-violent they would condemn violence. Peaceful, tolerant, conflict resolution does not resemble Eco-terrorism.

Green intolerance is everywhere. Eco-terrorists throw blood on innocent people because they are wearing fur. Greens justify this action as a punishment for a crime against nature. Wearing leather is now on the crime list and the message is: to protect the environment and animals, don't eat beef and don't wear leather.

These attacks are all part of the Green political strategy. The Animal Rights, Anti-Beef, Anti-leather message is intended to impact, then cripple businesses across America. The Greens want Americans to become so worn out with constant conflicts within our society that we become hostile toward our culture. This is when the Greens plan to present their political ideas as our salvation. Lenin's instructions for revolution include staging conflicts to keep society in a constant uproar so citizens will welcome change. Hitler used the same tactic. The nonviolent Greens are using violence, verbally attacking innocent people, laying traps for others and disrupting our society to put Americans in a frustrated, submissive state of mind.

Animal Rights

Animal rights are another example of the difference between public perception vs. actual group philosophies and activities within the Green movement. No one condones cruelty to animals. American pets are part of the family. Caring for animals is not the issue. Our love of animals does not equal approval for Green politics and terrorism.

Barry Clausen, a private investigator hired to infiltrate Earth First, obtained a copy of the Animal Liberation Front activist's handbook titled: *A DECLARATION OF WAR: Killing People To Save Animals And The Environment* By SCREAMING WOLF. Clausen states:

> *"They believe in a revolution to liberate animals and if necessary kill their oppressors -- HUMANS. The contents of this handbook on murderous terrorism is distinctly characterized by it's title and subtitle."*
>
> *Walking on the Edge*

The Greens goal to control our lives reaches far beyond Washington D.C. and environmental protection. The Greens, just like Hitler, stress citizen activism. The Greens justify abuse of their fellow Americans in the name of their cause. Activists are doing their Green duty by braving confrontations to declare their politically correct positions with Nazi-style fury. Like the Nazis, these people are not stopping to think about what they are doing. They are allowing themselves to become mean-spirited by allowing their standards to slide into uncivilized behavior.

America's future, including our environmental future, is far too important to leave up to the Greens just because they can afford excellent public relations. Hitler's propaganda machine convinced reasonable people to do unreasonable things. Excellent public relations do not equal excellent political decisions or developing sound public policy.

Animal Rights activists are a good example of how Greens are getting normal people to take aggressive action toward their fellow citizens. There is a difference between expressing a sincere concern for animal welfare and Nazi-style activism. The determining factor is in how people approach the situation. Nazi-style activists attack without qualification. They don't need facts. They assume they are right. Reasonable people take a different approach. They begin by talking to each other.

This author had a recent Green encounter. It began with a public announcement describing a car and asking the owner to report to the front of the store. Upon admitting ownership of said vehicle, a very angry woman began to share her opinion of how cruel it was to leave two small dogs in the car on a hot afternoon. Other customers did not have to strain to hear her remarks that included the fact that others were calling the authorities to take care of the situation.

This was embarrassing. Although briefly stunned, it was critical to respond to these accusations and stop the show. It was necessary to interrupt her to explain that although her concern was understandable the dogs were fine and well cared for. The explanation included these details: the dogs had just been shaved to keep them cool, they had water and this stop involved enough time to run into the store and pick up a receipt. The scene ended on that note.

Hindsight is always 20-20. What ought to have been added is that the dogs ride along because one pet has epileptic seizures if she gets upset. If she's home alone, she barks at every noise because she's nearly blind. That upsets her. She is much calmer resting in her basket in the car. If she has a seizure, medication and care are immediately available. If anything, these pets are over cared for.

Perhaps those people thought the dog was barking because she was overheating, but they could have asked instead of jumping to conclusions. There is nothing wrong with caring about animal welfare. The danger lies in the attitude and the way these situations are approached. People who have pets care about them. If a stranger is concerned about the feelings of animals, they ought to be just as concerned about the feelings of human beings. The Greens call for peaceful conflict resolution but in reality, do not display common courtesy or kindness.

If we were operating by usual American good manners, the woman would have discussed her concerns privately. She would have shown some respect for a fellow citizen. She could have asked how much longer the dogs would be in the car. This was not a respectful, friendly reminder. This person attacked without facts. The dogs were left in a cool car, where the air conditioner had just been turned off and windows opened. They were there for just a few minutes. They were not being mistreated. This was blind condemnation. The Nazis operated on blind condemnation.

People have no right to take action or assume someone is guilty without getting the facts. They have no reason or right to be rude. People need to reexamine and think about what they are doing. There is a difference between concern and blame. Concern is something you share with someone. Blame is something you do to someone. This confrontational approach to problem solving is a prime example of how Nazi-style Green political activism is being justified. It is becoming more common and it includes the destruction of valuable research data, scientific equipment and research facilities.

We all share a concern for animals. We can not allow ourselves to justify attacking innocent people in the name of animal rights or any other part of the Green movement. We need to remember there is a difference between assertive and aggressive behavior. To maintain a civilized society we must demand civilized behavior.

Industry must consider environmental issues. Environmental groups must consider industry issues. Industries can't be allowed to destroy the environment and the Greens can't be allowed to destroy America. We need honesty, communication, cooperation and compromise.

Basic Training Coming to a Mall Near You

So far, the Greens have played it safe. Eco-terrorists have been sneaking around at night disabling equipment, killing cows or stringing piano wire across trails when no one can see them. Now that they mastered the easy stuff, it's time to get serious and more comfortable confronting American citizens.

The Greens plan to take terrorism shopping. Coming to a mall near you, Eco-terrorists plan to start harassing Americans about the wrongs of capitalism and Christmas. In the name of the Green cause, you or a family member may be selected.

Many Americans agree, Christmas is commercialized but this is a different issue. American citizens ought to be safe in shopping malls. American citizens should not be exposed to terrorism in the name of anything. Is this military training for the Green troops.

This is one more example of the contradiction of the Greens professed non-violence and their activities. There are varying degrees of violence. Mainstream Americans must understand terrorism and citizen harassment is being cultivated by most groups associated with the Green movement.

Earth First took the lead on this one and told members to:

"go to the malls and: 'tear-it-up, shut-it-down and do-it-now'!"
From the Trenches
September, 1994

Beyond spending money for presents, how about eco-terrorism and it's effect on families. How long could your family eat if you could no longer produce income and there was no money coming in? Monkeywrenchers intentionally break expensive equipment some Americans use to make their living. No equipment, no work. No work, no income.

How can the Greens be honestly concerned about the life of a tree and not the life of a family? If you are a loving and compassionate person, how can you not care if a horse and rider fall down a mountain side? What caring person could set traps for motorcycle riders or timber workers that could result in their violent death?

If the Greens were non-violent, they would not invent violent things to do. Professed non-violence contradicts the violent acts of many involved in the Green Movement.

Contributing to the Delinquency of a Minor

Earth First is now recruiting students from high schools and colleges. Students are being targeted to join the cause and learn how to commit terrorist acts while they are young and above the law. Students are also easier to recruit than adults because they operate on emotion and are very naive.

The Hitler Youth were recruited at an early age to play political activists. They learned to be terrorists. Children were involved in a political movement. Hitler molded children into Nazis dedicated to the cause.

The Greens are using the exact same approach. They are recruiting children to be political activists. They are teaching children to be terrorists. The Greens have even popularized Hitler's slogan of the 'New Age' movement, with the Greens leading us into the 21st Century. America's children are playing political activist. They are learning to be dedicated to the environmental or Green cause.

So many books are out now pushing children to be politically active. One of these books is: *The Kids Guide to Social Action* by Barbara Lewis. The book covers issues like; recycling, gun control, protesting, writing legislators, how to get a bill on the ballot and even includes forms for students to copy. The book is a resource guide for child activists.

It includes a list of organizations for children to contact for assistance. Environmental groups listed range from the Sierra Club to Greenpeace. Political contacts are also listed. They include youth groups we expect to see and a surprise youth group, the Youth Section of the Democratic Socialists of America. Although calls for social change are not illegal, socialism is not the American standard. Listing this organization suggests to students that socialism deserves equal consideration with traditional political groups. This is a subtle devaluing of our system of government and the economic standard on which this nation is based. We are not a socialist nation. We are a capitalist and free nation.

3

Eco Child Abuse

"It takes a whole village to raise a child"
African Proverb

The idea *it takes a whole village to raise a child* is now being popularized in America. Greens promote this village concept and call for local communities and the world community to share the role of raising America's children. The village concept matches the approach Communists use to condition people to gradually accept their ideas. The Communist's goals include eliminating our traditional American family. The plan is to replace our tradition of private, independent child rearing with the Communist model where society plays a major role in child rearing. The village concept fits how the Greens are manipulating America in this direction. It is an African proverb.

Most Americans would not instantly embrace the idea that society ought to take control of raising their children. The American version might be, it takes a whole family to raise a child. The village concept is designed to come in the back door and prepare Americans to accept government becoming a part of family life by first encouraging Americans to accept non-family members or strangers becoming an influential part of the their child's life under the guise of benefiting America's children.

To understand how the village concept serves as a catalyst to advance this Green goal; read the following eco-philosophy on Green family values.

> *"No longer is it enough to speak of new techniques for conserving and fostering the natural environment. We must deal with the earth communally, as a human collectively, without the tramels of self-interest, profit, competition and property that have distorted humanity's vision of life and nature since the break-up of tribal society. **We must eliminate not only the hierarchy produced by our market-oriented society, but hierarchy as such; not only the patriarchal family, but all modes of gender and parental domination; not only the classes produced by our corporate society but all the social classes and elites."***
>
>
>
> *Murray Bookchin*
> Ecology and Revolutionary Thought
> Youth Greens - Left Green Network
> Sep. 1990 - Ecology, Anarchism & Green Politics
>
>

Note, this is from a 'Youth Green' publication. Murray Bookchin is a well-known activist in the Green movement and a forerunner in eco-philosophy. The Youth Greens work with the Student Environmental Action Coalition that is associated with the Democratic Socialists of America.

There is a difference between a volunteer program that addresses a specific issue area and being set up to give Green activists the chance to promote Green values to America's children. The tribal or village concept is a Green political tightrope. The Greens will attempt to gain control over American families by supporting efforts that give the government more authority over private family issues.

The village concept is part of African tribal lore. It serves as a handy tool for the Greens because it does not match the independent private way Americans raise their children.

Americans ought to think twice before letting Green strangers interact with their children. Americans normally teach our children to stay away from strangers because of the potential danger. It would be wise to continue that practice.

Parents have been set up to allow children to join in Green community (village) activities such as a hike, a field trip or an environmental youth conference. A false sense of safety has been created because it is an environmental activity. Parents feel good their children want to help clean up the environment. Some parents may welcome a break while their children learn about nature and are out in the fresh air. Most parents feel their children are learning how to be better people from these kinds of activities. Green activities seem harmless.

> *"The mission of the Hitler Youth is neither religious nor radical, nor is it philosophical, political or economic. It is entirely natural: **the young people should be led back to nature, they should recognize nature as the giver of life and energy**. And they should strengthen and develop their bodies outdoors, making themselves well and keeping themselves well. For a healthy mind can develop only in a healthy body and it is only in the freedom of nature that a human being can also open himself to a higher morality and a higher ethic."*
>
> *Adolf Hitler*
> Hitler, Memoirs of a Confidant
> (Bold Emphasis Added)

Hitler made youth activities sound wonderful. Hitler comforted parents by indicating their child's participation in the youth groups was not political or spiritual. Hitler lied. German parents made an error in judgment. They trusted the people, some strangers, involved in the Nazi movement with the hearts and minds of their children. German parents did not understand the personal and political ramifications that would follow.

German parents allowed their children to participate in Hitler Youth activities because it sounded like a healthy, non-political activity. German parents did not worry about their child's involvement. Others welcomed the organized activities. S.S.D.D. Same Stuff Different Decade.

America's children are being recruited into the ranks of the Green movement so they to can be indoctrinated with politically correct thoughts. America's children are involved in a national political movement. Green children's activities are nearly identical to those used to brainwash the Hitler Youth. The Greens have duplicated Hitler's approach to justifying children's participation in a national political movement. Using the same kind of emotional ploys, the political ideas of the movement are cemented in the child's mind because it is the core of all activities. Both Green and the Nazi youth:

- belong to special clubs
- have special badges or other propaganda items
- sing special songs
- say special new pledges
- get in touch with nature
- participate in parades
- meet leaders in the movement
- are recognized based on performance
- attend special youth conferences
- involve children at an early age

As early as age eight, America's children are writing letters to Congress. The Greens are using the call to save the environment as their excuse to grow loyal Green followers.

If Americans accept the village concept, then society will begin to play a bigger role in raising our children and shaping their opinions. America's communities have always played a role in the lives of our children. There is a difference between sponsoring a softball team and brainwashing.

Many programs currently operating such as Big Brother and Big Sister programs, mentor programs for at risk students or speaker's programs are not the same as the village concept. These programs are well run. Participants are screened, the programs monitored and someone is accountable to parents.

The village concept fits the Communist's ideology that society rather than families knows what's best for a child. The result is group-think instead of the spice of individuality produced by the traditional American family.

Recruiting small children into a political cause seems to be the trademark of dictatorships. German children were recruited into the ranks of the Hitler Youth at age ten, some as early as age eight. Russian children joined the Little Octoberist while in kindergarten and then the Young Pioneers by age nine.

Earth Day, The New Children's Crusade!

"If the millions of school kids who now raise Earth flags, plant trees and march in 'All Species parades' get their way, Earth Day will soon be bigger than Christmas."
Mike Weilbacher
E magazine - April 1993

Telling the American people Earth Day is a children's crusade is like saying Germany's children trained themselves to be little Nazis. Children did not organize the Hitler Youth, adults did. Children are not organizing the Green Youth movement, adults are.

'Greening' the schools is no accident. It is the Greens way to your child's heart and soul. Earth Day is the inroad. Children are being indoctrinated with Green ideology in schools across the country. When people realized what Nazi really meant, it was too late. Germany's children were already brainwashed to pledge their allegiance to Hitler. Hitler youth believed the future was up to them so they became Nazi activists.

Greens understand the concept. Children have no political past. They operate on emotion so their political opinions can be easily molded. America's children have been led to believe, just like the Hitler Youth were led to believe, that they are the only ones who can change the world. The future is up to them.

Political-Child Abuse

> "The execution of this great transformation must be left to youth."
> > Adolf Hitler
> > Hitler, Memoirs of a Confident

> "A lot of people think kids can't do very much work in the world. But I think kids might be the only chance."
> > Anna Brown, 11
> > Save the Earth - An Action Handbook for Kids

Pretty heavy load for an 11 year old child to carry. There is a big difference between children learning to be responsible and children being taught they are responsible.

Getting a Green education is very different from learning facts about the environment. Green teachers encourage students to react to environmental horror stories. Children are encouraged to get angry and to get politically involved. The Greens are scaring America's children into political action.

What are some ten year old children doing instead of playing? Some are gathering under trees to figure out how to fix the hole in the ozone. Fear drives them to do this. Children believe if they don't come up with the answer, they will have to dig holes and live underground like gophers.

Eco-Child Abuse is based on deception. Is it reasonable to put this level of stress on children? Where do children get these ideas? One example is found in a 1993 children's coloring book, *Helping Our Environment,* by Rudy Young. The author indicates this book represents a *'new trend of teaching'* and that it has *'great support from leading educators and teachers worldwide'.* The book deals with political and environmental issues. One topic is zero population growth. Zero population growth occurs when the number of births is the same as the number of deaths. To make a point, the author asks readers:

> *"Why might zero population growth be a good idea for the future?"*

The author gives these reasons for zero population growth.

> *"There will one day be so many people on earth that they will begin falling over the sides"*

> *"There will be so many people on earth that there won't be enough skateboards to go around"*

> *"There will be so many people on earth that it will get too heavy and fall out of orbit"*

> *"There won't be enough food to feed everybody"*

How can this kind of science get the support of leading educators and teachers? This is not science. This is emotional blackmail. This form of political science mixes a political issue with fear, to get a child to make an emotional decision.

This is not an uncommon approach to environmental education. The alternative to zero population growth is either starving to death or falling off the earth. Which sounds more pleasant? These simplistic choices are intended to convince children the only way to live is to support zero population growth.

Most Americans think learning about the environment is a simple process and a healthy experience. In concept, yes, in practice, no. Environmental education is complex. We must make a distinction between children learning about the environment and children learning to go Green or die.

The Green Emergency Room

Would we allow anyone to take a class of 8 year olds into a hospital emergency room and tell them it was their job to save a bus load of bleeding accident victims? What would they do? How would they feel?

Feeling it is their responsibility to save the earth causes the same kind of emotional trauma. Children are feeling it's up to them to save the earth. Just like the bus load of injured people, the life and death threat is too much responsibility for little people. Children have no frame of reference to draw from. It is a crime to put them in this position.

We can't continue to let the Greens send our children into the Green emergency room. The responsibility for that level of political and environmental responsibility belongs with adults.

Who's In Charge?

Seven year old children don't drive cars. They don't know how to steer, let alone, the rules of the road. Eight year old children don't run for office because they don't have the necessary life experience.

Why are seven and eight year old children expected to write opinion letters to politicians on political issues as if they are adults? This is an unreasonable level of student involvement in environmental issues.

Writing letters to politicians about environmental issues they can not comprehend and signing petitions about issues they do not fully understand, is wrong. Participating in Green public protest against our country is not what America's children ought to be involved in.

The distinction must be made between an eight year old parroting facts and an eight year old comprehending a complicated issue from a mature standpoint. Evaluating facts and forming intelligent opinions is part of the growing-up process. An adult grasp of a national issue or the political process doesn't occur by age eight.

If you don't have an eight year old handy, ask to see a friend's. Look at this little person and ask yourself; can this little person possibly understand these complex political issues? Should this child participate in national politics?

Like the Lion And the Cub

Like the lioness and her newborn cub, the lioness is unlikely to tell the cub, "Welcome to the world baby, now go catch dinner, show me how it's done." It would not be natural. The natural process is for the lion to nurture, teach and protect the cub until it can manage on its own.

If the Greens truly believed or were concerned with nature's way, they would never use children. They would not reverse the natural order of the role of parent and child. It is unnatural, unconscionable and unhealthy.

Children's hearts and minds are too precious to allow them to be used in this manner. The trend of parent-child role reversal is evident in Green theme television shows and motion pictures.

Who shall we thank for all this child activism?

"to what do we owe this recent surge of environmental responsibility among today's children? Many people believe that it begins with more activist-oriented ecology and conservation programs taught in schools. Kids are not only being trained to recognize potential environmental hazards in the home and their neighborhoods, but also are being taught to go out and do something about it. With this training comes a confident attitude that they can change old habits and long-standing public policy. "
1993 Earth Journal
Buzzworm magazine - Editors

The Greens intention and political motivation for using children to advance their political goals is obvious. The Hitler Youth was also trained, in school, to be politically active and with that training, they learned to feel confident about their political opinions.

The Hitler Youth also developed very confident attitudes about many things, such as:

- what they were doing was right
- their role in politics was essential
- today, rule Germany and tomorrow the world
- allegiance to Hitler and the cause came first
- Jewish people were their sub-human arch enemy
- learned to feel good about having power over Jews

As the saying goes, 'children learn what they live and live what they learn'. It doesn't matter if *what* they learn is based on false information, if they believe it to be true. Hate and anger can still be learned. It was child abuse then and it is child abuse now.

Materials for activists-oriented learning are offered free to teachers by all the large environmental organizations. Targeting children for political gain ought to be considered a child abuse crime, punishable by law. There is a difference between parents taking their child to a Fourth of July celebration that is pro-country and the Greens sneaking into the schools to brainwash children to be anti-country. Going behind parents backs and sneaking into the schools to get to the children is exactly what Hitler did.

Taking advantage of a child's innocent thoughts and emotions is like Green pornography. The Green assault on America's children is unacceptable and unforgivable. Many Americans are becoming increasingly concerned about Green assembly programs presented in our schools that send children home in tears.

Our Money, Our Children, Is This What We Pay For?

Environmental education is not what it appears to be.

> *"Members of Kids Against Pollution in Closter, New Jersey, have flown to many parts of the country to give talks about their work. They explain how they started their group in Mr. Byrnes's fifth grade class and how KAP has expanded to a network of 500 groups around the United States and in five foreign countries. The original KAP members are used to giving speeches by now, and they do it well. But some adults aren't too eager to listen to them - at first."*
> *Save The Earth - An Action Handbook for Kids*

How many school hours and tax dollars were used to pay for getting this children's activist's group going? How many teachers are being paid with tax payers money to start these groups across the country?

Children have no experience to form, fund or run a functioning national organization. Ten year old children don't establish international contacts and fly around the country all by themselves. It just doesn't happen.

Following Hitler's example, the Greens are taking children out of the classroom, involving them in fun events and setting up special conferences for children to attend. What child would not find this exciting? Hitler understood motivation. Exciting events without parent's supervision make children want to participate.

The Hitler Youth had to earn their way to Nazi political events. They were recognized and held a special place in the events. The Greens have duplicated this approach. Children are earning their way to Green youth events by participating in environmental events and becoming heroes for the earth. Green games, parades, songs, nature treks and personal 'adult-like' recognition are designed to become the preferred social life for a child so their political loyalties can be molded.

Recruiting The Little Green Army

Hitler built his youth groups using the same psychological approach. He used teachers to organize special outdoor activities. Children believed they were doing their duty to give of themselves to help save the sacred soil of the Fatherland from the evil Jews. Hitler lured thousands of children from their families and instilled in them firm political beliefs and unquestioning commitment to the Nazi movement.

> *"I never once during the Hitler years thought of myself as anything but a decent, honorable young German, blessed with a glorious future...none of us who reached high rank in the Hitler Youth will ever totally shake the legacy of the Fuhrer. Despite our monstrous sacrifice and the appalling misuse of our idealism, there will always be the memory of unsurpassed power, the intoxication of fanfares and flags proclaiming our new age...Today Germany belongs to us and tomorrow the world."*
>
> *Alfons Heck*
> Hitler Youth Leader
> A Child of Hitler

U.S. soldiers captured eight year old children, armed and fighting for the Nazi cause. Children were taught to act like adults and to have blind dedication to the Fuhrer.

There is nothing wrong with children learning to recycle. Everything is wrong with using children, like Hitler did, to mold them into political robots who did not question his visionary ideas.

The Greens would like us to believe small children are leading the Green charge for political activism. The reason for this facade is that it keeps the public's attention on children's concern for the environment and not on the Greens political motivation. This helps the Greens in several ways, they can:

- hide behind the environment as the excuse
- access and brainwash our children
- generate more public concern and sympathy

The October 30, 1994 edition of *Parade* magazine featured the story, *Kids Voting.* It is a new program to help young Americans learn the value of voting. This kind of program requires close attention. Following the election process is different than an in-school program promoted by an outside group. Pushing eight year old children to study a national issue to form a political opinion has questionable value. It may, as the article indicates, get more parents voting again, but the opportunity to influence the political opinions of young children poses a greater danger. If a child can not understand a national issue, they should not be expected to form an opinion on one. The promoters of the program indicate it is strictly non-partisan. The Green movement is also said to be non-partisan.

Since the Greens have targeted children, any school activity involving students and political issues ought to be monitored by principals, teachers, parents, concerned citizens and elected officials to ensure the Greens cannot use our schools the same way Hitler used the schools. School programs like this one must be carefully evaluated on their educational value versus the potential danger of children being manipulated.

Hitler Youth were indoctrinated by their teachers. They learned their parents were wrong if their parents did not agree with Hitler's ideas. Hitler preyed on children to create his little army of blind Nazi activists. Hitler also began his programming as early as eight years old.

We need to ask ourselves, is it wise and necessary to involve America's children in national politics? Is it in the best interest of our children to be involved in politics?

The January 15,1995 edition of, *Parade* magazine featured the article; *Mr. President, Here's Your Midterm Report Card.* The article described a program sponsored by, *Weekly Reader* that surveys children and asks them to set goals for the President. A follow-up survey is taken so the children can grade the President on how he's doing to reach their goals. Students surveyed were fourth, fifth and sixth graders. The top issue of concern was the environment. *Weekly Reader,* is now preparing the, *Election '96 Program.*

Education must encompass multiple subjects, politics included. It is disturbing that America's fourth and fifth graders are being encouraged to feel they are capable of passing political judgment on the President of the United States. Giving our President a report card complete with grades is arrogant and insulting.

Children are part of this nation's future. They may share the political concerns of their parents or teachers but concern is different than passing judgment or giving a political grade to adults, including the President. There is something wrong with this picture.

The Hitler Youth were taught they knew better than their parents and other adults. They were a part of Nazi politics. Hitler made sure they knew, he personally depended on them. Children learned to be arrogant and insulting political activists.

Politics and children don't mix. It is dangerous territory. Children learning about our political system is not the same as children learning they have an adult voice in politics. The real issue is these ideas are coming from environmental groups, radical teachers and Greens. America's children are not thinking of this by themselves. The tough questions on eco-child abuse are:

- Do students feel they have a choice?
- Was it a do or die message?
- Did the teacher use peer pressure to force action?
- Is it associated with grades?

Children are special little people. Their opinions and feelings are very important. Children need guidance as they learn how our country functions and how to be good citizens. We can not allow children to become political activists like the Hitler Youth. Children do not need to participate in national politics. Political interest groups should not be allowed to politically abuse children. Green education programs can have serious side affects. We need to protect our children by determining what is a reasonable dose of political issues in education and at what grade level. We need to reestablish the ground rules. We need to make a distinction between teaching about a political issue and using carefully selected information to mold students political opinions.

> *"The environmental movement is one of the subversive element's last steps. They've gone after the military and the police and now they're going after our parks and playgrounds."*
>
> Mrs. Clarence Howard
> Daughters of the American Revolution

The Greens will continue to use children as political pawns unless we change the rules. The first step is to recognize the Greens are coaching our children.

If the Communists were planning to brainwash America's young people, school would be the logical place to go. Children are there, all day long, by themselves. Children are so easily influenced by emotions. Being afraid of the dark is nothing compared to day and night end of the earth messages. Green movies, television shows, environmental studies, information provided to schools by environmental groups, Earth Day celebrations at school and other Green propaganda magnify the fear of environmental disaster in the eyes of children. The Greens intend to expand their opportunities to influence children.

> *"We support increased funding for education and a shift in decision making responsibility and funding control for education so that teachers are making most decisions about the curriculum, school goals and policies, specific students, school accreditation, and administrative and staff hiring, with significant involvement from parents, older children, and the local community."*
> *Green Party Program*

Why do teachers need this expanded level of authority? The Greens are pushing this so they can control the schools and ensure America's children get a Green education. Although the statement includes the line, 'significant involvement from parents' that is highly doubtful unless it's a Green parent. Make control possible by making control legal. The Greens have political support for their ideas.

> *"Grant expanded decision-making powers at the school level, empowering principals, teachers and parents with increased flexibility in educating our children."*
> *Governor Bill Clinton - Senator Al Gore*
> Putting People First

Perhaps President Clinton is not aware of the politics of the Green movement. Maybe the Greens copied his idea. Whatever the source, the Greens have targeted America's schools. We can't protect our children from something we can not see. The Green objective is to get children politically committed before parents figure out there is a difference between environmental education and Green indoctrination.

Teaching Children Away From Their Parents

During an educational activist's conference, one teacher told the group:

> *"no one knows what I teach my kids when I close the door and you've got to be willing to risk it."*

Statements like these epitomize the attitude of Green educators. This conference was a Green recruiting event. Many teachers who attended did not share that opinion, others did. Teachers who share this Green teaching philosophy are the teachers in question.

Radical teachers with radical ideas are influencing America's educational system. Dr. Pierce, a Harvard University Professor shared this idea on the teacher's role in promoting social change in the classroom. This statement was made at an educator's conference:

> *"Every child in America who enters school with an allegiance toward our elected officials, toward our founding fathers, toward our institutions, toward the preservation of this form of government ... all of this proves the children are sick, because the truly well individual is one who has rejected all those things and is what I would call the true international child of the future."*
>
> Dr. Chester M. Pierce
Educating for the New World Order

Why Rewrite American History?

Hitler taught children away from their parents, families, and friends by separating them from traditional values. Hitler used teachers and the educational system to brainwash the children. The majority of people first involved in the Nazi cause were teachers. The majority of the people first involved in the Green cause were also teachers. German children learned these ideas from their teachers:

- Don't tell your parents what you are learning
- German history is a lie
- Rewritten version of history is true
- German traditions are out-dated and old fashioned
- Your parents don't understand the Nazi party
- Children understand the Nazi party
- Jewish people are a blight on earth
- Germany's future depends on children

S.S.D.D., Same stuff, different decade. Radical Green teachers are giving America's children the same kind of permission and support to question authority as Hitler gave the Hitler Youth. The purpose of the rewriting history and attacking the idea Columbus was a hero is the Green way to get children to reject tradition. Children are learning:

- American history is a lie
- Not to believe official American stories
- American heroes are really liars and murders
- Children must raise a ruckus, protest
- Children understand Green ideas
- To be ashamed of being an American
- To condemn American way of life
- Parent's values and beliefs are old fashioned
- Children must make up for historical wrongs

Objective: influence children to embrace Green ideology by dissolving America's image in the eyes of her children.

"When an opponent declares. 'I will not come over to your side,' I calmly say, "Your child belongs to us already...What are you? You will pass on. Your descendants, however, now stand in the new camp. In a short time they will know nothing else but this new community."

Adolf Hitler
The Rise and Fall of the Third Reich

What's Wrong With Lies?

People believe them. Lies and revolutions are just like kidnapping. Kidnappers don't usually tell the victim what they are planning to do. If they were completely honest, people would have a chance to avoid becoming a victim. Nation-napping is no different. If revolutionaries were completely honest about their objectives, it would give people a chance to avoid that outcome. Beyond being deceitful, lies cause serious problems. People base their opinions on what they are told. They expect it to be true so they plan on it being true.

Children believe what their teachers, parents and other adults tell them. Children do not have an adult frame of reference. They do not understand what makes a society or government system work or what makes a society or government system fail. Children's books about the environment site capitalism and the American way of life as the primary cause of our environmental problems. Children are learning to dislike America.

'Rethinking Columbus'

A radical teacher's publication entitled, *'Rethinking Columbus'* basically explains how teachers can reinvent America by rewriting American history. They begin by writing off our past as a historical myth.

America needs to worry about the rethinking Columbus effort. The reason children are being taught to rethink Columbus is because the story of Columbus introduces our children to the first history of this nation. If American history is presented as myth or in a negative light, it will change children's values about America, our culture and our society.

There is a difference between exploring different aspects of history and deliberately focusing on one part of history and blowing it way out of proportion for political purposes. Green teachers are using American history to shame children into accepting the Green political position and taking political action.

Active Duty

Green teachers are using the environmental cause and related subjects like the story of Columbus to teach children to rebel against their country.

For example, one fourth grade class wrote to their U.S. Senator asking why he voted to spend money on Columbus and the quincentennial. He sent them a copy of the story of Columbus from the, *World Book Encyclopedia*. The children recontacted the Senator to inform him they believed:

- the story of Columbus was not true
- money should not be spent to honor Columbus

The Green subliminal messages twisted into this lesson are:

- Columbus didn't discover America, Indians were here
- Columbus was bad
- Columbus brought capitalism to America
- Capitalism is to blame for all environmental damage

The general idea is, if Columbus had stayed home, the world would be a better place because none of these things would have happened. Teaching this idea is wrong. No one knows what history would be if Columbus had not discovered America.

Changing the Definition of the Color Green

If you want to better understand Green politics, read a few children's books about environmental protection. Although the authors may not fully understand the political goals of the Greens, children's books teach Green political thought and stress political activism. The word Green is no longer defined for children as a color. Green is defined as:

> *"In recent years all over the world, green has come to symbolize sound environmental policies and practices."*
> Susan Milord
> Hands Around the World

This definition sets children and adults up to believe all actions or policies recommended by the Greens are automatically right. This message helps create blind Green followers. Some children's books portray children as violent, intolerant and aggressive towards capitalist polluters. Green lies depict all capitalists as one evil group using Hitler propaganda techniques. Some children's books contain outright lies. America's children are learning to see capitalism as opposite of environmental excellence. The Greens are creating the opinion socialism is better for the environment. Radical Green teachers are teaching Marxism.

> *"We are committed to the transformation of existing public school systems..."*
>
> *Green Party Program*

The Green strategy to bring about a cultural transformation involves America's standardized education system. New and separate teaching institutions would allow the Greens the freedom and isolation to teach the new Green knowledge. Public education is a key target for the Greens because now America's children are educated with standard information. If the Greens intend to control what children learn, it is to their benefit to do what they can to disrupt and discredit our current educational system.

Hitler used a similar approach to isolating children. Hitler organized youth camps and land service activities. According to Alfons Heck, German children did not rush to join the Nazis because of their dedication to saving the Fatherland. They joined to have fun, instead of working at home. Alfons also blames adults for not stopping Hitler.

> *"I developed a harsh resentment toward our elders, especially our educators from the Volksschule to university; not only had they allowed themselves to be deceived, they had delivered us, their children, into the cruel power of a new God."*
>
> *Alfons Heck*
> A CHILD OF HITLER

Freedom of Choice is Not the Issue

Most teachers are wonderful, caring individuals. There are obviously others who believe they have the right to impose their personal political beliefs on other people's children. That is not what the classroom is for.

The intent of this book is not to insult the integrity of the entire teaching profession. The purpose is to alert all Americans; teachers, parents, bus drivers, counselors, principals, everyone, about Green politics in education. We all care about children and we can not intelligently address the problem without alerting those involved at the source.

Curriculum content is not solely the teacher's choice. Teachers are responsible to the people who pay their salaries, the general public. Teaching personal or political philosophies to the public's children does not fit within the realm of their job description or public expectation.

Rewriting history vs. teaching American history, as written, is the issue we must address. Teachers are not hired to use their position of trust to take advantage of vulnerable young minds. That is not a job choice. People are expected to do what they are hired to do, as defined by the employer. Employers don't hire employees to do whatever they feel like doing.

The American people have not been asked if we want history rewritten. The American people, employ the educators. If the American people have not authorized educators to rewrite history, educators should not be teaching the rewritten version.

This is not a blanket indictment of educators. Educators may not be aware of the political objectives of the Green movement. This is as much a wake-up call for them as it is for other Americans. We need to work together to get the Greens out of our schools.

It is also important to understand teachers have to work with school boards. Greens are encouraged to become involved in local politics to quietly influence areas like education.

America's children are getting 'Greened' from all sides, including Green cartoons.

'Captain Eco'

> "Here's the picture, in a nutshell. Your planet's in serious trouble - from pollution, toxic waste and the loss of forest, farmland and fresh water....Your parents and Grandparents have made a mess of looking after the earth. They may deny it, but they're little more than thieves. And they're stealing your future from under your noses."
>
> Jonathon Porritt - Elllis Nadler
> Captain Eco - And the Fate of the Earth - 1991

This lovely thought comes from, *Captain Eco,* a children's book about saving the environment. The story is based around a cartoon character who comes from the soul of the earth to teach children how to save the planet. The story begins with a letter explaining to the reader that children took over in the 1990's and forced political leaders to support the Green Movement.

Other political leaders have blamed children's ancestors for political gain. From, *Hiler's Ideology,* by Richard Koenigsberg.

> "Our ancestors contributed to the catastrophic splintering of our inner being"
>
> Adolf Hitler
> Mein Kampf

Jonathan Porritt's story promotes Green political ideas throughout and criticizes everything about life on earth. Eating beef, eating fast food, bankers, people who drive big cars and others are singled out as ignorant, selfish sub-humans. Humans are all depicted as ignorant, lazy, selfish, boneheads. The politics of emotion are used to make children feel guilty, fearful, angry enough to resort to violence and finally, committed to being Green political activists.

The story suggests many things to young readers; eat less meat, buy organic vegetables, fight for animal rights, use human waste for fertilizer and join environmental groups. The authors draw many conclusions for children, such as:

- parents don't know what to do to save the earth
- children are the only ones who can save the earth
- children must teach their parents what to do

'Captain Planet'

The *Captain Planet* cartoon series is based on a similar theme. Gaia is the spirit of the earth. Five children and a green-haired super hero fight to save the planet from the bad guys like, *Hoggish Greedly* and *Looten Plunder*. The Greens always win, defeating evil capitalists. They use clever names and spread the anti-capitalist Green message.

The cartoon is a slick combination of Green messages: it hints at eco-violence. Gaia is the earth's spirit. Children learn to see the earth as a living being. It is like the movie, *Pocahontas*, that promotes Green spirituality.

If your children watch, *Captain Planet*, start listening. What messages are your child receiving about the environment, our culture and Green politics?

The book, *Captain Eco,* was written by Jonathon Porritt. Porritt is also the author of, *Seeing Green* and *Save The Earth.* *Save the Earth,* was published by Turner Publishing, Inc, a subsidiary of Turner Broadcasting System, Inc. Turner Broadcasting also created, *Captain Planet and the Planeteers.*

Repetition Is The First Law Of Learning

Children's books about the environment encourage children to join environmental groups. Environmental groups want children for members because it gives them multiple opportunities to encourage children to go Green. Memberships in Green organizations serve the following purposes:

- put Green propaganda in the hands of children
- keep Green propaganda in front of children
- instruct children on what to think and what to do
- gives Greens more money
- gives Greens more political power

During a political show and tell, it's a numbers game. The more members you can hold up, the more chance politicians will pay attention and vote green. Are all Green group members voting age?

At School, Are Halloween And Earth Day The Same?

Halloween is an event:

- one day
- kids dress up in costumes
- community involvement, trick or treat

Earth Day is a celebration designed to promote cultural and social change. Earth Day is the vehicle to foster public acceptance for Green ideas. Earth Day is a ceremony filled with Green ideology. It has been expanded to Earth Week.

The Earth Day celebration.

What goes on:	What it means:
• day, week, month	• environmental programming
• all species parades	• reduce child to species
• multi-culturalism	• abandon melting-pot
• fly the earth flag	• replace American flag
• sing earth anthem	• replace America's anthem
• honor earth heroes	• replace American heroes
• public celebration	• recruit new Greens
• earth is being	• Green spirituality, earth worship
• child fun-time	• Get into Green social circle
• Earth Pledge	• replace our Pledge of Allegiance

Why is it so important America's children accept the Green concepts of, All Species and One People? Communists believe people are no more than animals. The political motive behind All Species is to raise children to see themselves as no more deserving than other species or animals. Children raised with this mentality will not expect to be treated any differently than animals.

The Earth Pledge of Allegiance:

> *"I pledge allegiance to the Earth, and to the flora, fauna and human life that it supports, one planet, indivisible, with safe air, water, and soil, economic justice, equal rights and peace for all".*

The Greens political purpose for One People, One Planet is to condition our children to see themselves as global citizens instead of American citizens. Children raised with this mentality will lose their independent streak. Independence is the heart of America.

Group-thinking followers and drones is the objective. It would be much easier for drones to obey Communists than it would be to try and force an independent American to submit.

Earth Day is also the vehicle the Greens are using to introduce new symbols, values and traditions for children to identify with. The Greens need children to sever connections with our past and culture so they will accept a new one without question.

To accomplish this the Greens rely on Hitler tactics again. The Greens have manufactured Hitler's, *historic dishonor* by rewriting our history. Our children are learning America is something to be ashamed of. The Hitler Youth learned to be ashamed of Germany's past and proud to participate in the new order of the Nazis. Our children are learning to accept:

- new world order
- new Green symbols
- new Green heroes
- new Green pledge of allegiance
- new Green belief system
- new Green culture

There is a difference between teaching children values most Americans can agree with and teaching children new values many Americans don't know about.

One Earth Flag company helps clarify the purpose of the Earth Flag by advertising a message that suggests we should not burn the American flag, just replace it with the Earth Flag.

Earth Flags come with a copy of the earth pledge of allegiance. Some schools fly the Earth flag all year, giving it the same status as the United States flag. The message is, both flags are equal, but they are not.

Everyday people want peace and everyday people want a clean earth. If we do not fly a peace flag all year, why should we fly the Earth flag all year? The Earth flag is not our nation's symbol. It is not equal to the flag of the United States of America. Leaving the Earth Flag up all year is intended to give it equal status in the eyes of our children. It will be easier for the Greens to replace our flag if the Green flag is already accepted.

Environmental protection should not include creating a gray area regarding the symbol of our nation.

Greening School Sports Programs

School sports programs are another target for the Greens. Competition needs to go. The Greens want our schools to shift from a focus on competitive team sports to programs that emphasize cooperative play.

The Greens believe competition divides people into winners and losers and that is not acceptable. The Green goal here is:

- nullify pride of achievement for those who excel in sports
- eliminate competitiveness, accept everyone is the same
- comfort children who have less or no athletic ability

Personal development and lessons learned from participation in competitive sports are invaluable. Physical skills, physical fitness, self-discipline and team work are lessons used repeatedly throughout the course of a lifetime.

Why eliminate such a wonderful opportunity for those who are gifted athletes and others who just love to play? There is a difference between a personal choice not to participate in organized sports and not having the opportunity to compete in sports.

Is this the result of the Communists applying rule number one of the, *Communist Rules for Revolution?*

> *"Corrupt the young; get them away from religion. Get them interested in sex. Make them superficial; destroy their ruggedness."*

Is this attack on sports and competition designed to destroy our children's ruggedness? Competition is healthy. This is another effort to force us to be the same, eliminate individualism and turn us into Green drones with no ambition.

Would professional sports be impacted by the Greens emphasis on cooperative play vs. sports competition? Professional athletes are trained from childhood in their respective sport(s). Without this training-ground (for replacement talent), the quality and entertainment value of professional sports would diminish and eventually die-out. The multi-million dollar sports industry would not be exempt from the Greens goal to control the people and the economy of this nation.

Wild Animal Rights

The make-believe Indian white wolf myth and real life wild wolves are not the same. Children learning they can depend on wolves or safely swim with sharks is unhealthy. America's children are being told wolves and sharks are their friends.

Sell that to someone who has been attacked by a wolf or had a loved one killed by a man-eating shark.

As children, most of us were taught to stay away from things that could hurt us. We did not learn wolves were friendly creatures or insects were just like us, bugs with feelings. The Green idea we are all the same creatures, who respond to each other in the same way, is insanity. If a mountain lion had feelings for people, it would not attack and mutilate people. It would not attack defenseless children in campgrounds.

Animals do what animals do. Snakes and bees bite, even if we'd like them not to. The Greens are preying on children's emotions so children will write letters that parrot Green political messages on endangered species, animal rights and wolf reintroduction. Children are not toys. It is a crime, pure and simple, to diminish their natural sense of fear of wild animals. Self-preservation is a natural instinct. Taking this away from children is unnatural and is another Green contradiction to natural law.

Little Red Riding Hood

> "At last some scientists began to wonder if wolves really were dangerous. They went deep into the forest to study how the wolves live. One scientist was walking in the forest when he met two wolves by accident. One wolf ran away. The other wolf walked right up to him. The scientist was scared. But the wolf just licked his face and trotted away! The scientists learned that healthy wolves do not attack people."
>
> Wild Wild Wolves
> Joyce Milton

Greens indicate healthy wolves are not a threat to people, but what if a person meets an unhealthy wolf? Can a child tell the difference? The message the child gets from this story is, do not fear, wild wolves will lick your face.

This is unconscionable disregard for a child's safety. Wild wolves are not the same as the family pet. There are multiple children's movies out which depict wolves as the mystic protectors of children. Children need to understand this is a fantasy, not a fact.

Some may argue, this is a child's fiction story. What harm can one story do? It's not this one story that will do irreparable harm. It is the sum total of Green programming that creates the problem. Children receive Green messages about creatures and the environment from school, movies, cartoons, coloring books, television specials, environmental clubs and stories like this one. It would be easy for a child to believe the message is real, not fiction, and that is what is dangerous. It is not safe for children to think they can talk to wolves.

Wolves are now being reintroduced into populated areas. What happens if a child gets lost in one of those areas and disturbs a pack of wolves? What will the child do? What will the wolves do? The wolves may run away but what if one was hurt or rabid? That innocent child would be in big trouble and may, because of Green programming, die a painful death. At least, if the child understood wild wolves were not the family pet, that child might not make its presence known and have a chance to climb a tree or sneak away. The child has no chance if it runs right up to the wolf, asking to be attacked.

Recently, a rabid mountain lion took on four adults and their dog. They managed to kill it with a kitchen knife and all survived the attack. They had a critical advantage. They were smart enough to be afraid of a mountain lion.

A woman was brutally attacked and killed by a mountain lion near Sacramento, California. She was jogging and the mountain lion was hungry. Sightings of mountain lions in populated areas, such as Sacramento, have increased since the ban on mountain lion hunting was passed by voters. Mountain lions are also showing up in southern California neighborhoods. A teacher was attacked and killed by a mountain lion while hiking.

Wild animals are unpredictable. No one can be 100% sure how a wild animal will respond to people. The animal's response depends on its circumstances at that particular moment.

The instant Green response to the mountain lions coming into cities is that too many people have invaded the mountain lion's habitat, forcing them to relocate. This sounds logical on the surface, but think about it. The lions are being forced out of their habitat because there are too many people living there. To get away from people, the lions decide to relocate to a metro area?

Some people believe the reason the lions are showing up in populated areas is easy food. Because of the hunting ban, the mountain lion population has grown and that would lower the populations of those animals they prey on. Supply and demand may be forcing the lions to look for other prey, like dogs, cats and people.

Oregon just passed a law that bans hunting mountain lions and bears with dogs. According to seasoned hunters, it's almost impossible to find the illusive animals any other way. Since the ban, several incidents involving mountain lions have occurred in the state. Early August brought two more sightings of lions in populated city areas. One involved a mountain lion that attacked and killed a cat in a back yard one evening. The other, involved a male mountain lion that was seen stalking a group of children as they played in a backyard pool. The lion was on the other side of a chain link fence until the family dog chased it away. What if the family had no dog? If mountain lions will change their illusive behavior and start looking for food in the city limits, so will wolves.

Too much competition in their natural habitat may be causing the lack of natural prey available to the lions. If some lions were relocated to less populated wilderness areas or their numbers thinned, nature would have time to recuperate and balance out.

It seems logical, if we can put a man on the moon, we can find reasonable and effective solutions to correct environmental problems, including these kinds of sensitive habitat issues. Child safety must be the first priority. The best way to combat Green propaganda is to make sure children understand that wolves and other wild creatures are not tame, safe playmates.

Wisdom of the 60's, Shall We Try Some More?

Do we have the maturity to admit that as individuals and as a society we've made a few errors in judgment? The counter culture of the 60's has produced some very harmful results. Our children are hurting. The early drug culture has led to our current drug crisis. Teen sex and teen pregnancies have sky rocketed. Is this the result of the Communists applying rule number one of their *Communist Rules for Revolution?*

> *"Corrupt the young; get them away from religion. Get them interested in sex. Make them superficial; destroy their ruggedness."*

Have we been set up to abandon traditional American values?

4

Facts or Fabrication ?

The American people are not getting the straight facts on serious political issues. What we are getting is a lot of Green Communist propaganda.

> *"The press is our chief ideological weapon."*
> *Nikita Khrushchev*
> Washington Post - 1957

What is preventing us from getting good information? The Greens have systematically 'Greened' the media by convincing journalists it is their duty to go beyond reporting the news and use their position to:

- advocate the Green political position
- manage facts to control what Americans hear
- 'Green' public opinion
- help save the planet

The Greens have motivated journalists to accept this as their duty based on the idea, time is running out and only they can help the ignorant masses understand what needs to be done. If journalists do not help sway public opinion, part of the blame for catastrophic environmental ruin will rest on their shoulders.

This is not a new tactic. Lenin and Hitler used it. Nazi propaganda and doctrine were spread by public information.

Hitler controlled the airwaves. People heard what Hitler wanted them to hear.

The Greens operate on the end justifies the means. Slanted stories or out-and-out lies are acceptable. To intelligently move forward, we need to make a distinction between fact and fabrication. This distinction begins with our public information sources and extends to all the environmental information we have received to date. We need to understand the 'Greening' of our public information sources is a three stage process. First, the Greens have successfully pushed the press to go beyond reporting facts to advocating the Green position. The second step was to get the media to go beyond advocacy and begin concocting news stories to increase public support for Green politics. The third step is Green control of mass communications. Then we will hear only what the Greens want us to hear. We are now in stage two and rapidly approaching stage three.

> *"The press should be not only a collective propagandist and a collective agitator, but also a collective organizer of the masses."*
> *Lenin*
> New York Times - 1955

This statement by Lenin explains why the Greens targeted the media and pushed them to go beyond reporting the facts on environmental issues and pressured them to help shape public opinion. The Greens used the emotional pull of a pending environmental 'crisis' to manipulate the media into what amounts to conning the American people.

According to James Tyson, author of the 1981 book *Target America,* there are thousands of Communist propaganda agents working in the United States. Tyson explains the Soviets allocate over $240 million per year to fund these agents worldwide. Tyson backs up this estimate with information provided by an undercover agent for the FBI who was a member of the U.S. Communist Party. The Communist agents operating in America are known as 'Pro-Cells'. Pro-Cells are professionals such as journalists, advertisers, lawyers, doctors and other influential people.

On October 21, 1994, the *Associated Press* reported that Aldrich Ames, the CIA agent arrested as a spy, was paid more than $2.5 million by the Soviets. Mrs. Ames claimed she participated under duress. According to this *AP* story, after she was told where the money was coming from, she and Aldrich went to New York and spent 6,000 KGB dollars over the weekend.

Why are we spending millions of dollars to rescue the Soviet Union when it appears they have plenty of money to spend financing Communist efforts in the United States? Are we financing our own demise?

Creative Journalism

Creative journalism was evident in a 1993 *NBC* report on the condition of the Clearwater National Forest in Idaho. The story addressed accusations that heavy logging posed a threat to fish populations. *NBC* news showed photos of apparently dead fish lying in water and a scan of a large clear-cut mountain area. This was apparently to confirm to viewers that logging was killing fish. The clear-cut served as the background image for Anchorman Tom Brokaw.

Senator Larry Craig, (R-ID) publicly challenged *NBC* on the truth to the story and that resulted in an apology to viewers. Brokaw explained that the fish *NBC* featured were not actually dead, they were only briefly stunned for testing. According to one report, *NBC* never responded to Senator Craig's charge that the clear-cut shown was also false information. Senator Craig indicated the clear-cut was really a burn area in a forest in Washington state and not located in Idaho's Clearwater Forest.

Tom Brokaw may have taken the heat for the creative journalism of an *NBC* staff writer. Mr. Brokaw may not personally research the stories he reports. Maybe he is just handed a script to read. There is a difference between reading and writing the news. This story was contrived, the evidence created and it advocated the Greens political position.

Tom Brokaw and other journalists could help put an end to 'creative journalism' by publicly advocating a renewed commitment to accuracy among his peers. *NBC* is not alone in creating biased news reports.

Networks ought to report the news. Citizens ought to be allowed to form their own opinions. Mismanagement of the facts is a violation of the public trust. It ought to embarrass those who consider themselves professional journalists.

Americans who did not hear *NBC's* apologies may still believe the fish were dead because of timber harvest. We need to make a distinction between a news report and a news story.

- a news report is based on real facts
- a news story is make-believe

We can not form intelligent opinions if what we are told is based on fabrication. In the past, there was a significant difference between the sleaze rags and the evening news. Now the tactics and integrity levels appear to be the same. Where do professional journalists draw the line? What do they want to be known for, truth or trash?

Journalists are expected to adhere to the same level of honesty they expect and need from their fellow Americans. Journalists must be able to trust what their surgeon or auto mechanic tell them. Their health and well being depend on the integrity of other professionals.

If journalists can depend on the word of other Americans, then other Americans ought to be able to depend on the accuracy of their words. We rely on journalists as our news source and our emergency broadcast system. We have every right to expect to be well informed, not misinformed.

Apologies after the fact don't fix the problem. Striking it from the record is useless if the jury already heard the remark. The media ought to better police themselves and penalize those who do not practice responsible public broadcasting. If a network representative is accused and is found guilty of intentionally lying to the American people, it ought to result in penalties such as:

- fire the person (s) responsible for the false information, the reporter, the writer and/or the researcher.

- fine the networks a substantial amount or take the show off the air until a commitment to honesty is made.

This would be a major step toward restoring the trust of the American people for this profession.

Green leaders also have an obligation to be honest with the people of this nation. It is not acceptable to further political goals by lying. The American people deserve more respect. Deliberate lies or creative journalism, is fraud. Public information, like news reports, impact people's lives and influence political opinions.

False information about the environment can:

- cast a vote for a Green candidate
- lower public opinion of fellow Americans
- create support for a Green organization
- justify Eco-Terrorism

Big Con Jobs Begin With Little Con Jobs

The speech by Chief Seattle, made famous by the Green Movement, is not based on what the Chief said. The Chief's speech is a victim of creative journalism. It was improved by a film writer who thought the changes would create a stronger message for an environmental film.

The improved version of Chief Seattle's speech has been repeated in environmental publications, children's books and Earth Day events. Greens continue to use the improved version, aware it is enhanced, because it has more political value. Chief Seattle's speech is also featured on the cover of a Green party brochure. Altering the facts or not revealing all the facts is dishonest.

Green Rules of the Game, Manipulate the System

"...but there was a political decision that was made by those who introduced the Ancient Forest Protection Act, that by introducing a national bill at this time, you may have more enemies than friends...

... A lot of our strategy is to nationalize this issue, and if every Senator in the country could see that their state would be affected directly, they might not be willing to protect what we are saying is a very special and different, unique, ecosystem in the Pacific Northwest...

*...all native forests do deserve protection, they would all
be protected, as well as native grasslands and native
woodlands and native coastlines and so on under the
endangered ecosystems act."*

Marc Liverman, Attorney
Conservation Director Audubon Society - Portland
LAW Conference 1991

This statement shows those involved have no problem
intentionally deceiving our Senators, other political
representatives or the American people. The language used
by the Audubon attorney, *'protect what we are saying is special'*
is interesting. The choice of words is significant. The language
suggests other areas have already been targeted and the
political plan is to over emphasize the value of this particular
ecosystem to establish a legal precedent to control ecosystems
across the nation. They are getting political support by not
sharing all the facts.

*"Manipulation is persuading people to make up their
minds while withholding some of the facts from them."*

Harold Evans
British Journalist,1971

Hitler lied whenever it suited him. The most important thing
to remember is, this is the mentality of the Greens. This is not
to suggest that every person involved with the National
Audubon Society is a liar or a Green Communist. It is to
confirm manipulating the truth in this manner fits 'the end
justifies the means' mentality of the Greens.

The Greens:

- violate the public trust
- take advantage of the public's financial support
- use the reputation of environmental organizations
- manipulate the public, politicians and political system
- get by with it if they can

The Audubon Society was very involved in the Spotted Owl issue. From the beginning, one of the key reasons given to stop all logging was that Spotted Owls could only live and survive in old growth timber. The 1982 edition of the *Audubon Society Encyclopedia of North American Birds*, indicate something different. It indicates the spotted owl is flexible. It can live in tree cavities, on the floor of caves, on the ground near large rocks and even takes over nests other birds have abandoned. We were 'set up' to believe otherwise.

> *"... with the spotted owl, there was two years invested in doing nothing but press, public relations and media work before any litigation was filed, that's critically important.* The other important thing is that you never emphasize your legal theories to the press; you emphasize what you're saving. *The legal theory never appears as attractive to the public than the fact that you're saving big, old trees.*
>
> Andy Stahl
> Sierra Club Legal Defense Club
> Seattle Office: Resource Analyst
> Western Public Interest Law Conference - 1988
> (Bold Emphasis Added)

The end justifies the means. The Green Movement continues to prey on emotions to achieve immediate political reactions and increase the size of their bank accounts as they continue to advance their political agenda.

> *"The Northern Spotted Owl is the wildlife species of choice to act as a surrogate for old-growth protection and I've often thought that thank goodness the spotted owl evolved in the Northwest, for if it hadn't, we'd have to genetically engineer it. It's the perfect species to use as a surrogate."*
>
> Andy Stahl
> Sierra Club Legal Defense Club
> Seattle Office: Resource Analyst
> Western Public Interest Law Conference - 1988

The purpose for nationalizing Spotted Owl and timber harvest issues was to put control of the industry in the hands of the federal government. Slick public relations campaigns and media coverage across the nation created the impression the federal government had to step in or the owl would go extinct and timber harvest would cause severe environmental damage. Instead of a state issue to be settled by the state, it became a national issue that had to be settled by the federal government. That was the goal, to set the precedent for the federal government to intervene and control the situation.

We need to keep in mind; our government is not the problem. The Greens are using our system to bring down our system and they created this situation. Communist leader Gus Hall indicated in 1972 that one of their political goals was to nationalize American industries and demand those industries be controlled by federal laws (Public control).

Americans had no reason to doubt the facts presented on the Spotted Owl or any other environmental issue. If no one questions the Greens, they can simply move on to their next target and do the same thing. That is how the Greens operate. The Spotted Owl was never the issue. Taking control of one state economy at a time is the objective. The following statement made by Gus Hall in 1972 clearly defines this goal.

> *"Socialism corrects the basic flaw of capitalism. It sets human society on a new path. **The means of production, factories, mines and mills become the property of the people.** They operate and produce only to fulfill human needs. They are not motivated by profits. **This is the foundation for a new set of priorities, for new values...What is involved is a conflict of values."***

> Gus Hall
> Ecology -1972
> (Bold Emphasis Added)

Just Off the Internet

Control of production and distribution is communism. The Green Communists are using the environmental cause to hide their efforts to control industries and individuals across America.

> *"Tired of the same old system: Join the Communist Party, USA*
>
> *Susan Wheeler wrote the following, excerpted from People's Weekly World: Fledgling efforts to approach logging in the Northwest in a new way that respects the requirements of whole ecosystems, already tentative and frail, are in imminent danger of falling victim to timber corporations' appetite for raw material to turn into profit.*
>
> *Both houses of Congress have passed a measure that will open national forest up to new assaults and essentially nullify the Clinton administrations's feeble Northwest forest plan and efforts to save salmon. 'Salvage' operations are touted as measures to remove untidy 'dead or dying' timber, thus improving the health of forests, although environmentalists have long pointed out that dead timber plays a crucial role in the life cycle of forest ecosystems.*
>
> *In particular, seven of the sales are within Oregon's Ten Mile Creek watershed and neighboring watersheds. Ten Mile Creek is the site of a unique research experiment designed to restore wild salmon runs by recreating the conditions that foster successful spawning."*

This article was featured in the 'From the Internet' section of the July/August 1995 edition of *Ecologic* magazine. It is easy to see from reading this statement that Wheeler has a more than passing interest and working knowledge of timber harvest and environmental issues. Wheeler promotes the Green idea of managing entire ecosystems which includes not removing any timber, dead or alive, from the forest. This suggests the Communist Party is well informed and very involved in this issue.

Obviously the Communists have been working to achieve their 1972 goal to gain control of mill production. The federal government is directly involved in environmental decisions regarding timber harvest. The Communists have been successful.

Green Communists are using the environmental cause to justify their calls for Americans to change our 'values' and to accept their values. Green values amount to socialism and 'compulsory Green living.' The Greens need to convince Americans to surrender control of production and distribution to the federal government. Years of planning and propaganda were used to prepare the public to support the Greens taking legal control of the timber industry.

Public or government control of production and distribution is Communism. If we continue to accept Green control of business and industry in America, the Greens will continue to take control, one business at a time. Greens are also attacking individual rights. This is why environmental laws are the center of a growing debate across America. Environmental protection is not the issue. The issue is Green control of industries and individuals.

Wheeler's article uses the environmental cause to suggest:

- capitalism is bad for the environment
- ecosystem management is good for the environment
- Green values and Communist's values are the same
- becoming a Communist will save the environment

If Americans continue to allow the Greens to use the environmental cause to force government control of free enterprise, the Greens will have successfully manipulated Americans into volunteering for communism.

Since the Spotted Owl issue made the news, more owls have been found. The Greens avoid that topic. They intend to advance communism by keeping the public focus on loss not gain. The Greens are not concerned with the facts, only with accomplishing their political goals. We have been set up to accept what the Greens say is true. We have been lulled to sleep. When an individual person or business is accused of an environmental crime, Americans need to say, prove it!

The Greens have spent hours and thousands of American's hard earned dollars convincing us to trust that they are acting in our best interest. We need to realize, we are seeing the goals of the Communist Party carried out. We need to stop trusting the Greens and start looking at environmental issues from a cautious political standpoint.

Create-A-Crisis

The ideas the Greens are promoting are based on a pre-set political agenda. Many of the environmental issues we are dealing with were outlined as political objectives years ago.

The World Conservation Strategy was put together in 1980 and outlines how the Greens believe the world ought to be run. According to the conservation time line, the World Bank called for action on forest in 1989. That fits the time frame for the Spotted Owl crisis and setting the public up two years in advance of the alleged crisis.

Whittaker Chambers is a former Soviet agent who defected to the United States in the late 1940's. Chambers was a Senior Editor of *Time* magazine. During that period, he states in his book *Witness* that Henry Dexter White, Secretary of the Treasury helped create the World Bank and later ran the organization. Chambers states that he knew that Henry Dexter White was a Soviet agent. It is not hard to believe this is true considering career CIA officer Aldrich Ames was arrested and convicted as a Soviet Spy in 1994.

Greens want Congress to endorse the World Conservation Strategy and use it as a guide for environmental policies in the United States. The World Conservation Strategy includes this objective:

> *"set out a plan of action to bring about the required political decisions and allocations of financial and other resources."*

In other words, the end justifies the means. Do whatever it takes. Set us up and manufacture support for the 'required political decisions'. The Pacific Northwest, according to the World Conservation Strategy, is a world heritage site and requires "careful allocation and management of timber concessions". To set us up to support the 'required political decisions', to gain control of the timber industry and the economy of the region, what had to happen?

- World Bank called for action on forest
- Manufacture crisis to make it a national issue
- Spotted Owl becomes federal issue
- State economy controlled by federal government
- Government involved in production and distribution

Control of production and distribution is how business under communism functions. The timber industry explained the Spotted Owl was a surrogate to conceal the political objective to control the industry and stop logging. Green attorneys openly admit the owl was used to help make logging illegal.

*"The special role of disinformation is enhanced by the aggressive and ambitious character of communist external policy. This aims at **promoting and establishing communist regimes in noncommunist countries throughout the world by giving support to the extreme left-wing opposition, by gaining temporary political allies, by exploiting and deepening whatever internal crises may occur, and even by creating artificial crises.**"*

Anatoliy Golitsyn
New Lies for Old
(Bold Emphasis Added)

Pick A Number, Any Number!

Speaking of disinformation, how many species are really going extinct? According to Green groups there is no exact number; one source sets the number at over 165,000 a year, another 500,000 by the year 2000. Another research source indicates that the United States has recorded only 7 species, perhaps 13 total, which might have gone extinct since 1973.

There appears to be a *slight* discrepancy. Are we losing 13 species in 21 years or 165,000 species per year? What estimate is true?

Where is the scientific data and list of species to support these claims? Science is absolute. If there are that many species dying, we ought to have a list of what they are, where they are and a record of how many there used to be. Without scientific documentation, it is impossible to form an intelligent opinion.

Where do the Greens get these numbers? The Green approach to science appears to be: pick a number, any number, the bigger the number, the better.

What Are the Facts?

There is no question we have some major environmental
messes to clean up. These extinction numbers are just too far
apart to be above board. Something is wrong. Losing 7
species over a 21 year period vs. losing 165,000 species per
year makes a big difference in how we respond to the
situation.

We either have a catastrophic problem or a manageable set of
circumstances we can correct by making different and better
choices. Wild claims don't cut it. Documentaries by Green
groups don't reflect the overall picture. What America needs
and deserves, is an in-depth look at the issues in question.

Before we can help determine what direction this country
takes, we need accurate information. Our future depends on
it. What television network is willing to help Americans
uncover the truth? An on-going public debate would give us
time to understand the environmental issues.

It is important to repeat, those involved in environmental
careers, like any group of professionals, must be accountable
for what they advocate. They must be able to back up what
they are 'saying' with documentable facts.

Huge discrepancies in claims, lack of unbiased public
information and the subversive approach of the Greens
continue to support the theory that environmental issues are
being exaggerated to further the Greens political aims.
Americans are willing to do our share to correct
environmental problems. We need accurate information to
effectively address the tasks we face.

Incompetence or Dishonesty?

Environmental organizations have created the impression they are the most reliable sources for environmental information. Most Americans don't question their facts.

The 1995 book, *The True State Of The Planet,* edited by Ronald Baily, challenges current reports concerning the environment. This book is the combined effort by some of America's leading environmental researchers. The authors present what they believe is an accurate interpretation of environmental science. The authors seek to make distinctions between environmental activism and environmental science. The book offers up to date information and disputes many of the claims made by the Green Movement. It is worth reading.

Americans who care about the environment recognize the reason environmental groups are presenting false information to the public. Roberta Parry, of the U.S. Environmental Protection Agency, wrote this letter to the Sierra Club. It appeared in the April 1995 edition of the magazine.

> *"In 'Conservation a la Carte',* **Paul Rauber incorrectly states that pesticide runoff into streams and rivers is the primary cause of water pollution in the United States** *....While pesticides have been detected in some drinking water supplies, nitrate, a nitrogen compound is by far the chemical contaminant most responsible for violations of drinking-water standards.* **Pesticides (which affect 27 percent of impaired stream miles) often seem to be used by environmental groups to gain the attention and dollars of the public,** *while the major causes of water pollution are ignored."*
>
>

Roberta Parry

Agriculture Policy Branch,
Office of Policy, Planning and Evaluation,
U.S. Environmental Protection Agency
(Bold Emphasis Added)

This is not a mere violation of the public trust. It is blatant disregard for the truth. The article 'Conservation a la Carte' was written by *Sierra* Senior Editor, Paul Rauber. Mr. Rauber may not do his own research, but when it's published, *Sierra* magazine and their staff are responsible for what is written. With the resources available to the Sierra Club, the vast network of environmental facts and information that includes the EPA, there is no excuse to present inaccurate and misleading information.

We can only draw one of two conclusions. This error is due to incompetence or dishonesty. If environmental sources are incompetent, we can't rely on them. If environmental sources are dishonest we can't rely on them. How much more inaccurate information have we received on critical environmental issues? Correct information is essential if we are serious about taking care of the environment.

The environment is like a patient who needs help getting well. If we were the patient, we would want a diagnosis and treatment plan based on fact, not fabrication. Misrepresention could put our life at risk. Like an illness, the diagnosis and treatment plan for a healthy environment require competent, honest information or we are putting the environment at risk.

What can we learn from this?

- Green groups are not always a reliable source for environmental information.

- Sensationalizing false information is okay if it increases membership and financial contributions.

- It is more important to increase public support for the Green political agenda than it is to tell the truth.

- Environmental protection is not the goal. If it was, groups would try to stop water pollution by using their dollars to get the real contaminant out of the water.

Misrepresentation is counter-productive. If we accept the end justifies the means mentality, the Greens will continue to put political goals first. Do we want to stop pollution or fund a revolution? Like a wolf in sheep's clothing, many Americans don't see these groups as the political animals they are.

As the saying goes, necessity is the mother of invention. How much of what we are hearing is true? What has been manufactured to serve the Greens political agenda? Before we set public policies that will turn our society upside down and put an end to individual freedom in this country, we ought to get the facts. Gradual Green control will occur if Americans continue to trust what the Greens are 'saying' needs to be done. It's just a matter of time.

We have environmental problems and we have to decide how to handle them. We can't allow Green *Chicken Little* messages to put us in a crisis level mentality. The Greens need to create an unreasonable sense of urgency so Americans won't have time to consider the issues or the facts.

Panic Politics

America needs good laws, not more laws. There are too many bills presented for consideration each session. Over 260 pieces of Green legislation alone were introduced in the 101 and 102 Congresses. That is too many bills in one subject area. How can they receive adequate review?

This legislation overload is partly to blame for the problems we are experiencing within our government system. Third parties won't fix this. The two party system works, but it's gotten off track and needs our assistance to correct the problems.

Our political officials are overworked. They meet with constituents, serve on committees, vote on bills, make numerous personal appearances and campaign if they run for office again. What happens with that kind of schedule? The daily workload is divided among the staff. House and Senate staff review bills, listen to lobbyists and then report to the Congressman or Senator.

Solution

If we put a limit on the number of bills introduced each session we could slow down the process and regain control. The avalanche of legislation gets laws passed before they are adequately scrutinized. The crime bill, for instance, was about 2000 pages long. Just days before the vote, some political leaders had not even received a complete copy of the bill.

There was pressure to get it passed before the end of the session. The big push came from the administration. Lobbying groups started the routine. Trading favors and trading votes got it passed.

Where is the fire? Why do we need to be in such a hurry to pass this kind of precedent setting legislation? If politicians had more time to personally study proposed legislation and then discuss the ramifications with the people they represent, this kind of political insanity could be changed and avoided. Politicians ought to focus on correcting and improving our nation, not stumbling through piles of proposed legislation.

Political leaders ought to have plenty of time to study the issues and pass necessary laws, not more laws. Then they could determine whether or not the law compliments our constitution, preserves our freedom, protects our culture and ensures our national security. Bills that don't meet these basic standards ought to be referred to the people or thrown out.

We, the people, share the responsibility for creating some of these problems. Running for political office has become a popularity contest rather than a race based on who will do the best job for the country and the people.

Many politicians end up being celebrities rather than concentrating on being effective legislators. The public expects politicians to make hundreds of public appearances while in office. Qualified people leave office due to the constant demand on their personal life.

After a day on the job, politicians are expected to give up their evenings and weekends to meet the demand for public appearances. Politicians, like the rest of us, ought to have time to re-group and relax. A number of public appearances are part of the job, but if legislators had time to ponder proposed legislation and go home at days end, they would probably do a better job.

Legislating Population Control

Population control and natural dying are also on the Green agenda. Natural dying and assisted suicide are meant to accomplish the same thing; lower the population. Like Hitler, the Greens are redefining life and death issues. The Greens are making death a political issue to diminish the value of life, from abortion to assisted suicide. The choice to use or not to use technology to save a life is a personal decision. Greens suggest using technology to save a life ought to include consideration of the value of the life in question.

Assisted suicide is considered an environmental issue because if the people who have been diagnosed as terminally ill or permanently disabled were to choose to die, it would reduce our population. In premise, the idea of choice is not completely unreasonable. Caution must to be exercised to ensure, if someone chooses to check-out, it is their decision, not legalized murder.

Hitler took control of life and death issues based on his values of the quality of the life to be saved. He began by ordering retarded children and the mentally ill put to death because they were considered 'useless eaters.' The same mentality was applied when the Jews entered the death camps. The Nazis divided them according to their labor value. The Jews were either sent to the left or the right. This was an instant sentence to live or to die based on someone else's judgment of a person's value to society.

German citizens allowed themselves to become immune to the pain of their neighbors. Hitler created a death culture using fear, terrorism and manufactured hate. He legalized murder.

The Greens are affecting our culture. They are making their ideas legal. We need to pay close attention to state ballot initiatives. The Greens, in 1991, specifically identified the strategy to use the ballot initiative process to:

- publicize their alternative ideas
- challenge the two party system
- advance Green politics

The Greens are using ballot initiatives to get pieces of their political agenda legalized. Voters don't know the initiatives are part of the overall Green agenda. This is another Green set up. The Green plan is to cause the transformation of our society one initiative at a time. The Greens camouflage their politics because they don't want Americans to vote or campaign against the initiatives. Every initiative they can slip by takes us one step closer to a Green future.

Jeremy Rifkin, author of the book *Entropy*, suggests we need to reduce our population to the level it was in the Solar Age to maintain the earth's carrying capacity. Rifkin estimates that population was about 1 billion people in 1800. After that time period, we changed from solar based to extraction based energy consumption.

Rifkin indicates the world's population should reach 8 billion by the year 2015. How many of us, worldwide need to go, to reach a Solar Age population? If we understand correctly, it seems we need to reduce the human population by 7 billion people over the next 20 years to reach 1 billion. Rifkin suggests these steps to reduce the population:

- License parents for no more than two children
- Penalty for more children is higher taxes
- Citizens volunteer to limit families to two children
- Sterilization programs, force could be necessary

David Brower, of Earth Island Institute and Free Willy fame seems to agree with Rifkin. Brower stated:

> "childbearing should be a punishable crime against society, unless the parents hold a government license...all potential parents should be required to use contraceptive chemicals, for the government issuing antidotes to citizens chosen for childbearing."
>
> Dawning of the New Age of the New World Order

Hitler shared the concept of superior people and population control. He eliminated the Jews, the retarded and others because they were, in his opinion, not fit to live. He considered them vermin and an enemy of the Fatherland, Motherland.

> "We in the Green Movement aspire to a cultural model in which killing a forest will be considered more contemptible and more criminal than the sale of 6 year old children to Asian brothels."
> Carl Amery
> Greens

Earth First founder Dave Foreman has an interesting point of view on population control. He seems to share Hitler's mentality of extermination. During an interview with Jerry Mason, Foreman was asked what his three main goals were.

> "my three main goals would be to reduce human population to about 100 million worldwide, destroy the industrial infrastructure and see wilderness with it's full complement of species returning throughout the world."

The population of the United States is about 261.6 million. If there was no one else in the world, the U.S. alone would have to reduce our population by 161.6 million to reach Foreman's goal for world population. Another population thought from Dave Foreman:

> "Aids is not a malediction, but the welcome and natural remedy to reduce the population of the planet...should human beings disappear, I surely wouldn't mind."

Public information sources indicate that Dave Foreman came up with the idea for Earth First while on a camping trip. According to the authors of *Trashing the Economy*, Ron Arnold and Alan Gottlieb, in 1979, Dave Foreman was actually propositioned by the Wilderness Society and the Sierra Club to form a radical environmental group that they would finance. The author's informants report Foreman accepted that deal.

Earth First became what mainstream groups publicly referred to as the radical fringe. Earth First went public and became the visible, radical arm for the Green movement. The terrorist activities of Earth First make the politics of mainstream groups seem mild. Earth First helped to:

- sensationalize environmental issues
- nationalize environmental issues
- make the politics of the mainstream seem rational

This is another set-up. Trick the American people into supporting the political ideas of mainstream groups because they are less radical than Earth First. This does not mean the political ideas of the mainstream groups are reasonable. It means, when politicians compare demands, the mainstream groups now appear to be the lesser of two evils. This political hoax was also used to:

- increase public concern for the environment
- increase public support for Green politics
- increase public contributions

It worked, but picking the lesser of two evils is not a good way to set environmental policy.

What does this tell us about the integrity of these mainstream environmental groups? Betraying the trust of the American people is acceptable. The end justifies the means.

Taking Terrorism Mainstream

The Sierra Club has in the past publicly distanced themselves from groups like Earth First. A May 1995 article for *In These Times* magazine reveals Dave Foreman has been named to the elite 15 person Sierra Club board. Foreman is also on Sierra Club's five member executive committee for 1995-96. This ought to make it clear, radical politics and terrorism are acceptable to the mainstream groups. According to the article, Foreman will play a leading role. This also shows us the radical fringe was never really the radical fringe.

David Brower, founder of the Earth Island Institute, was also named to the Sierra Club board. He was once ousted by the Sierra Club for being too radical. Obviously, times have changed.

We ought to be concerned that Dave Foreman is a part of the leadership of one of the largest mainstream environmental groups. It indicates that radical ideas are a part of the Green agenda.

The Nazi movement began as a tiny band of radicals. Those radicals gained recognition and then took their radical ideas to the mainstream. The masses began to accept those radical ideas and terrorism became a part of mainstream politics in Germany. The Greens seem to be following the same path.

The Greens have their own set of radical ideas they are now taking mainstream. Although the Greens have not publicly revealed plans to exterminate people to lower the population, they have called for voluntary human extinction.

As a people and as a nation, we can not ignore the facts. Reminiscent of the Nazis, participants in the Green movement are lying to the masses and using terrorism to gain political power. Radical politics and acts of terrorism will not solve environmental problems.

Environmental efforts ought to focus on restoration and taking responsible steps toward preventing further problems. The current focus on spending millions of donated dollars on litigation or to finance terrorism is not the most effective way to solve environmental disputes.

These groups ought to focus on cooperation and spend those millions of dollars helping businesses and individuals correct the problems. They could be taking creative and cooperative steps to help boost our economy by paying unemployed citizens to replant burned areas or clean up riverbanks. Instead, these groups focus on lobbying and law suits to change public land use policies to legally force their ideas on the American people.

The goal is not cooperation, it is control. The problem is three fold. First, the Greens are not the only Americans capable of understanding an environmental issue. Greens are not the only Americans who can think. Second, American citizens are loosing equal representation to a growing eco-dictatorship. The third part of the problem is citizens do not realize the Greens have created this eco-monopoly to gain control of land use in America.

The Green movement has become an eco-monopoly. An eco-monopoly is different than the number of people in America who support a healthy environment. An eco-monopoly is this author's term for Green control of public information regarding environmental issues. From 'spendy' Green documentaries to the daily news, the Greens have all but eliminated American's opportunity to hear both sides of an issue.

There is little difference how the Greens are controlling public information to sway public opinion and how the Nazis used public information to sway public opinion. One sided propaganda convinced Germans that the Jews were materialistic scum who were no longer fit to live as they had been living. One sided propaganda is convincing some Americans to believe others are materialistic scum who are no longer fit to live as they have been living.

The greatest problem with this eco-monopoly is that it dominates environmental decision making on the national level. The opinions of other American citizens aren't getting the attention they deserve because they can not compete with the financial resources and the media prejudice the Greens have set up.

Almost everything we hear and see regarding environmental issues is based on information provided by environmental groups. Green groups are calling for radical change in America based on their ideas of environmental protection. Americans need to find a way to hear both sides of an issue before political decisions are made.

A few people resisted Hitler's lies. Those in the resistance movement made up their own minds. They fought the Nazis and saved thousands of innocent people in the process. They approached this political mine field from the standpoint of what could be done instead of what couldn't be done.

Every American wants to do what is necessary to protect the environment. Like most issues regarding the environmental cause, we do not know what is true. The only way we are going to find out is to get both sides in front of the people and figure out who knows what they are talking about.

Some population experts suggest we do not have a major population problem. Population issues affect us all and so will an oppressive government system. If the future of our nation and the world is at risk, isn't it time we found out what is going on?

Green Is Extreme

> *"The elimination of beef and other meat from the human diet is now required if we are to have any hope of saving the planet and ensuring our children's future."*
>
> *Jeremy Rifkin*
> Biosphere Politics

Rifkin is a political leader in the Green movement and is aggressively pushing this part of the Green agenda in Washington D.C. The Greens want control of production and distribution. This includes controlling our natural resources, economic base and food supply.

What would it take to get control of, or put an end to beef production? Find a way to prevent ranchers from raising and supplying beef to the American people.

Can the Greens actually eliminate beef and other meats as a food choice in the United States? Consider the 'Big Guns' involved in this Green coalition, all targeting the individual rancher.

The beef business is a prime example of Green politics in action.

*"What everyone likes is the Big victory you load them
cattle trucks for the last time and they go driving off
into the sunset and they never come back. "*

*"But you can win a lot more victories than that ultimate
one, you can win a lot more victories by making him
(the rancher) pay for what he does out there and by
making it so expensive in his operation and making so
many changes for him to continue to run his cattle on
the public lands that he goes broke, he can't do it, he
has to come up with other ways to be a rancher. "*

*"When you get right down to it, the boots and the hat,
boy for them guys, its a way of life."*

*"The ultimate picture is of course, the last cattle truck
driving off into the sunset, but that's not how you
win."*

*"How you win is one at a time, one at a time, he goes
out of business, he dies, you wait him out, but you
win."*

Roy Elicker
National Wildlife Federation Counsel
(Bold Emphasis Added)

Does this sound like a sincere plea to protect the environment
or a plan to put a ranching family out of business? To end
production you have to destroy the producer. Make control
possible by making control legal.

It sounds like the Nazis secretly discussing the fate of Jewish
businesses, but this is the type of heartless dialogue common
among Green activists. Elicker's message goes on to point out
how activists can use endangered species to put cattlemen out

of business. These mean-spirited attitudes are carefully concealed from the general public.

This does not mean all representatives of the National Wildlife Federation are Communists. It does mean that this is an example of how the Greens are using concern for the environment to destroy the beef industry.

Put A Little Green In Your Life

Would you burn down your own home? That's the idea the Greens are selling to the American public to justify the end of beef production.

Why would a rancher destroy the land that feeds them? If cattle can't eat, they die. If what the Greens say is completely true, the rancher would have put themselves out of business a long time ago. To produce beef for this nation, generation after generation, they had to take care of the land.

Put yourself in the same situation. Put a little green in your life. Boy, for you guys it's the football, your computer, your music, your clothes, your career, *'boy for you guys, it's a way of life'*. Yes, it is. It's a matter of freedom and personal choice.

According to this Green political logic, your choice of clothes (and other personal preferences) makes you automatically guilty of being an anti-environmentalist. It doesn't make sense, but what if people believed it? By the same token, ranchers should not be labeled or judged automatically guilty because of their chosen profession and dress code.

Ridiculing personal preference to imply guilt, as opposed to addressing the issue in question, is asinine. You might hear that approach on a playground. Kids use the saying, 'you're ugly, and your mama dresses you funny'. When was the last time, in a political discussion, an adult accused you of having cooties?

Why are the Greens attacking cowboy clothes? It is an effective manipulative tool for the Greens. The purpose is to cloud the public's judgment. There is a method to the madness. A few, well-placed remarks dehumanize the issues.

Greens have mastered the Communist art of diverting the public's attention. The tactic is called character assassination. It prevents people from discussing the issue in question. The Greens do not give people the facts or explain the consequences. Instead, the Greens keep the jokes flying and people laughing. The result is, the audience forgets the issue, likes the Green comedian, and leaves with a strong dose of the Green political perspective. It is a very effective method to avoid the factual and the human side of an issue.

America needs to take a step back and re-evaluate these issues: Health care, animal rights, anti-hunting, gun control, population control, natural dying, privatization of our educational system and political correctness.

The objective is to get Green political ideas legalized before we understand there is a difference between concern for the environment and being coerced into supporting Green politics. If allowed to go unchecked, America's response to environmental sensationalism will give Green Communists time to accomplish their mission.

It doesn't matter what is true. It matters what people think is true. It's all a matter of perception. The Greens are good at creating false perceptions.

Most big businesses are made up of small, individual businesses. Beef production is the result of individual ranching operations. If the Greens put one rancher out of business, the industry will not be destroyed. If the Greens are successful putting many ranchers out of business, one at a time, it adds up to the end of an industry. That is a big deal. We have lost a food choice. Families have lost their independence and their income. America has lost economic strength.

The National Wildlife Federation representative spelled out the Green strategy. The end justifies the means. The objective is to put Americans out of business one at a time. The big victory comes from little victories. That's how the Greens plan to win.

This has nothing to do with the environment or the Greens would focus on the environment, not issue blanket (dehumanizing) orders to put people out of business.

What's to win?

Is this a game or a war? It's a war against America being waged on one citizen and one group at a time. If we accept government control of other peoples lives, we begin to sacrifice our freedom. Gaining control of one person, one group, one step at a time, is the political strategy.

> *"We're in a war, the war of industrial civilization against the natural world"*
>
> Dave Foreman
> 1991

Recent reports indicate the 'Unabomber' revealed he was part of a group that wanted to break down society and divide it into smaller units. The Greens have a similar goal. They want to create bioregions and establish small communities.

The Unabomber stated in a story by the *Associated Press* on April 26,1995 that the goal of his group was:

> **"the destruction of the world wide industrial system.**
> *Through our bombings we hope to promote social instability in industrial society and give encouragement to those who hate the industrial system."*
>
> (Bold Emphasis Added)

The goal to completely transform our society is also a Green goal. The Communist strategy is to cause chaos within our society to destroy American's desire to fight for our country.

> **"Visualize Industrial Collapse"**
> *Earth First*

> *"my three main goals would be to reduce human population to about 100 million worldwide, **destroy the industrial infrastructure** and see wilderness with it's full complement of species returning throughout the world."*
>
> *Dave Foreman*
> Earth First Co-Founder
> (Bold Emphasis Added)

The political messages of the Unabomber, Earth First and Dave Foremen seem to be the same.

Success does leave clues. Hitler realized before the people of a nation would accept a new set of cultural values, the old set of traditional images and patriotic symbols had to be systematically devalued in the eyes of the people. This is about our collective American 'ways of life' and our culture. It is about our freedom to choose whatever we would and could be. We are being set up to believe that attacks on our society are accidental grassroots cries for environmental protection. We are being set-up to accept our past isn't worth preserving so we too will accept new symbols and traditions. The Green objective is to change Americans values about, cowboys, meat, business, society and American history. Cowboys represent a key part of American history. They are a symbol of our pioneering spirit, individuality, ruggedness, the wild west and our national pride. Cowboys played a big role in creating our culture and traditions. Even traditions like hamburgers.

The Greens are using environmental protection as an excuse to put ranchers out of business and gain control over what we eat. We are to live happily ever after eating roots and rice. Whatever the issue, hamburgers or endangered species, we need to participate in the political process. We need to recognize when we are being set up for Green Communism or the Greens will continue to manipulate us.

Using Your Imagination

Writers, producers and directors are being asked to further the environmental cause by using entertainment to help sway public opinion. Most of these Americans do not understand that behind the environmental cause lays the Green movement. Some do.

The fall of 1989, *In CONTEXT* magazine featured an article on 'Redefining Entertainment'. The article focused on how entertainment could be used to transform values and promote social change. Entertainment was a miracle tool to:

- popularize the transformation of society
- attract masses to concept of change
- unite audience and create a following
- create anger toward enemies presented on screen
- send subliminal messages to sway political opinion
- change the world

Norman Fleishman was interviewed for this article. Fleishman is known as the conscience of Hollywood and indicates he was influenced by Joe McCarthy. He states:

> *"I was around the progressive movement as a child, so I agreed with McCarthy only about one thing: that the storytellers were the most powerful people in the world. He went after the storytellers, had many of them blacklisted in Hollywood, because he felt their power. **In a sense I followed in his footsteps,** only **I've taken the opposite tack. I do what I can to assist and support them and inspire them, if I can,** by way of these meetings I've held over the years."*
>
> (Bold Emphasis Added)

Excuse me? Joe McCarthy's mission was to stop Communist storytellers from using entertainment to spread propaganda and subliminally influence the American people. Fleishman indicates he has 'taken the opposite tack'. The opposite of stopping Communist storytellers from using entertainment is helping Communist storytellers use entertainment to spread propaganda.

Later in the article, Mr. Fleishman states:

> *"**So we need to popularize these things that we believe in, add the element of entertainment-** the gripping, the holding, the entrancing....I'm not saying this is an iron-clad plan to change the world, but I do believe in the possibility of transformation."*
>
> (Bold Emphasis Added)

Is Mr. Fleishman saying he helps Communist storytellers or is he saying he uses the power of entertainment to impose his political beliefs for social transformation on unsuspecting Americans?

America, we must stay mentally alert for subversive messages woven into entertainment. What Fleishman is advocating is not honest. It is based on deception. It is more like a con job or a sting operation. Entertainment is supposed to be entertaining; a performance, a party, something people do for amusement. Americans do not expect entertainment to be used as a political tool to change their values and political beliefs.

It is significant to mention that issue of *'InCONTEXT'* was sent to then Governor Bill Clinton. The Winter 1990 magazine printed this letter to the editor:

> *"Thank you for sending me a copy of your recent issue of* *'InCONTEXT'.* **I enjoyed the article featuring Norman Fleishman on 'Redefining Entertainment'. His behind the scene's work has educated many Hollywood writers about the important social and environmental issues** *that are increasingly the concern of the 'middle'.* **I wish you continued success in your goal to make the major cultural shifts our world is now experiencing to be as graceful and as positive as possible."**
>
> Bill Clinton
Governor of Arkansas
(Bold Emphasis Added)

What major cultural shifts was Governor Clinton speaking of? Mr. Clinton indicates he supports using 'behind the scenes' tactics to manipulate the American people and use entertainment to spread biased political messages.

Most Americans do not expect entertainment to be used to brainwash them into accepting new political ideas for social transformation. Political ideas are like any other product. Quality products and ideas are sold on their merit and value to the buyer (honesty). Shoddy products or questionable ideas can't be sold on merit. Shoddy ideas or products require conning the buyer into accepting a product or idea by using misleading information (deception). It's like beach front property in Arizona. After you buy it, it's too late.

Many writers, stars and producers are unaware the Greens have long courted Hollywood to promote their political ideas using news and entertainment sources. This is why news includes make-believe facts and make-believe entertainment is used for Green political brainwashing. This is completely unreasonable.

The environmental cause and Hollywood stars are not to blame. The 'Greening' of Hollywood is the problem. 'Behind the scenes' politics take unfair advantage of trusting Americans. Using entertainment to indoctrinate unsuspecting consumers, including children, is underhanded.

> *"A red cancer is gnawing at the vitals of this nation and the world. The Communists are working at being Communists 24 hours a day. Let us work at being Americans 24 hours a day."*
>
> *Cecil B. deMille*
> Movie Director -- 1948

Case In Point

In one episode, the television program *SeaQuest* focused on a crew member, who craved a mouth-watering hamburger. The crew member had to get the meat illegally. He had to smuggle it on-board and secretly prepare the hamburger.

Just as he was ready to take that first bite, the captain walked in and ordered the crew member to surrender the hamburger. The captain justified this action by reminding the guy meat consumption was illegal and it was his duty to enforce the law.

Earlier in the show the audience learned that meat had been outlawed by the government. It was determined meat was bad for public health, so meat had been banned and was no longer a food choice.

As soon as the captain was outside the door, he decided the hamburger looked good, so he took a couple of big bites, then tossed the remainder in the trash. He deprived another, but indulged himself and wasted the rest.

Case in point: Do as I say, not as I do. In a Communist country, the privileged few get what the masses are denied.

Where Do We Draw the Line?

There is a difference between life in a capitalist free society and life in a Communist society.

Support for environmental protection does not equal American's support for a political revolution and a switch to communism. When Green political objectives become public knowledge, the people who continue to publicly support the Greens ought to be the first to walk their talk. They ought to stop their lives, give up their wealth, their property and live by the Green rules they are trying to force on others.

Communism is based on a double standard. Do as I say, not as I do. Russian leaders preached equality to the masses and went home to live in private luxury. 'Do as I Say, Not as I Do' is the Communist double standard.

Examples of do as I say and not as I do by those involved in the environmental cause can be found across the nation. Here are two examples.

The Sierra Club played a key role in nationalizing the

Spotted Owl issue to stop logging in the Pacific Northwest. According to a 1994 story by the *Associated Press,* William Arthur, the regional director for the Sierra Club, made this comment during panel discussions with President Clinton criticizing the timber industry:

> *"We cut like there's no tomorrow and tomorrow caught up with us yesterday."*

This statement would suggest to most people that Arthur believes too many trees have been cut and that no more should be cut down. Think again.

Soon after he successfully helped close down small mills and puts hundreds of loggers out of business, specifically because cutting down trees was harmful to the environment, Arthur cut down 70% of the remaining trees on his property. The money Author made was designated for home improvements. According to the report, twelve years ago Arthur cut down enough trees to put himself through graduate school. Arthur justified his reverse political position, stating:

> *"the Sierra Club doesn't have trouble, with logging when it's appropriate."*

According to the report, Ken Kholi, a spokesperson for the timber industry indicated that Arthur, representing the Sierra Club was among eight other environmental groups suing the Colville National Forest. These groups were suing them for not protecting old growth trees. Kholi indicates Arthur cut down some of the same kind of old growth trees he was suing to protect.

According to an article in *Ecologic* magazine, May 1995, Jon Roush, President of the Wilderness Society harvested 80 acres of old growth trees on his property. The Wilderness Society

President sued the U.S. Forest Service in 1983 and prevented them from logging in the Bitterroot Forest due to the harm it would cause to the environment. Roush owns a ranch in the Bitterroot area. It borders the land he prevented the Forest Service from harvesting. According to the article, the Roush ranch is worth $2.5 million.

There's nothing wrong with cutting trees on private property. There is something wrong with making sure other Americans don't have the same right. That is the do as I say, not as I do, difference. There is no excuse, no clever justification, for this misuse of power. These environmental protectors are hypocrites. They accept donations to prevent others from logging and then log themselves.

Some things just aren't right. Judge Helen Frye awarded the Sierra Club Legal Defense Fund of Seattle, Washington and the Western Environmental Law Center of Eugene, Oregon $1,005,512 in November, 1994. This money was paid to reimburse these groups for the dollars they spent on the Spotted Owl case. This is all perfectly legal under the Endangered Species Act. This allows all Americans to help fund Green groups. First, the Sierra Club Legal Defense Fund uses the money donated to them. Then, they reach into every taxpayers pocket to pay them back for the money they spent to stop timber harvest in the Pacific Northwest.

> *"You can't save a forest and cut it down too."*
> *William Arthur*
> Sierra Club - February 1994

The Sierra Club guy can harvest his trees and make a profit. The Wilderness Society guy can harvest his trees and make a profit, but other Americans should not harvest trees for profit. Do as I say, not as I do.

Things Can't Get Any Worse

That's exactly what the Jewish people thought. The Jews kept trying to be reasonable, to work with the situation, to comply, until things got back to normal. That didn't happen.

Hindsight is always 20-20. What the people did not realize is that Hitler and his Nazis were lying, unreasonable people. Reasonable people dealt with Hitler like he was a reasonable person. That was a critical mistake.

People don't treat known enemies in a trusting manner. They keep their guard up. America's guard is down because of our genuine concern for the environment. The Greens refer to the environmental cause as a war.

Americans have tried to reason with the Greens. It is a waste of time. We need to take Green politics and ideology seriously. We must realize we are dealing with a fanatical, unreasonable minority. We need to recognize it is a war.

People tried to reason with Hitler. It was a waste of time. Hitler played for power while others played fair. Hitler was serious about his Nazi ideas. The Greens are serious about their ideas. Hitler didn't play fair. The Greens don't play fair. The Greens want it their way or none.

A Dangerous Message

Recently, the film, *The Last Supper* with Jason Alexander, (co-star on Seinfeld) was reviewed. The movie is about college students who kill people they determine are not politically correct or are anti-earth. The movie is supposed to be a comedy about getting rid of the people who bug you.

Another comedy film with a Green twist is *Serial Mom* starring Kathleen Turner. This movie is also about how a seemingly ideal suburban Mom gets carried away with killing people who bother her. This movie includes a scene where Mom and garbage men are discussing the neighbor who doesn't recycle. The conversation concludes that someone ought to kill that neighbor to help save the environment.

These movies are intended to be funny and entertaining. The underlying social message is not humorous. It promotes extreme intolerance toward other people.

The distinction we must make is between free speech and accountability. The message the public hears is the responsibility of the writers and others in this area of movie making. Fostering hate towards our fellow Americans and suggesting those people ought to be killed because they are not politically correct is where Hitler began.

It takes just as many strokes on the keyboard for a writer to express ideas in a positive rather than a negative manner. If the script was not about a serial killer, the writers might take this approach. The Mom states she will never give up trying to teach her neighbor the value of recycling. Mom could enlist the support of the garbage guys to help the neighbor learn to recycle, even if the three of them had to do it for her.

Justifying killing people to protect the sacred soil is what Hitler did. According to the book, *The World Must Know*, Hitler and his propaganda minister Dr. Joseph Goebbels understood he needed the masses to, *'unite them behind his rule'*. They began by lying and manipulating the masses to:

- believe they had an evil enemy
- believe it was a question of life or death

They accomplished this by using:

- Hitler's speeches and personal drama
- managing public information press, radio or film
- all information was presented with Nazi slant
- played on sympathy and fear
- demonstrations had religious, tribal ceremonial quality
- repeated Jews were savage, greedy, vile creatures

Hitler made the Nazi cause the center of public life. He played on emotions to adjust public opinion to agree with his solution to his manufactured political dilemma. He used propaganda to enlist support for all Nazi ideas from economics to saving the sacred soil of the Fatherland. This decade, public information and entertainment are being corrupted to enlist support for the Green cause and adjust public opinion to save Mother Earth.

A recent episode of *Seinfeld,* featured the character Elaine dating a Communist. Several times during the show, her lines expressed how 'cool' it was to date a Communist. Is it just a joke or a subliminal political message that Communists are cool?

Actors and actresses are not Communist because they deliver a line. Entertainers are not responsible for the content of a script unless they write it. Actors and actresses perform. The question isn't about performance, it involves using performances to create a specific public perception.

The entertainment industry has to take a serious look at it's responsibility factor in American politics. The industry must address what is fair use of their product and what is misuse. Integrating political messages and using emotional appeals to get consumers to take a political position is not fair use. It is a conflict of interest and a violation of professional ethics.

This is not about censorship, it is about ethics, responsibility and recognizing this art is being abused for political gain. There is a difference between entertainment and indoctrination.

Powerful Allies

The environmental movement enjoys the support of some very powerful allies who may have no idea what they are really lending their names to.

Robert Redford is a good example. He's been involved in the environmental cause for years. A 1989 article on the Greens indicated Mr. Redford might even be the Green white house hopeful. He indicated he was not.

The official Green Party program came out a few years later. Mr. Redford may be one of many Americans who doesn't fully understand what he is supporting. It appears he may not.

Every American needs to understand the Green's political plans. What happens in this country affects each and every one of us. We won't be able to protect the environment if we lose our freedom to take action. We don't have to stop caring for the environment to stop a Green revolution.

When Robert Redford discovers he would lose control of Sundance under the Green political system, he may want to publicly withdraw his support for the Greens.

Greens want to end private property ownership. The Greens don't want any more land speculation or development. Robert Redford built a beautiful resort in an undeveloped area. He cut down trees, but he proved capitalism, concern for the environment, development and capitalist success can go together. They compliment each other.

Our American Culture

A culture is what is created when a group of people develop a certain way of living or 'way of life'. A way of life includes traditions and those are then passed on from one generation to another, creating a lasting culture.

Where we live and how we live is part of who we are. Freedom is the ability to make personal choices about our lives. Some people love life in the big city. Surfers live for the beach. Other Americans thrive on life in the suburbs. Some prefer the country. Each life choice carries with it the joy, challenges and responsibilities connected to living in that particular place.

Hitler proved you can destroy a culture right in front of people's eyes. Although Nazi domination seemed to occur overnight, it occurred step by step. Hitler took control gradually, step by step, until he had complete control of the nation and the people. He made control possible by making control legal, one law at a time.

Earth Island Journal is published by Earth Island Institute. Americans were encouraged to donate to Earth Island in a promo just before the movie *Free Willy* began. Earth Island Institute is directly associated with the Green Party and promotes their efforts.

Earth Island staff also serves as faculty members for seminars on Deep Ecology (earth worship) education. These training sessions are offered to teachers, Green activists and community organizers.

Earth Island founder, David Brower is once against sharing his talents with the Sierra Club as a new member of their Board of Directors. Brower also founded the League of Conservation Voters and Friends of the Earth. Jonathon Porritt used to be executive director of Friends of the Earth. James Tyson, author of *Target America*, identified Friends of the Earth as an affiliate of the NLG, National Lawyers Guild. He indicates affiliate organizations promote Communist ideas and help form other groups to do the same.

Tyson summarizes the political purpose of these organizations with this quotation from an NLG leader:

> *"I am a double agent, I want to use the System to bring down the System."*
>
> William Kunstler
> NLG Convention - 1971

That fits making control possible by making control legal. Earth Island works on multiple environmental projects. For example, *Earth Island Journal* editors surveyed various environmental groups to get ideas for 50 more things Americans could do to save the earth. *Trilogy* magazine published this list in its 1990 Winter issue. Nine ideas from that survey are listed below.

Before reading the list; imagine if membership in any of the environmental groups surveyed may be associating you, or even lending your financial support to help further any or all of these objectives.

Does your support for environmental health equal support for the following political ideas?

- Be a total vegetarian
- Disconnect your power lines
- Don't have children
- Live on $140 a month
- Set a maximum wage
- Don't own pets
- Let domestic cattle go extinct
- Don't use batteries
- Use washable cloth instead of toilet paper

Are the individuals who developed this list using washable cloth instead of toilet paper? Are they living on $140.00 a month? Have they disconnected the power lines at their offices? If not, it's do as I say, not as I do politics. We ought to take these goals seriously because the Greens take them seriously. The Greens plan to attain these goals by using different excuses to justify specific legislation. They don't have to propose it themselves. They can get others to do it for them.

For example; setting a maximum wage is a socialist step to communism. Congressman Ron Dellums bill; *A Living Wage, Jobs for All Act* supports the Green goal. Americans are not expected to notice Dellums bill is a step toward socialism or that the political goals of the Greens and the Democratic or Eco-Socialists match.

Americans who are involved in environmental efforts for personal rather than political reasons may not understand the Green agenda. It's hard for Americans to see what's going on politically if their attention is diverted to other issues.

A key to Hitler's success was he operated like a magician. He kept people paying attention to the wrong things so no one noticed what was actually happening. Hitler kept his message simple and repeated it often. The bigger the lie and the sensationalism, the better.

The Greens have imitated Hitler's technique. The Greens keep their message simple and repeat it often: Save this, Save that, but Save it! The Greens also play on fear and hype to motivate the public and the politicians to support their cause. Like Hitler, the Greens intend to make control legal before Americans know what is happening.

> *"It is possible to lead astray an entire generation, to strike it blind, to drive it insane, to direct it towards a false goal. Napoleon proved that."*
>
> *Alexander Herzen*
> Russian Journalist - Political Thinker

5

Shades of Green

The Green strategy is to bring about a massive shift in our values by using different issues and avenues to either create conflict or send subliminal Green messages to the American masses. The idea is to gain support for Green ideas without being obvious. These ideas come in many 'shades of Green'. Each plays a part in eroding American traditions and values.

The Greens have been working 'behind the scenes' planting and cultivating alternative ideas to challenge our standards and public policies. The Greens use different issues to camouflage their political agenda, including:

- Third Party Politics
- Rewriting American History
- American Indian Rights
- Green Spiritual Politics

These shades of Green are like playing a game of cards with a stacked deck. The players think they are playing by the same rules with the same odds of winning, but that is not the case. The deal looks fair but, the dealer knows what cards he's getting and how he's going to play them. That leaves the rest of the players at a definite disadvantage. This is how the Greens are advancing their program. They have stacked the deck and the American people don't realize they are being deceived and cheated. Here are some ways the Greens have set Americans up to lose.

Third Party Politics

Many of us are ready to do almost anything to help stop the decline of America. We are tired of watching others devalue the standards and ideals on which this country is based. We have even considered supporting a third political party.

Part of the Communist assault on our country includes weakening our system of government. The Greens are promoting third party politics to change our two party system and divide the vote to put their candidates in power. How have the Communists arranged to run their independent candidates? According to an article by Joelle Fishman entitled; *"Impact of the 'Independent Plus' in the Election of '88,"* featured in the January 1989 edition of Political Affairs.

> *"To break the two party lock on the system, the Communist Party joined in coalition with a number of independent parties to support the Uniform Federal Voting Act sponsored by Rep. Jon Conyers Jr. This bill would liberalize ballot access laws for independents and new parties. It demands full support of the 101st Congress along with the Universal Voter Registration Act introduced by Sen. Alan Cranston."*

> *"The Communist Party...decided not to field a presidential ticket in 1988...Instead the National Committee urged all state organizations to reach out to other independent forces and strive to run Communist candidates, where possible, on independent or coalition tickets..."*

> *"the idea of electing left and Communists independent candidates to public office is now on the agenda. The groundbreaking campaigns of 1988 opened the way"*

Political Affairs - Marxist Journal - January 1989
(Bold Emphasis Added)

Fishman was, at that time, the chairwoman of the Communist Party of Connecticut. It is worth noting that Senator Cranston was also identified as a Green legislator by the Rifkins in their book, *Voting Green*. Senator Cranston has since retired and is now involved with Mikhail Gorbachev's environmental organization that are indirectly linked to Green Communists activities in the United States. Former Senator Cranston may, like most Americans, not be aware of the Greens plans to 'use our system to break down our system'.

Lying about their politics allows Communists to sneak in the back door and trick the public into voting for a Communist camouflaged as a Democrat or an independent.

> *"Just as **Communist, left and progressive independent campaigns found common ground with the 'progressive wing' in the Democratic Party in the effort to defeat Bush, so the common ground widens to shape the course of the country under the incoming administration.** Many of the independent campaigns related to, or found their beginnings in the **Jackson movement. The Rainbow Coalition** and labor-based coalitions...provide the arena for ongoing grassroots organizing toward the 101st Congress, future elections and political empowerment."*
>
> (Bold Emphasis Added)
Political Affairs - Marxist Journal - January 1989

According to a report in the July, 1995 issue of the *McAlvany Intelligence Advisor*:

> *"Former Communist Party Vice Presidential candidate, Angela Davis has been named as the new executive director for Jesse Jackson's Rainbow Coalition. Davis has also served on the Central Committee of the Communist Party U.S.A."*

Independent candidates are part of the Communist's plan to divide the vote and disrupt our electoral system. The Greens are also setting us up to support proportional representation to again, 'use our system to bring down our system' and make control possible by making control legal.

> "it's very difficult for Greens and kindred spirits to overcome the virtual two-party monopoly of the political process. What we need in the United States is the proportional representation that Europe has (i.e. if 18% of the people vote for Green Senate candidates, then 18 percent of the Senate would be Greens). Greens around the country are beginning to talk this up and may well make proportional representation a battle cry for the 90's."
>
> John Rensenbrink
> National Spokesman, Greens

Third parties and ideas like proportional representation is easier to resist when we realize the Green purpose is to destroy our system and set us up to put Greens in office.

If we can not get our political leaders to carry out the will of the American people, then a third party may be necessary. Before we commit to that solution, we ought to consider the following.

Our government is based on the two party system for good reason. Multiple parties create division, confusion and upset the checks and balances of our government system. Imagine what life and taxes would be like if we experimented with different political philosophies every four years? Third parties sound enticing but they could create more problems.

Mr. Perot said some things Americans wanted to hear in 1992, but he dropped the ball at critical points in the campaign. Many people, discouraged with the leadership offered by the Democrats and Republicans, voted for Perot. There could not have been a more effective way to put the current administration in the White House. This is not to suggest Mr.

Perot is a Communist. It is to point out how third parties can influence an election by splitting the vote.

The two party system may not be perfect but it gives us a choice of two distinctly different concepts of how America ought to be governed. The Communist's strategy involves encouraging multiple parties because it disrupts and breaks-down our electoral process. Multiple parties put America on shaky ground. America can not risk sending a Watermelon, 'Green on the outside, Red on the inside', to the White House.

John Drakeford, author of, *Red Blueprint for the World,* noted:

> *"In a democracy Communism's objective is to destroy everything that gives stability to the highly developed capitalist state. The legislative, judicial and executive branches of the government must all be destroyed to prepare for the next form of government. William Z. Foster, the former chairman of the Communists Party in America, stated it very clearly when he said:"*

> *'No Communist, no matter how many votes he should secure in a national election, could, even if he would, become President of the present government.* **When a Communist heads government in the United States - and that day will come just as surely as the sun rises - that government will not be a capitalistic government but a Soviet government, and behind this government will stand the Red Army to enforce the Dictatorship** *of the Proletariat.'*
>
> (Bold Emphasis Added)

Wishful thinking, or is this part of the calculated political effort by the Soviets to take over our country? We must be careful whom we elect and the laws we support. The founding fathers gave their lives to give us a legacy. It was their love of liberty and extraordinary wisdom that produced the Constitution, the Declaration of Independence and our system of free government. It is visionary now, over 200 years later.

Our system of government is not the problem. The problem is the people in office who are abusing the system. We ought to stick to the two party system unless we are convinced beyond a shadow of a doubt that it is our political system, instead of the people in office, that is to blame for our problems.

We don't need to reinvent government. We need to clean up the one we have. It is like a priceless antique. With a little elbow grease it will be as good as new. Throwing it out would be a tragic mistake. America is the envy of people around the globe. Our culture, freedom and system of government are the reasons. The Green goal to devalue our system of government is no different than their reason for devaluing our past. If we dislike what we have, we will be more likely to try the Green alternative.

Rewriting American History

> *"The German people have in the year 1936, in the fourth year of the National Socialist regime, ended the period of their historic dishonor.*
>
> > *Adolf Hitler*
> > My New Order

The Greens often use Hitler's tactic of bringing up and dwelling on injustices of the past to justify calls for change in the present. Hitler ignited the Nazi movement by:

- ridiculing Germany's past and traditions
- presenting new traditions for a new order
- nature theme of save sacred soil of the Fatherland
- rewrote a politically correct history

Hitler devalued Germany's past so he could offer his ideas for a new and brighter future. The German people accepted their past was dishonorable and anxiously left it behind to support Hitler's new order and world conquest. They choose not to protect their traditions and culture.

The Greens are igniting the Green movement by:

- ridiculing America's past, legends and heroes
- rewriting history, a politically correct version
- nature theme, save Mother Earth
- producing 'historic dishonor'

The Greens want us to accept America's past as dishonorable so we will agree to leave it behind and support a Green world order, or world government. The Greens hope Americans will not choose to protect our traditions and culture.

The Greens are effectively eroding our feelings about our past by 'Greening' American history; rewriting it to be Green and politically correct. An example is the current Disney hit, *Pocahontas.* The movie presents a historical figure in a new light. *Pocahontas* is portrayed as a mythical, eco-feminist champion of nature who talks to trees. Richard Corliss made this comment in his review of *Pocahontas* in the June 19, 1995 issue of *Time* magazine:

> *"GREEN POWER: As teacher of the land's bounty with John Smith as her student, Pocahontas becomes the first eco-feminist."*

There is no question, Pocahontas was a heroine. The question involves using the power of entertainment to spread the Green idea of eco-feminism and Green spirituality. This is the link to Green politics. This movie is an example of stacking the deck. Americans think they are enjoying a simple boy meets girl fantasy but in reality, the mix of fantasy and fact promotes three parts of the Green political agenda that are:

- Green version of American history
- Green spiritual values
- Green eco-feminist heroine

American history was modified to promote Green values by using a politically correct version of that event. Good entertainment has a lasting effect. When children study the true story of Pocahontas in school, will they identify with the 11 year old Indian girl who did not have a romance with Captain Smith or will they identify with the story of the 20-something Indian maiden who became romantically involved with Captain Smith? Will they see Pocahontas as their Green heroine and accept her spiritual values? Will they think they ought to talk to trees?

> *"I developed a harsh resentment toward our elders, especially our educators from the Volksschule to university; not only had they allowed themselves to be deceived, they had delivered us, their children, into the cruel power of a new God."*
>
> Alfons Heck
> A CHILD OF HITLER
> (Bold Emphasis Added)

This decade, the 'God' is Green. Children operate on emotion. They do not understand the difference between fantasy and fact, unless it is explained. Entertainment, like anything children are exposed to, can have a lifelong affect. The distinction must be made for children that fantasy is based on imaginary things, like daydreams, but facts verify actual events and depict the truth. *Pocahontas* may be billed as a fantasy, but because it tells a story about an actual historical event, it is viewed by many children as real. When facts are distorted and mixed with fantasy it can create confusion and incorrect assumptions. Richard Corliss noted the movie message included:

> "the standoff with the white man is one of eco-heroes vs. strip miners, defenders of an idyllic homeland against greedy invaders."

The concept of 'defending an idyllic homeland' mirrors the environmental message Hitler used to change peoples values. Hitler also mixed fact and fantasy to motivate young children to see him as a hero and want to be Nazis. Hitler understood children can learn politically correct beliefs and behavior. The movie, *Pocahontas* also conveys the idea of 'greedy invaders'. That reinforces the Greens goal to discredit our past by depicting Columbus as a bad guy. Mixing seemingly harmless fantasy with revolutionary opinions is a dangerous trend. It is the Green, 'behind the scenes' way to change our attitudes toward our past, our present and our future.

Hollywood has a free hand. It's still a free country. Hollywood leaders need to understand the Green agenda or they will continue to be used as the Green 'mouth-piece'. They don't have to make Green movies. To turn this around, every American needs to recognize Green propaganda.

There is a difference between positive and negative interpretations of the American past. We ought to keep in mind negative representations of American history serve the Green agenda. There is a difference between ideas that encourage national pride and images designed to destroy it.

Disney Studios is not to blame. Like other Americans, they probably do not realize the Greens are using the magic style of Walt Disney to help transform our society and change our values. If they did, they probably would not integrate Green politics into future films.

Discovery Happened

The Greens would like us to believe we can turn back the clock by rearranging American history and turning our society upside down. Greens claim this will save the earth. We need to remember the Green goal is first socialism then communism. The Greens political strategy is for Americans to become emotionally attached to the *feeling* of eco-topia so we support eco-socialism.

The Greens hope we will take leave of our senses, abandon our past and support the Green movement like the Germans supported the Nazi movement. The Greens are romanticizing Indian lore to devalue the contributions of other Americans from Columbus to the cowboys.

Christopher Columbus was not a bad guy because he sailed over and discovered America. Going out and discovering things was what people did back then. It was not an easy job either. It took courage, dedication and amazing fortitude. Put yourself in place of Columbus. Can you imagine waiting years to get on a ship manned by a bunch of convicts (because no one else would go) and set sail across uncharted waters to prove the world was round? It was a major risk and a major accomplishment. Columbus is a hero.

Our Cup Is Half Full, Not Half Empty

We can't pretend to have the ability to put things back as they were before Columbus discovered America. We don't have those options. We can only work with what we have. The best we can do is take a look at the environmental situation to see what we can do, then do what we can to prevent harm and correct damage.

The Green purpose for condemning Columbus is to:

- increase positive focus on the American Indian
- increase negative focus on pioneers
- magnify environmental issues
- blame capitalism for all evil
- create shame for America's past

What if another empire had stopped by first? What if aliens beamed the Indians to Mars? What if cannibals landed first and ate all the people? Things could have been worse. This land mass, known as America, would be discovered by people at some point in time. Those people might have chosen other ways to stop the Indian wars. They could have completely eliminated the tribes instead of placing them on reservations. Although this was not a perfect solution, it was better than complete annihilation. History is not perfect. No one can assume to know what would have been better for the American Indian. Like our own lives, we can focus on what makes our cup half empty or we can focus on what makes our cup half full. Many wonderful things have occurred since Columbus discovered America.

The Green attack on Columbus encourages Americans to court the Indian culture and end our historical relationship with cowboy legends and western culture. The number one rule in the 'Communist Rules for Revolution' includes the aim to destroy our ruggedness. American culture is based on rugged individualism. The cowboys are our heroes, American symbols of strength, bravery and honor. The Greens intend to destroy our individuality, our ruggedness and our culture.

> *"Every time I hear the word culture, I release the safety catch on my revolver."*
>
> *Hermann Goring*
> Known as the # 2 Nazi
> Psychopathic God

Culture presents a revealing contradiction between what the Greens say they support and what the Greens practice. If the Greens truly respected multi-cultures, they would respect our culture. America is the melting pot. People came to America to become Americans and blend into this unique culture. America is the culture of one, based on the contributions of many. The Greens are pushing multi-culturalism. That creates marked divisions and promotes individual cultures instead of a united culture. If the Greens truly respected different cultures, they would not be trying to systematically destroy ours. Part of the Green plan to erase our culture involves erasing different pieces of it. For example, a few ways the Greens are trying to erase our pride and history include:

- insult the cowboy image: ridicule it
- devalue frontier traditions; horse racing to rodeos
- soften American's toughness
- use environmental excuses to change land use policies
- gain control of rancher's ability to produce beef
- replace cowboy heroes with eco-heroes
- replace our values with Green values

The Indians are also victims in this Green assault on our past. As a minority group, they were targeted by the Communists years ago. The Greens pretend to help the American Indian by promoting Indian issues. The Green Communists are actually using the Indians to advance their political goals.

The Indian wars present many opportunities for the Greens to bring up injustices of the past and use as emotional hooks to sway public opinion on current political issues. Greens focus on 'bad' so we'll believe 'bad' is all there was. The Greens follow the Hitler theory; if you say something long enough, people begin to believe it. Environmental themes take first position in Indian issues, then Green political goals come into play.

The Cowboy and Indian wars were an unfortunate consequence of westward expansion. People can judge and pretend they would have handled the situation differently, but they were not there. We ought to remember, it's a two way street. Both the Cowboys and the Indians did things to be ashamed of.

According to one documentary, the Indians tacked living children to trees and then left them to die. Certainly scalping wasn't a pleasant experience for the cowboys, but it is what the Indians did. Cowboys destroyed villages and killed men, women and children. The Indians burned down homesteads and killed men, women and children. It was war. People on both sides lost their lives. Nothing we feel will ever change the situation for those who got scalped or burned at the stake. We can not alter the events that shaped that time in history.

History is a part of our everyday life. Everyone can look back over their lives and say; *'gosh, wish I'd handled that differently'*. We don't have time machines so we can't go back and do it over. We can't teach people hundreds of years ago how to behave; not Columbus, the cowboys or the Indians. We ought to pay attention to what went right, instead of allowing the Greens to magnify and judge the evils of every historical action. The Green assault on our past goes way beyond the Indian wars. The Greens are attempting to create shame for every part of American history, from the cowboys to the bombing of Hiroshima.

For example, John Wayne is an American legend. John Wayne played the role of the good guy, the cowboy who fought the Indians, but his movies usually included a healthy respect for keeping his word with the Indian warriors, in spite of the fact they were viewed as an enemy.

On screen, he loved this country. He usually played parts where he stood out as the good guy who drew a line between right and wrong. He could be pushed just so far, then he stood up to the liars, manipulators and the rest of the bad guys. John Wayne's character on screen usually reflected a fair, honest, independent person who did what was right. Off screen, John Wayne was an American patriot.

Those attitudes and national pride are heartfelt and characteristic of the American people. These ideals are an intricate part of our nature and our culture. Those attitudes reflect our character. Americans are strong, independent people who will stand-up for what is right. The Greens are trying to destroy our character, make us weak and cloud our judgment of right and wrong so we will accept their values.

Rewriting history is the Green way to destroy our national pride. It is a political tactic we can't ignore. Playing up the Indian culture is designed to make a mockery of our past. Hitler created his new Germany using the same approach. He diminished the value of Germany's past. He rewrote history as if it began with the Nazi movement. The Greens are rewriting history to create a brand new America by diminishing the value of our past. Pitching our past is not necessary, if the goal is to clean up the environment.

Indians are being used in other ways to help disrupt the way our society functions. Recently, two Indian boys were found guilty of nearly beating a delivery man to death. This case received national attention due to the question of how the boys ought to be punished. Instead of being sentenced according to the law, a tribal leader pleaded with the Judge to allow the punishment to be based on tribal law and tradition instead of 'white man's law'. The tribal leader was granted his request. Instead of going to jail, the boys were to be banished to a remote island to survive off the land for 18 months.

Dateline, NBC featured an in-depth follow-up report that revealed the following:

- banishment was never part of that tribes traditions
- restitution promised to the victim has not been paid
- boys on an island 15 minutes from their homes
- boys were not living off the land
- boys parents provided them with food and supplies
- tribal leader was not keeping track of them as promised
- one boy applied for a drivers license during banishment

Most Americans honor their word, some don't. The tribal leader used emotional arguments like, tribal tradition, honor, alternative to prison and a guilt trip about 'white mans law' to con the Judge. The tribal elder did not honor his word. He lied about banishment being a tradition. The boys did not receive the punishment agreed upon.

No matter how our emotions are twisted; America can't afford to start playing favorites when it comes to enforcing the law. We can not use a different set of laws and punishments for every sub-culture in America. It would create massive turmoil and more frustration.

Another way the Greens are using the American Indian involves the spiritual dimension of the environmental movement. The Greens are using Indian lore to tempt Americans away from traditional religious beliefs. The Greens promote Indian beliefs because it is a clever way to manipulate other Americans into accepting Green values without being obvious.

The Greens have built their political power by combining forces with small special interest groups such as the Indians. The political goals of these groups are carefully intertwined into the politics of the environmental cause to create a stronger political force.

Many little groups supporting each other's goals equal one large lobby pushing the political goals of minority groups. The Greens use unsuspecting people to advance their goals. The Greens are using Indian beliefs to promote their spiritual politics and alternative land use ideas.

Chief Seattle's speech is a prime example. It is recited on Earth Day, put on posters and is generally hailed as the guiding light of the environmental movement. These are the words created by scriptwriter Ted Perry in 1971. Although the words are attributed to Chief Seattle, in 1992, they were proven to be mostly a forgery.

> *'How can you buy or sell the sky, the warmth of the land?*
> *The idea is strange to us. If we do not own the freshness of the*
> *air and the sparkle of the water, how can you buy them? Every*
> *part of the earth is sacred to my people.'*
> (Bold Emphasis Added)

The spoken words are beautiful and anyone who loves and respects nature understands those sentiments. If we put our feelings aside, what is the Green political motivation? The Chief's message is used by the Greens because it promotes the idea people cannot or should not own the earth. The Greens are using these words to set Americans up to accept socialism. The Greens use the Chief's speech to:

- repeat idea that private property ownership is wrong
- suggest private property ownership harms earth
- infer shared ownership is better for the earth
- subliminal message: change to socialist land use

If we accept 'no one can own the earth', we accept the Green goal to end private property ownership.

It is worth noting that recent reports on tribal life indicate that it was actually quite hard on the environment. The Greens use the Chief's speech as an emotional ploy to plant the idea of shared or socialist land use so the Greens can continue moving us down their path to communism.

Here's where the *bait and switch* comes in for Indian tribes. The Greens indicate they support treaty rights and Indian's right to own their lands. Remember, revolutionaries operate on 'the end justifies the means' mindset. If socialism is legalized and communism follows, the sacred places of the Indian nations would be lost right along with the property rights of every other American.

How can Green promises be broken? Read the 'Green fine print'. It allows them to change the rules because they have reserved the right to change their program.

> *"The Green Program spells out in considerable detail the values, policies, and forms of governance that compose a Green alternative to the current order.* ***It is a living document that remains open to further democratic development and change.****"*
>
> Greens

Tribal Ways

The Greens use Indian myths to make living off the land seem like an easy romantic journey. The great white wolf is portrayed in movies as the spirit guide that will save, guide and protect people. The Indian mythical white wolf rescues humans lost in the wilderness.

There is a political purpose to promoting this Indian myth. It helps the Greens gain more public support for:

- government to create more wilderness areas
- reintroduction of wolves in populated areas
- spiritual idea we are one with animals and nature

This is the Green way to convince Americans to associate a tribal or communal lifestyle with environmental excellence. The political purpose for glorifying primitive ideas is to set us up to accept group status over independence. Accepting group or tribal status would make it easier for the Greens to impose 'compulsory Green living'. The Greens also want Americans to finance their ideas for international environmental protection. Communist Rules for Revolution, number six, the Greens intend to break us financially. To head us in this direction, the Greens suggest we:

- disconnect our power lines
- reduce our quality of life
- share our wealth equally with the Third World

Redistributing wealth helps Third World countries protect the environment by improving their quality of life because now:

- wood is used for cooking and heating
- electricity would prevent more resource depletion

Part of this makes sense. Helping Third World countries stop depleting their resources by introducing electricity as an alternate energy source makes sense. What does not make sense is the Green ideas to disconnect our power lines. If we disconnect our electricity, we would be creating the same situation in America the Greens say we need to correct in Third World countries? Solar power is an option, but not every American can afford to install a solar system.

The Greens objective is to condition Americans to view primitive as progressive. This is part of setting us up to accept a major reduction of our quality of life as the only way to save the environment. Remember, the Green goal is 'compulsory Green living'.

> "*Indeed one of the biggest obstacles to the Global Marshall plan is the requirement that* **the advanced economies must undergo a profound transformation themselves**....*The new plan will require the wealthy nations to allocate money for transferring environmentally helpful technologies to the Third World...however, any such effort* **will also require wealthy nations to make a transition themselves that will be in some ways more wrenching than that of the Third World,** *simply because powerful established patterns will be disrupted.*"
>
> Senator Al Gore
Earth in the Balance
(Bold Emphasis Added)

This indicates Mr. Gore's idea of a Global Marshall plan goes way beyond sharing wealth and technologies with other nations. A transition '*more wrenching than that of the Third World*' is anticipated for advanced economies like ours. If Third World countries will face a difficult transformation up to advanced technology, what is a '*more wrenching*' transition for advanced economies?

Anatoliy Golitsyn, an ex-KGB officer who defected to the United States, warned Americans in his 1984 book *New Lies for Old,* that world communism was still the goal of the Soviets. The epilogue of *New Lies for Old* by Larry Abraham states the Communist plan is to merge the United States with the Soviet Union so our resources can continue to support them. Abraham states:

> "*There is only one way: Increase their standard of living, while drastically reducing ours.*"

The Greens call for this 'redistribution' of American's wealth in the name of environmental justice.

It is part of the Communist scheme to convince Americans to:

- support the Green call for world government
- support the Green call to change all our values
- support the Green call to abandon capitalism

After the government has control of our property, our paycheck, our weapons, our lives and our country, it will be too late to debate the issues. Americans will be in the same position the Jews were in Nazi Germany. They were at the mercy of the those in power. Again, the Greens copy Hitler's propaganda tactics:

> *"The sacrifice of personal existence is necessary to secure the preservation of the species."*
>
> *Adolf Hitler*
> Mein Kampf

Another note on the tribal lifestyes; if we eliminate our system of food production and distribution, where will we get our food? If we accept the Greens idea that becoming a vegetarian is the best thing we can do to save the environment, it will be much easier for the Greens to transform our food system to 'compulsory Green living' and rationed lentils. It is cheaper to feed the masses roots and rice.

People in Third World countries also hunt wildlife for food and pagan rituals. That has reduced wildlife numbers. Americans, on the other hand, have developed sophisticated alternative food sources to keep our wildlife in healthy numbers. If wildlife protection is the goal, ranchers and hunters ought to receive praise instead of condemnation by the Greens. Many initial efforts to protect and enhance wildlife habitats were initiated by hunters and ranchers.

Think It All the Way Through

Another Green idea to improve our lives and the health of the environment includes the opportunity for city-dwelling Americans to volunteer to be relocated to rural areas and do socially useful work in smaller communities.

Although this idea sounds great, it requires additional consideration. Remember, the Greens have copied many of Hitler's tactics because they worked. The Greens, like Hitler, call for a major reduction of our population. It would be wise to be wary of relocation programs to move people out of densely populated areas to work in rural America. The Jewish people didn't think relocation to work farms in the country sounded too bad.

When the Nazis needed the Jewish people to cooperate they promised them better conditions at the other end of the trip. The Nazis also favored starvation as a way to control large numbers of people and curb resistance.

The Greens want to transform America's food system. The Greens are promoting the romantic idea of buying only locally grown foods to help save the environment. That may sound like a good idea and it could help local businesses. Before agreeing this is a good idea, take a trip into the Green future. Remember these Green political objectives?

- limit services to local area
- limit production and distribution to local area
- terminate trucking
- eliminate private automobiles
- shut down most airports
- non-consumptive uses of wildlife

What if the Greens achieved these goals and the locally grown products were not enough to feed the people? What if the crops failed? What if there was a natural disaster? People could not fish or hunt for food because consuming wildlife would be illegal. Supplies would run out at the local market and people could not get in their car and drive to another state to get food. It would leave people at the mercy of those in power.

American farmers have organized a method of production and distribution that ensures a constant food supply. If floods destroy the California crop, other states can balance out the loss by selling their crops. Animal rights, endangered species and wetlands' issues are the excuses the Greens are using to justify political action and government control. The Greens are working hard to cripple the following food industries.

- Beef
- Fishing
- Poultry
- Farming
- Hunting

The Greens are out to control these industries; one business at a time. From a local perspective it may appear to be insignificant. From a nationwide perspective the result would be a complete departure from the way American food is supplied. How many people in this country depend on the grocery store for the products we put on the dinner table?

Never happen? It is happening. Fishermen can't fish. Ranchers are losing grazing permits and farmers are besieged by animal rights activists. Other Green issues like wetlands and endangered species are affecting these businesses as well. One by one, the Greens intend to gain control of these industries using environmental protection as the excuse to take control.

These Americans feed this nation. We all depend on them doing their part to produce and distribute our food supply. These Americans have developed the sophisticated method of producing large quantities of food. They produce enough food for us to share with other nations in time of crisis.

If the Greens are successful in their campaign, what will we eat and where will we get it? The time to ask those questions is now, before the Greens put these Americans out of business. The Greens are disrupting our food supply system to justify the need for more government control. Think the Green plans all the way through. We ought to protect these businesses, as if our life depended on it.

If we accept government control of these peoples lives, we are beginning to accept control of our own lives. Hitler proved you can destroy a culture right in front of people's eyes; one person, one group, one step at a time. He made control possible by making control legal.

Those businesses and industries who have not yet been impacted by the Greens will not be exempt. They are just lower on the priority list. The Greens want it all. They want legal control of your life.

Political VooDoo

Hitler realized, before people would accept a new set of cultural values, the old set of traditional images and patriotic symbols had to be systematically devalued in their eyes.

The Greens have created a spiritual side of environmental protection for many reasons. Land use and private property rights are the hidden political targets. It is important that all

Americans, religious or not, understand this part of the Green set up.

Karl Marx summed up Communism with the single sentence, *'the abolition of private property.'* The spiritual dimension of the environmental movement can be summed-up in one word, *atheist*. Communists are atheist. This is why the Greens want to de-value organized religion in America. This is why they are promoting ideas that reject or challenge traditional religious beliefs and encourage paganism.

The Greens are using myth, magic and the environmental cause to entice Americans into earth worship and joining the Green movement.

How are the Greens using religion to advance the goal of creating atheists? The Green plan to transform American's spiritual values is a step by step series of gradual changes. Each small step de-emphasizes existing religious focus on the creator and shifts the focus to creation. The process is already in motion. The Greens have manipulated religious leaders to use their influence on people to help save the world from environmental disaster. The following progression shows how the shift to atheism is to occur:

- Include nature as part of current religious focus
- Get Americans to accept nature as part of worship
- Increase religious focus on creation instead of creator
- Use fear of human survival to increase nature worship
- Get Americans to accept the need to put nature first
- All Americans are set up to become atheists
- Communists are atheists
- Communism is the faith of Communists

"We say the name of God, but that is only habit. We are atheists."

Nikita Krushchev

Religion is the Green enemy. Communists believe it is the opiate of the people and must be eliminated. This is why the Greens promote alternative pagan belief systems. The Greens have infiltrated traditional religious ranks to:

- promote Green ideas as environmental protection
- use religious leaders and network to sway voters

The Greens are using the environmental cause as a recruiting tool to con Americans away from traditional moral principles and into believing in Green spiritual principles. The Greens political motivation is:

- weaken America's moral fiber
- increase number of Greens in America
- increase acceptance of Green politics
- increase political clout on environmental issues
- promote socialist policies
- lessen resistance to communism

The Greens are accusing Americans of not caring about the environment to challenge us to prove how much we care. We can prove we care by blindly accepting Green values and political recommendations. The more Americans who fall for the spiritual side of Green politics, the easier it will be to sell socialism as the other half of the environmental solution. It would be far easier for the Greens if Americans volunteer for 'compulsory Green living'.

Green religion includes various belief systems like Deep Ecology or Spiritual Ecology with fundamental links to pagan ritual, occult and Indian myths. Another way the Greens are setting Americans up to accept Green spirituality and it's role in 'compulsory Green living' involves Spiritual Ecology and Eco-Psychology. A good example of the connection between these two concepts is found in the January 1, 1995 issue of Parade magazine. The following article was from *Self*:

> *"Feeling depressed about the planet? Perhaps you need a couch session with an eco-therapist. Eco-psychology, a new trend in psychotherapy, helps people deal with their anxieties about problems like endangered species and deforestation. What's the best therapy? According to one eco-shrink, daily walks in the woods and establishing a relationship with a tree."*

Following is this author's summary of Spiritual Ecology and the Council of All Beings ritual outlined in Carolyn Merchant's book *Radical Ecology*. According to Merchant, spiritual ecology was invented by Joanna Macy and John Seed. It is not something that has been passed down for generations. It involves a ritual where the beings of the *Three Times* are summoned. That means those beings who have helped the earth, are helping and will help the earth in the future.

This ritual is referred to as the *council of all beings*. The basic idea is all beings are given a voice and the opportunity to share their concerns about environmental issues and how they are affecting them. Humans form a circle and wear masks that represent specific beings. They can be a fox, a river, a tree or any other element of nature. They take turns role-playing beings and listening as humans.

The *council of all beings* ends with humans requesting help from all beings. Each being responds, removes their mask and becomes human again by entering the circle where all the humans bond together then disperse for merry making. This ritual is to raise our consciousness about other beings' feelings on environmental issues. Accepting toads and trees as equal beings is part of the message. Earth Day parades give the Greens the opportunity to spread this concept by using little children to wear the mask of one creature or another to display they are equal to animals. Big Green people dance around as trees, fish or other beings. If we put this in perspective, we can see the Greens purpose is to change our traditional beliefs by changing our focus to:

- fear of environmental disaster
- feel we are equal to animals
- interest in pagan traditions

Hugging a tree will not help solve environmental problems or reduce anxiety about deforestation or endangered species. Doing something positive for the environment would be better therapy than doing something useless like finding a tree and hugging it.

Cleaning up a beach or river bank would help the person feel positive, like they had some measure of control. They would learn to think of positive ways to help the environment. They would learn to focus on feeling helpful instead of feeling helpless. They could see the result of their efforts instantly by focusing on positive actions. That would be a feel-good prescription. Advising someone who is worried about deforestation to go find a tree to be friends with would magnify their problem. Being friends with a tree suggests trees have human qualities, like the tree in *Pocahontas.* The person who was only worried about deforestation now has an added problem of talking to trees. This advice increases the focus on deforestation because it increases the focus on trees by establishing trees as personal friends. This eco-advice could lead to complications. It could lead to an eco-obsession.

What happens if the tree dies or is struck by lighting? The patient would feel like a friend had died. Professional therapists would see this pitfall. They would find productive ways to address environmental concerns and avoid recommendations that could backfire.

Giving depressed people the impression, hugging trees will help them feel better and will curb their concern about deforestation is not healthy. There is a substantial difference between having a healthy respect for the magnificence of trees and unhealthy, boderline insanity. Vulnerable people are easy prey. This is not to suggest that all psychologists and therapists are Green. This advice was given by one eco-therapist. This is to show the Greens political motivation behind eco-therapy. The Greens have many reasons to introduce eco-therapy. It encourages Americans to equate tree hugging with environmental health. That is like, *The Emperor's New Clothes*. The Greens may get a few people to run around like fools, but most Americans will see through the hoax. Remember, mandatory tree hugging on Sunday is also part of 'compulsory Green living'. This is another way to set us up for Green communism. Eco-therapy helps the Greens:

- promote nature as our mother, a human being
- condone fanatical behavior as a normal part of life
- nature worship is solution to environmental issues
- convince normal people to do abnormal things
- create and recruit fanatics

The Greens are using Hitler's approach to mental health. Hitler got the masses to abandon traditional values and:

- reconnect with the sacred soil of the Motherland
- feel a religious dedication to the Nazi cause
- equate being a Nazi with saving the Fatherland

The Greens are programming Americans to:

- re-connect with nature and the earth
- have a religious dedication to the Green cause
- equate being Green with saving Mother Earth

Hitler also used trees to cement a commitment to the Nazi cause; he sent children out to pick the bugs off of trees. The Greens send adults and children out to hug trees. Same stuff, different decade. Hitler also convinced normal people to do abnormal things. We can avoid repeating the German's mistake by not falling for the same emotional traps.

June 16, 1991, The *San Francisco Examiner* carried a story by Richard Powelson entitled *"Religious leaders see green, Agree to take up environmentalism."* Powelson reports:

> *"Sens. Albert Gore D-Tenn., and Tim Worth, D-Colo., active environmentalists in Congress, helped organize meetings with religious leaders June 2-3. Paul Gorman, executive director of The Joint Appeal in Religion and Science in New York, the name of the coalition of religious leaders, said the leaders now will get more involved in Congressional action, such as seeking to testify at hearings on environmental action. "They won't be talking about fuel efficiency standards or how much global warming there is," Gorman said."*

If they aren't talking about specific environmental issues, are they talking about spiritual environmental issues? Church leaders and other Americans ought to start making specific distinctions between religion and environmental protection. They are two different issues. Communists are atheist. Greens need to destroy religion because it is a fundamental link to America's strength and moral foundation. The Greens have re-created many of the elements Hitler used to entice a nation. The following list reminds us of the ideas Hitler used to sell Nazi politics to the masses. The Greens have merged all his ideas into key parts of their calls for environmental protection and social transformation.

- transformation of society
- new age, new order
- one people
- protect the sacred soil
- paganism
- earth is living being

We need to recognize the combination of politics, earthly spirituality and visions of a new age are the exact same psychological traps Hitler used. Hitler was insane but people fell for his idea that a completely different society would equal a better life. Curiosity killed the cat.

Many Germans rushed to become Nazis without thinking. Many Americans are rushing to be Green. Some have jumped off the deep end into Nazi-like environmental fanaticism. Just because they've gone Green, doesn't mean they have to stay Green. The Greens have promoted the environmental cause as the politically correct thing to do. It was politically correct to become a Nazi. Think it through.

Hitler grounded his Nazi movement in a quasi-religion. He convinced people to abandon their moral and religious beliefs and to put their faith in the Nazi cause. The Hitler Youth denounced their faith in God when they pledged allegiance to Hitler. Hitler lured people from all levels of society to join the Nazi movement. The Greens are on the same wavelength.

Those involved in the environmental movement promote the idea of transformation and the need to create an earthly faith to solve environmental problems.

> *"To look for a technological solution to the ecological crisis would be a lethal mistake. Scientific analysis points, curiously, toward the need for a quasi-religious transformation of contemporary cultures."*
> *Paul Ehrlich*
> 1993 Earth Journal

Paul Ehrlich has been very involved in the environmental cause for years. He is best known for his predictions on the population crisis. Many of his predictions are reported to be wrong.

The Greens are approaching their goal to eliminate religion and transform our culture from multiple angles. Look at what has been popularized in America. Psychic readings, numerology, goddess mythology, occult, deep ecology, witches, tree hugging, reincarnation and a tremendous focus on Indian myths. These are only some ways to tempt Americans to abandon traditional beliefs.

The August 7, 1995 edition of *U.S. News & World Report* featured the story; *Yeltsin's eyes and ears,* according to the article; Russia's top officials receive *'horoscopes and advice on the occult'* and a psychic *'corrects his karma'.*

Children are learning drumming in school. This is intended to be a spiritual experience to introduce children to an alternate belief system. Greening religion also establishes parental support to allow their children to participate in Green environmental events without knowing the religious agenda of the Greens. The Greens also use quotes from the bible to convince churches to include environmental messages in their sermons. Protecting the environment does not need to include social transformation, earthly spirituality or any other form of Green political voodoo. America's religious leaders need to realize Greens are advocating:

- organized religion is an out dated addiction
- adherence to dogmatic beliefs is religious escapism
- blame Judeo-Christian religion for environmental ruin
- ideas about God must be shattered and erased
- a new religious paradigm and a new faith is needed

*"Once the ruling power is in our grasp, we must seize the evil in Germany by the root and tear it out, **to make way for the new faith, for the new religion.**"*

Adolf Hitler
Memoirs of a Confidant
(Bold Emphasis Added)

Like Hitler, the Greens call for a new faith and a new religion. Like Hitler, the Greens have added spiritual values to politics. Deep ecology is part of Green spirituality. The March, 1991 issue of the Earth First Journal featured the Eco Depth Gauge. Readers were instructed to read each definition until they reached the one they did not agree with. The category above that was their commitment to environmental protection. Here is that Earth First Eco-Depth Gauge. Where do you fit?

Superficial	We should take good care of our planet, as we would any valuable tool.
Shallow	We have a responsibility to protect Earth's resources for our future generations.
Deep	Wilderness has a right to exist for its own sake.
Deeper	Wildlife has more right to live on Earth than humans do.
Profoundly Deep	Humans are too great a threat to life on Earth.
Radically Deep	Human extinction now or there won't be any later for this planet. A painless extermination is needed.
Abysmally Deep	A quick annihilation is too good for humans. A horrible, fatal illness from outer space is only fair.

It is important to understand the Deep and Deeper levels are evident in Green spiritual politics. Deep ecologists believe the only reason to use any part of nature is to meet a basic need and protecting nature requires a major reduction in human population. They claim this is required if human life and non-human life are to continue to co-exist.

> "If I were reincarnated I would wish to be returned to Earth as a killer virus to lower human population levels."
> Prince Philip of Great Britain
> Leader, World Wildlife Fund
> From the Trenches, 1994

Other issues impacted by Green spirituality are:

- natural resources
- economy
- assisted suicide
- wildlife reintroduction
- recreation
- ecosystems, biodiversity
- population control
- endangered species

Earth Day is a holy day for the Greens. It's a day to honor the spiritual connection to Mother Earth. Earth First publishes its journal on pagan nature holidays. An environmental group that organizes Earth Day event's year round is called Sun Day. Since many Americans associate Sunday as the day of worshipping the creator, the name Sun Day connects those earth activities to a religious day, but shifts the emphasis to worshipping creation. The Unitarian Church advertised these discussions and rituals:

- Gaia, a Living Being
- Animal Rights
- Deep Ecology
- Native Religious
- Greens and Bioregionalism
- Ritual and Action
- Creation Spirituality

The Green Movement is introducing this kind of religious combination to set us up to become atheists.

> "Spiritual ecology, in contrast to utilitarian ecology, pays homage to the awe of nature and the wonder of creation."
> Jeremy Rifkin
> Biosphere Politics

Synonyms for utilitarian are: practical, functional and workable. In other words, practical and functional utilitarian environmental policies are different than spiritual ecology.

The principle focus of spiritual ecology is to pay tribute, honor or even worship creation or the environment. Rifkin's distinction between utilitarian and spiritual ecology fits with the concept to set environmental policies based on spiritual values not on what is practical or workable. This gives the Greens one more way to justify policies and laws that do not have to make sense. It makes control possible by making control legal.

> *"The task of saving the earth's environment must and will become the central organizing principle of the post-Cold War world."*
>
>

Senator Al Gore
Putting People First

Other political leaders have demanded for society to be transformed and organized around a new set of ideas.

> *"Our ideology is intolerant ... and peremptorily demands ... the complete transformation of public life to its ideas"*
>
>

Adolf Hitler
Psychopathic God

The Vice President demands saving the environment must become our 'central organizing principle'. There is no question we must protect the environment. The question is, on what principles will our environmental policy decisions be based? Will the decisions be based on functional, workable utilitarian principles or based on the spiritual principle of worshipping creation?

> *"Indeed, it may now be necessary to foster a new environmentalism of the spirit."*
>
>

Senator Al Gore
Earth in the Balance

Freedom of Religion is not the issue. The issue is, Green spiritual principles are influencing our political leaders ability to render fair judgment about environmental policies.

Consider our land use policies (public and private), our economy and our population policies. Biodiversity plays a major role in most issue areas. The Biodiversity Treaty that President Clinton has indicated he will sign has the support of many of our political leaders. What is biodiversity?

Biodiversity means the value for all organisms on every part of the earth except for humans. Human activity is blamed for the loss of biodiversity. One solution to preventing the loss of ecosystems and biodiversity is wilderness areas where human activity is limited or forbidden. Our government is expected to increase the amount of protected areas to preserve our biodiversity. Why does biodiversity affect each and every American? The September 1994 report from *EnviroScan*, a Canadian report on business and environmental issues used this quotation to explain the meaning of biodiversity:

> *"...the point of radical environmentalists protests and actions is the preservation of biological diversity. A term from the science of ecology, the **biological diversity of a place is, in a nutshell, its resemblance to what it looked like before people interfered with it**...Biodiversity might be more properly called ecological diversity, because, as radical environmentalists use the term, **it refers to not only plants and animals but to mountains, rivers, oceans as well - the non living and living aspects of an ecosystem...Human interference tends to lessen this biodiversity.**"*
>
> Rik Scarce
Eco-Warriors
(Bold Emphasis Added)

EnviroScan emphasized the meaning of biodiversity, stating:

> *"Clearly, **the preservation, maintenance and enhancement of biodiversity** (biological diversity) - as encouraged by radical environmentalists - **means returning the environment to its condition before any human involvement or impact. Biodiversity demands the elimination of human participation in the environment."***
>
> (Bold Emphasis Added)

EnviroScan is published by Public Relations Management Ltd. of Ontario, Canada. Greens call for a substantial reduction in human population. Americans need to pay attention to what our political leaders are thinking about issues such as biodiversity.

> *"Ultimately there isn't a chance of persuading people, civilizations and countries to take biodiversity seriously **unless they first understand, from the depths of the human spirit, the need to relate to Creation, to be sensitive to the realities of suffering and mistreatment, and to have a larger holistic spiritual view of what Creation is about."***
>
> Bruce Babbitt
> Secretary of the Interior
> From the Trenches - 1994
> (Bold Emphasis Added)

Our immediate problem is that Green spiritual ideas are affecting America's public policy because they are affecting America's policy makers. We have a major problem.

> *"**To some, the global environmental crisis is primarily a crisis of values.** In this view, the basic cause of the problem is that we as a civilization base our decisions about how to relate to the environment on premises that are fundamentally unethical."*
>
> Senator Al Gore
> Earth in the Balance
> (Bold Emphasis Added)

Before we move forward, we need to decide what principles we are basing our decisions on. Are they Green principles or the principles in our Constitution? We need to make a distinction between environmental policies based on facts and good judgment vs. setting public policies based on Green spiritual values and Green politics.

As If By Magic

'Magical Blend' magazine promotes the idea that our society is going to experience a major social transformation. The purpose of the magazine seems to be to prepare people to deal with the transformation, to help them reach a higher level of spiritual awareness.

The April 1994 edition of 'Magical Blend' featured an article by Vice President Gore regarding the relationship between the people and the planet. The Vice President shares the idea we are global citizens, we must reconnect with nature and that we need *new* leadership.

The Clinton-Gore ticket gave America new leadership. What new leadership is the Vice President talking about? The Vice President also indicates in his article that readers ought to help force political change by lobbying representatives. Vice President Gore also suggests America needs:

- new attitudes
- a new model
- new stories to pass on to our children.

Vice President Gore writes that our political leaders can't do this alone and suggests the readers begin pushing for change. Gore indicates the push ought to come from the bottom-up, from the grassroots. He suggests politicians can help, but support shouldn't be coming from the top-down. Support for new leadership is not coming from the bottom-up if the Vice President is generating it from the top-down.

'Magical Blend' magazine comes complete with ads for celtic pentagrams, witchcraft, voodoo, soul retrieval, pagan rituals and other adventures in magic. 'Magical Blend' is a curious place to find an article by the Vice President of the United States. It is a unique audience from which to seek political support for change, a new faith and new leadership.

> *"Regardless of how high the cultural importance of a people may be, the struggle for daily bread stands at the forefront of all vital necessities...To be sure, brilliant leaders can hold great goals before a people's eyes, so that it can be further diverted from material things in order to serve higher spiritual goals...The more primitive the spiritual life of man, the more animal-like he becomes until finally he regards food intake as the one and only aim of life."*
>
> *Adolf Hitler*
> Hitler's Secret Book

Deep Ecology mirrors Adolf Hiltler's concept of spiritual manipulation. It is a primitive spiritual way of relating to the earth. The idea to take nothing more than you need is universally understood. It also diverts people's attention from material things to serve higher spiritual goals.

> *"We want you to join this common effort to unite our country behind a higher calling."*
>
> *Senator Al Gore*
> Putting People First

When political leaders ask us to answer higher callings we ought to think twice.

The Green Bible

A quotation from Vice President Gore appears in the *Green Bible*, right along with religious leaders, deep ecologists and Green activists. This is a free country. It is not a crime to be included in the Green Bible. It only indicates, those who complied the series of quotations believe the Vice President thoughts compliment Green spirituality.

The Vice President has written forewords to books that discuss and seem to support ideas like deep ecology. One book titled, *Climate in Crisis* includes this statement by then Senator Gore.

> *"The solutions we seek will be found in a new faith in the future of life on Earth after our own, a faith in the future that justifies sacrifices in the present, a new moral courage to chose higher values in the conduct of human affairs, and a new reverence for absolute principles that can serve as stars by which to map the future course of our species and our place within creation."*
>
> Senator Al Gore
> Climate in Crisis
> (Bold Emphasis Added)

What are the higher values and absolute principles? Are they rules, laws or religious values? Are these the central organizing principles? These are some of the questions Americans must answers before they respond to a higher calling or try a new faith or new ideas.

The author of *Climate in Crisis,* Albert Bates, suggests solutions to environmental problems require worldwide reorganization of the way we live and relate to nature.

Bates indicates saving the earth will require Americans to reconsider these values:

- individual rights
- creation of wealth
- private property rights
- reproductive rights
- patriotism

Bates indicates a new paradigm is needed to solve our environmental problems. Bates new paradigm includes:

- elimination of individuality
- eliminate acquiring wealth (capitalism)
- receiving uniform income
- sharing wealth equally
- equalizing worldwide standard of living
- adopting ecological world view

The reason for this massive social transformation is to protect the environment. What Bates calls for seems to be the end of capitalism and the establishment of world communism. Believing we all share this earth and must lend a helping hand to those in need has long been an American tradition. Americans volunteer to share their wealth and talents with others. The key to our success and generosity is freedom.

There is no question that we can always improve the way we operate. We can consume less and alter behaviors to correct environmental problems. What Bates describes sounds like 'compulsory Green living'. Why will world communism solve the ecological challenges we face?

The Vice President recently recommended a new publication called: *Macrocosm USA, An Environmental Political and Social Solutions Handbook with Directories.* Before the Vice President would recommend a book, certain steps would usually occur. The office of the Vice President would first review the publication to determine if it was something Mr. Gore would want his name associated with. After initial scrutiny, it would be passed on to Mr. Gore for his approval or disapproval.

We would expect the Vice President to review the contents before providing a personal endorsement. At the very least, prior to printing; approval of the page on which the Vice President's quotation was to appear would surely require checking spelling and placement.

> *"There are many crucial challenges that await us in the next few years...I need your help now as we work to build a better future for all Americans. I appreciate your expression of support and generosity. Thank You for Macrocosm USA."*
> *Vice President Al Gore*
> Macrocosm Insert

Praise for the publication indicates the Vice President agrees with the purpose of the book that is promoting progressive ideas. We can always use innovative ideas. The question of endorsement regards the insert page where the Vice Presidents quotation is located. The page highlights the contents of the book. Features include an article by the radical environmental terrorist group, Earth First! The Green party is also listed on the feature page. Other groups listed in the publication include: Eco-Socialist, Democratic Socialist, the Communist Party of the United States and other controversial groups. The book does offer a mixed bag of controversial and mainstream groups.

It is not a crime to promote change in a free country. It is not illegal for the Vice President to lend his name to this book. We need to ask ourselves if it's appropriate for the Vice President to endorse a book that identifies Earth First as a selling point?

The current administration has just condemned terrorism as the new legislation suggests. Why did the Vice President endorse a book featuring a terrorist group? Doesn't this endorsement communicate to readers that the politics of Earth First are acceptable? It is hard to imagine anyone involved in environment issues would not understand the radical politics of Earth First!

The book is a resource guide for alternative and progressive political opinion. The authors want to revolutionize politics, cultivate social change by promoting alternative ideas for social transformation in America.

Listed on the insert along with the Vice President's quotation is the Green Party and Green ideas such as Bioregionalism, co-housing, economic conversion, vegetarianism and land trust. The Green Party is briefly discussed in the book. One article indicates that is because it is still too soon to bring up Green politics in America. The book offers these ideas on religion:

- existing religions are old fashioned
- due to global changes, religion, will die out
- this will occur for a new vision of God to reign

We can learn from the mistakes of others. The German people did not take Hitler's plans to reduce the population seriously. They did not think it could really happen. They were wrong. Hitler was dead serious. He made it happen.

What every American needs to realize is that Green spiritual politics are not really about an earthly religion. The Green faith is Communism. The Green Communists are doing everything they can in any way they can to destroy our way of life, our economy and our strength as a nation. America is under siege. It is time our political leaders do what they were elected to do, protect and serve all the American people based on our constitution and our principles, not the Green minority faction.

> "If we are to give the leadership the world requires of us, we must rededicate ourselves to the great principles of our Constitution...our nation needs the services of organizations who will remain vigilant in the defense of our principles."
> President John F. Kennedy

6

Sold Out

Are Americans being mentally prepared to accept drone status? Recently PBS aired a program called *Human Quest*. The idea seemed to be; humans smile when happy, cry when sad and that means people around the world are the same. The idea behind this concept was; if we reeducate ourselves to think differently, we can live as one people. We could all fit into the same mold. One speaker suggested we could go to *'re-training camps'* to learn to think properly.

This is a Green message. This idea has been fine-tuned by Communists. It's called brainwashing. People who did not agree with Lenin or Stalin were sent to slave labor camps to complete a *'re-education'* process. If they were lucky, they came back from Siberia, politically correct.

Individuality and independent thinking are not part of the Communist vocabulary. This is not to suggest the *Human Quest* program or its speakers are Communist. It's to point out the Green message. If Communists plan to control Americans, it will be much easier if we accept drone status in advance.

Another step toward a Green future involves gardeners and farmers, from gardening enthusiasts to those who make a living tilling the earth. The Greens targeted these Americans, encouraging them to get involved in the environmental movement. The Greens play on pride and emotion, using the idea that these Americans love the earth and the soil. They are the best people to protect it and help others understand the

Greens. The Greens are also encouraging backyard gardens as a way to reconnect with nature. Growing gardens and taking care of the soil is great. It is also the exact same tactic Hitler used to manipulate people into joining the Nazi movement.

> *"Hitler found the farmers some of his strongest supporters. He singled them out as guardians of the holy soil."*
> *Alfons Heck*
> A CHILD OF HITLER

Guilty Man Flees When No One Pursues

When people have something to hide, many times, they accidentally draw attention to it. Criminals often volunteer information they could not know unless they participated in the crime. Generally, this is the theory behind guilty man flees when no one pursues. Guilty people can give themselves away by pointing out what they don't want anyone to know.

Recently, the EarthWorks Press published, *It's a Conspiracy, The National Insecurity Council.* It's a subject way outside the realm of their normal environmental publications. The book looks at different conspiracy theories. Considering their focus is environmental protection, it is extremely unusual for this group to spend time and money writing or worrying about conspiracy theories.

There is a logical explanation. The book suggests conspiracy theories are silly and Americans are just insecure. Conspiracy theories have nothing to do with the environment, so why are the Greens drawing attention to the subject? The Greens are trying to counter being exposed for conspiring to use environmental issues to overthrow our government by setting us up to dismiss the possibility.

Guilty man flees when no one pursues.

Apply the 'guilty man flees' theory to the following statements made by well known environmental activists. Gaylord Nelson, the founder of Earth Day recently gave a talk about Earth Day and the environmental movement.

He brought up an odd point and discussed it at length. It was the idea, some Americans had twenty years ago, that April 22nd was chosen for Earth Day because it was Lenin's birthday. Nelson got the audience laughing and joked away any connection.

After twenty years, why is this an issue? Earth Day has the national spotlight on April 22nd. Most Americans don't even know it's also Lenin's birthday. If Lenin's birthday is not an issue, why bring it up? Guilty man flees when no one pursues?

There is another interesting point relating to Communism and Lenin's birthday. To rekindle the Russian spirit and commitment to Communism, Krushchev, in 1955, ordered April 22nd to become the day to remember Lenin. This act changed the focus from the day Lenin died to the day he was born. This gave Leninists an opportunity to celebrate Communism instead of mourning the death of Lenin. April 22nd, is the day Communists celebrate Communism. Now, it's the day the Greens celebrate Earth Day!

Nelson's advice to the audience included this thought.

> *"Think Green, and then you will do what's right."*
> *Gaylord Nelson*
> March 1995

Do guilty women flee when no one pursues?

> *"Now that the Cold War is over it appears that some Americans are searching for a new scapegoat to blame for the current chaos in the country. Environmentalists have quickly become the new target for the right. Although it is dispiriting to be assailed as the destroyer of the American way of life, the backlash is not necessarily a reason to despair."*
>
> Carol Grunewald Rifkin
> Co-author - Voting Green - 1992

The American people have shown overwhelming support for the environmental cause. What does the Cold War and chaos in our country have to do with environmental activists?

Senator Al Gore points out in his book, *Earth in the Balance* that Americans are:

> *"hostile to the messengers who warn us that we have to change, suspecting them of subversive intent and accusing them of harboring some hidden agenda, Marxism, or satism, or anarchism. ("Killing the messenger," in fact, is a well-established form of denial.)*

Subversive intent? Marxism? A hidden agenda? Killing the messenger? What does Marxism or satism have to do with the goal to clean up the environment? Guilty man flees when no one pursues? There is no question we have to clean up the environment. Do we need to transform our society to accomplish the task?

Having different opinions is what a free society is all about. A democracy is not intended to be a one way or none operation. The Greens are setting Americans up to feel sorry for them to keep our attention off critical political issues. The Greens are planting the idea they are being treated unfairly to discredit in advance, those Americans who question Green political ideas. Why do questions about Green solutions to environmental issues pose such a threat to those whose professed goal is environmental protection? If Americans are asking questions about environmental issues and suggesting options, it ought to be considered a positive. Asking questions means people care and want to help make good decisions.

Democratic problem solving involves a 'give and take' attitude toward finding solutions to complex problems. That is how win-win agreements are reached. If environmental excellence was the goal, discussion would be welcome. There is a difference between welcoming different opinions and pretending to welcome different opinions.

The Greens use the anti-environmentalist label to discourage discussion. *Greenpeace* even put out a book, *The Greenpeace Guide to Anti-environmental Organizations.* The Green thought police are trying to make it a crime to question the Greens. This suggests the Greens believe they alone have all the right answers. This fits Porritt's vision of Green dictators. The Greens have one primary solution for all environmental problems. It is the complete social transformation of America. Shouldn't we get a second opinion? We could tap into the collective American brain. It is a vast resource of intelligence and ingenuity. Why should we trust our lives and our future to the opinion of an intolerant minority? That is a dictatorship, not a democracy. It's Green communism.

> *"John Wayne. One of two great symbols of American machismo and proponents of a belligerent national posture, especially toward communist states, was actor John Wayne; the other is Ronald Reagan."*
> *Anne H. Ehrlich, Paul R. Ehrlich*
> Earth - 1987

Why are environmental activists pointing out Mr. Wayne and Mr. Reagan were belligerent towards Communist nations who abused people and were considered a threat to our nation? These Green statements continue to stand out as guilty man flees when no one pursues. Perhaps those who do not think it is correct to fight communism, believe we ought to welcome communism. Criticizing John Wayne and Ronald Reagan is another attempt to discredit our past.

The environmental community, like any other group of professionals must be accountable for what they advocate. There is a huge discrepancy between the Green practice of demanding accountability of others and the Green practice of not being accountable to others.

The Greens have an intolerant approach, not a cooperative spirit toward problem solving. The Green concept of 'no compromise' clearly illustrates their idea of negotiation. Communists operate on the, my way or none, approach to politics and power. The Greens manipulate themselves out of accountability using poor-me tactics and shifting the burden of proof to those who question them. Are the Greens infallible? Professionals, from surgeons to insurance adjusters, recommend people get a second opinion.

Bad Guys Do What Bad Guys Do

Despite the Green idea that Americans are lame to be concerned about communism, the emergence of Russia's Vladimir Zhirinovsky ought to have thinking people thinking. He is radical, mean and politically dangerous.

> "I say quite plainly, when I come to power, there will be a dictatorship. I may have to shoot 100,000 people, but the other 300 million will live peacefully"
> > Vladimir Zhirinovsky
> > July, 1994

There is a difference between cultures. Many people around the world have kind hearts, others do not. The Olympics prove people from different cultures can get along with each other. Believing Mr. Zhirinovsky thinks like we do, is a mistake.

Zhirinovsky probably isn't kidding about slaughtering 100,000 people. The Greens profess we are all one people. It is a nice idea, but it is simply not true. Every culture is unique. Different cultures grow different attitudes. Every nation has good guys and bad guys. Bad guys do what bad guys do.

The explorers who discovered the cannibals and the headhunters can serve as a reminder to the rest of us. The explorers may not have anticipated the particular habits of those tribes when they first met. After initial encounters, they understood. Those people had a different set of values.

International Cooperation or International Domination?

The Green movement is not about cooperation and sharing. It's not about science. It's not about the environment. It is about Communist control of America and the world. Look at the environmental conditions in other parts of the world. Their resources are in bad shape because they have not been cared for. In contrast, Americans have developed our resources. If we had not used our intelligence to do so, who would help the less fortunate? Who would bail out the starving Russians? We need to make some changes and correct environmental errors, but that does not require the complete transformation of our society.

For years, volunteers have joined the Peace Corps and helped developing countries learn how to manage their resources so they can help themselves. Citizens of the United States already share our wealth, information, food, people and financial resources. Many American volunteers have been repaid for their kindness with hostile acts of brutality, like beatings, rape and murder.

There is a difference between international cooperation, which we already do, and international domination. Can we do more to work with other nations? Sure, but we can't help the world, if we can't help ourselves. Choice is the determining factor. Freedom and independence are the only reasons America is not in the same environmental condition as other countries, including Russia.

We have been free to use our brains and our backbones to stand up for, care for and build our resource base. Capitalism and the desire to make the world a better place is the reason. During the process of developing our resources, mistakes have been made. Americans want a healthy environment. The question is; does achieving our goal of a healthy environment require submitting to a Communist world government?

Self-fulfilling prophecy is when people believe what they are told, even if it is not true. If good students are treated as if they are stupid, grades usually go down. The opposite is also true. If poor students are told they are intelligent, grades usually improve.

We don't have to fulfill the Greens prophecy and accept world government because they say we must. We can make up our own minds. Some futurists suggest Americans will accept subordination to Japan, Europe or the Greens gracefully. This forecast is due to both our foreign policies and internal conflicts that are weakening our nation. The same futurists suggest America can avoid domination if we change our focus from external affairs to internal affairs.

We need to make the future of our country our first priority. That sounds like awfully good advice. We ought to be able to focus on America and correct our internal affairs without hurting the rest of the world. This would not mean America would ignore world affairs. It means we would cooperate with other nations without being controlled by other nations.

A healthy nation is like a healthy family. If the family is the last priority, it will break down. A family can't base their future on what is best for the neighbors. They don't have to ignore or fight with the neighbors to make sure their family is healthy. A nation is no different. We must focus our attention on internal affairs if we intend to get America healthy and keep America healthy.

Our Greatest Enemy

We do not have to continue on this Green path to hell. We can work together and support each other like we have in the past. We can regain control of our lives and help get this nation back on track.

Our greatest enemy is ourselves. Americans are famous for practicing a live-and-let-live attitude. We need to realize we are dealing with a radical and intolerant political ideology that is pushing tolerant people to the limit. We can not continue to allow the politics of special interest groups to shape America's destiny.

We've got to take a stand and take responsibility for our future and the future of our country.

Basic Ingredients Of A Revolution

Revolutions stem from a conflict of values. Principles and values are what guide the people and the governments of nations. If a group decides to change the values of a nation, it is because their values conflict with the existing principles, ethics and morals that guide that nation. If this group is allowed to impose their values on that nation, revolution has occurred. Then new values and principles will guide that nation. The wisdom of John F. Kennedy is worth repeating to illustrate how important our principles are to this nation.

> *"... we must rededicate ourselves to the great principles of our Constitution...our nation needs the services of organizations who will remain vigilant in the defense of our principles."*
> *President John F. Kennedy*

When one group decides to impose their principles and values on a nation, the group:

- devise plans to overthrow government
- develop ways to build public support for new ideas
- use support to gain political clout, then seize power

'Subvert the Dominant Paradigm' is the Greens revolutionary call to overthrow our governing model. The Greens plan to impose their political ideas on this nation. If the American people do not stop them, Green principles and values will become the guide for the way our government and our society function.

You Decide

The following represents a summary of the strategic aims of the CPUSA, set at their national convention in 1969, in contrast to the political aims of the Green movement.

U.S. Communist Party Objectives and Strategies.

Mission: Seize permanent power over the American economy and government system. The Communist's plan of attack included these ideas.

- Build alternate political party, rival two party system
- Build or infiltrate a cause American masses support
- Reform capitalism and society, use minority issues
- Build alliances with all radical, anti-establishment groups

1995 Green Movement, Green Party Political Profile

- Greens are a radical alternative third party
- Green environmental cause has America's support
- Greens reflect Communist's goal to destroy capitalism
- Green movement represents multiple radical causes

To achieve their goals, the Communists had to invent a reason for Americans to accept our society ought to be changed and organized around an economy where businesses operate to meet the basic needs of the people instead of a society organized around personal profit and free enterprise. The Communists had to find a way to justify economic conversion.

To convince Americans capitalism is a flawed system in need of change, Communists focused on these points:

- Capitalist system creates have and have-nots
- Capitalism is only good for a few and hurts most people
- Present socialism as a better alternative

How do the Greens use environmental issues to promote anti-capitalism?

- The earth can not afford capitalist system
- Environmental problems can't be solved under capitalism
- Capitalism is cause of environmental ruin around the world
- The only solution is a new society based on Green values
- Utopian socialism is best plan for people and environment

Communists had to find a way to convince Americans that:

- Public control of production and distribution is better
- Produce only what is needed, stop consumerism
- End capitalism, put people before greed or personal profit

What do the Greens insist will save the environment?

- Public (government) control of economy and business
- Public (government) control of all natural resources
- Public (government) regulates production, based on need
- Public (government) controls distribution of goods, services

Lenin used the idea, *'People not Profit'*. The Greens use the idea, *'People Before Profits'*.

To convince Americans to change our way of life, the Communists outlined these ideas to persuade us to try socialism because our society was no longer adequate.

- Riot against society, create chaos, justify in name of cause
- Create strife between classes, promote a classless society
- Program masses, plant Communist ideas whenever possible
- Challenge Americans to try new ideas, higher values
- Goal is revolution but only talk about it until ready to act

Green political activities match those Communist goals.

- Eco-terrorism excused in name of environmental cause
- Greens are working to create a classless, genderless society
- Greens push socialism as an environmental imperative
- Ecological future depends on changing all our values
- Greens talk about Revolution, because they plan one

Subvert the Dominant Paradigm or Overthrow the Governing Model.

Green politics and ideology fit the Communist goal to seize permanent control and impose their values and principles on our society. The environmental cause is being used as their path to power.

United States Communist Party Goals Set in 1930.

- Eliminate American Pride
- Eliminate patriotism
- Patriotism out of schools
- Diminish individualism
- Teach Marxism

Have those Communist's goals been achieved?

- Rewriting American history, degrading our hero's
- Where is American patriotism?
- Pledge of Allegiance and other events out of schools
- Global citizen focus over U.S. citizen and individuality
- Green teachers are teaching Marxism

Coincidence, or the result of a calculated political effort?

Review the *'Communist Rules for Revolution'. How* many more symptoms can we identify? Who started these trends?

1. Corrupt the young; get them away from religion. Get them interested in sex. Make them superficial; destroy their ruggedness.

   - recreational sex, free contraception
   - males speaking in feminine tones
   - males wearing earrings & hair barrettes
   - drugs, alcohol and gangs

2. Get control of all means of publicity. Get peoples' minds off their government by focusing their attention on athletics, sexy books, plays and other trivialities.

   - Green journalism
   - Green entertainment
   - Televised trials

3. Divide people into hostile groups by constantly harping on controversial matters of no importance.

   - Multi-culturalism
   - Labeling: Hyphens before American
   - Anti-environmentalists vs. environmentalists
   - Politically correct speech

4. Destroy the peoples' faith in their natural leaders by holding the latter up to contempt, ridicule and obloquy.

   - Ridicule of America's historical leaders and legends
   - Columbus
   - John Wayne
   - Cowboys Bad, Indians Good

5. Always preach true democracy but seize power as fast and as ruthlessly as possible.

   • Greens are working behind the scenes for more government control under the guise of environmental protection.

   • Sweeping calls for major legislation and change:

     • Healthcare
     • Crime Bill
     • Terrorism Bill
     • NAFTA/GATT
     • National Biological Survey
     • Biodiversity Treaty

6. By encouraging government extravagance, destroy its credit; produce fear of inflation, rising prices and general discontent.

     • United States Government Budget 1.61 Trillion
     • EPA budget 6.6 billion
     • Deficit
     • Foreign aid: 1995 goal, over $7 Billion

7. Foment strikes in vital industries; encourage civil disorders and foster a lenient and soft attitude on the part of government toward these disorders.

     • Eco-terrorism
     • Animal Rights terrorism
     • Baseball, Airlines

8. By special argument cause a breakdown of the old moral virtues; honesty, sobriety, continence, faith in the pledged word, ruggedness.

     • Special Argument Number One: Environmental cause
     • Pre-Nuptial Agreements
     • Law Suit Mania

- Opening Adoption Records
- Sexual Revolution

9. Cause the registration of all firearms on some pretext with a view of confiscation of them and leaving the population helpless.

- Crime bill
- Gun control
- L.A. riots
- Koresh, Weaver, Lamplugh
- Anti-Hunting
- Wildlife protection
- Public health or security
- Oklahoma Bombing

We can not attribute all these events to Communist activities in America, though many events are probably connected. We need to focus on protecting the principles and values that are America's foundation. The *'Communist Rules for Revolution'* help us see the kind of traps Communist's use. Communists are committed to achieving the Party's goals.

> *"The policy of the Leninist Party, it's wisdom and conscience, correctly express what is realized by the people, it's thoughts, aspirations and hopes. And we are convinced that the great cause of communism, to which the Party has devoted itself, is invincible."*
>
> Mikhail Gorbachev
> 1985 - Speech

Advance Means Retreat, Retreat Means Advance

Another tactic used by the Communists is retreat really means advance. They fake being weak when they are strong and act strong when they are weak. This strategy keeps their enemies misinformed so they can be caught off-guard. After 20 years of service, a veteran officer in Russia's KGB, Anatoliy Golitsyn, defected to the United States and wrote the book, *New Lies for Old* in 1984. He warned the Communists were using disinformation, meaning putting out false information, to mislead us. Disinformation is used to divert attention from what is really going on in the Soviet Union. According to recent press reports, Russia's military is disorganized and weak. Other researchers contend the Russians are building their strength while we continue to downsize our military.

> *"Idealism did not stop Hitler; it did not stop Stalin. Our best hope as sovereign nations is to maintain strong defenses. Indeed, that has been one of the most important moral as well as geopolitical lessons of the 20th century. Dictators are encouraged by weakness; they are stopped by strength. By strength...I do not merely mean military might but the resolve to use that might against evil."*
>
> Margaret Thatcher - March 1995
> (Reprinted by permission by IMPRIMIS, the journal of Hillsdale College)

During a 1994 interview with *Audubon* magazine, Gorbachev referred to Communism as *'ideological garbage'* and indicated Communists had made a mistake trying to impose their values on others. Advance through retreat? Many Americans feel Communism appeared to die a very sudden death and have been slow to trust the Communists. Some Communists must have foreseen or planned the event.

> *"the August '91 coup was totally staged for Western consumption is evidenced by the fact that the **papers for the Gorbachev Foundation were filed with the California Secretary of State in April '91, four months before the pseudo-coup.**"*
>
> McAlvany Intelligence Advisor - March 1995
> (Bold Emphasis Added)

Anyone who has been involved with the legal process of creating a foundation or business understands it takes months of advance planning and documentation prior to filing papers with the State. Another consideration is these things cost money. Who financed Gorbachev?

The environmental movement is funded largely by the Environmental Grantmakers Association (EGA) which is supported by 138 foundations and groups, including:

- Ford Foundation
- Pew Charitable Trusts
- Rockefeller Brothers Fund
- Rockefeller Family Fund

The Gorbachev Foundation has received long term financial commitments from the following foundations:

- Ford Foundation
- Pew Charitable Trusts
- Rockefeller Brothers Fund
- Rockefeller Family Fund

The prologue for, *New Lies for the Old,* was written by Larry Abraham. He states, in 1953, the Director of Research for the House Special Committee on Tax Exempt Foundations was Norman Dodd. Dodd learned during a meeting with H. Rowan Gaither, Jr., then President of the Ford Foundation, that the Ford Foundation was *"following a covert plan"* and working directly with the White House to achieve this goal:

> *"we shall use our grant-making power to so alter our life in the United States that we can be comfortably merged with the Soviet Union."*
>
> H. Rowan Gaither, Jr.
President - Ford Foundation
(Bold Emphasis Added)

According to Abraham, Dodd asked Gaither if the American people would be informed of this. Gaither told Dodd:

"We wouldn't think of doing that, Mr. Dodd."

This is a significant point. It appears there are some very wealthy people who believe in the 'Do as I say, Not as I do' Communist philosophy. They also believe, they alone know what is best for the American people, world communism.

Seemingly unrelated issues reveal disturbing facts and direct links to what we are experiencing in America today and the political objectives laid out by:

- Russia's Communist Leaders
- Leaders of the Communist Party U.S.A.
- Ex-KGB Agents that Defected to the United States
- American Grant Makers, Foundations
- Prominent American Citizens, Pushing Social Change
- Mikhail Gorbachev
- Environmental - Green Movement Leaders
- Green Party
- United Nations

It is the opinion of this author that those Americans involved in this effort are either working with the Soviet Union because they are Communists, because their beliefs parallel Communism or because they have been duped into accepting the philosophy of communism under a different name. This is possible. The new name given to Communist values back in the early 70's was 'humanistic values'.

When comparing the concept of 'humanistic' political ideas in John D. Rockefeller's book released in 1973, *The Second American Revolution,* Gorbachev's vision for Green Cross International, the goals of the Green movement and the Green Party Program, the political objectives are unmistakably the same. Rockefeller's book looks like the outline of the Green Party Program and most of the goals set by the CPUSA. Some of the ideas Rockefeller promoted to bring about the second American revolution are also evident in Green politics and communism. They are:

- Planned Society
- Guaranteed Annual Income
- Public ownership of business
- Physical needs provided for citizens as basic human right
- Redistribution of the wealth
- Economic conversion
- Reconsideration of social classes
- True democracy
- Degrading American history
- People before profit
- Diversity, community
- Socially useful work
- Atheist instead of traditional religion

Rockefeller uses the terms, basic human rights and financial insecurity to justify the call for a guaranteed income and other basic needs. Those are the terms Congressman Dellums uses in his promotional information for: *H.R. 1050, A Living Wage, Jobs for All Act*. It is also the language of communism.

Rockefeller made this statement:

> *"there are many who have doubts about a guaranteed annual income, fearing it would create an enormous class of drones... but I am confident that there will be far fewer drones than many of us think..."*

Citizens living under communism are many times referred to as drones. The confidence in his statement: *there will be far fewer drones than many of us think,* suggests that Rockefeller and others intend to impose these ideas on unsuspecting

Americans. He states in the affirmative: *there will be far fewer drones,* as if it's only a matter of time.

The environment is severely degraded in Russia. Why? Communism is the reason. Russian citizens may have been concerned about environmental issues, but they did not have the freedom or desire to take steps to correct the problems. When the government has control of people's lives, people lose hope. People stop caring and operate like drones, completing their daily tasks. They know they do not have the power to change anything so they exist in a form of slavery. They depend on the government to provide the basics. They work and the government decides what they earn and how they live.

> *"They pretend to pay us and we pretend to work"*
> *Soviet Workers Joke*

It may be a joke in Russia, but it isn't very funny when it appears this way of life is planned for the American people. Rockefeller's ideas for promoting this kind of humanistic revolution in America include many of the same ideas the Greens are calling for today such as:

- need new leadership to head America in this direction
- get to accept utopian socialism or humanistic socialism
- calls for social change
- calls for citizens to develop higher consciousness
- call for decentralized government

The values Rockefeller outlines match the socialist to Communist transition and the Green ideas to revolutionize our society.

Like the Communists, Rockefeller infers the problems we face can't be solved with our traditional values of:

- family ties
- patriotism
- conventional view of success
- traditional religion

To fully understand the extent to which Americans have been set up, take a closer look at Rockefeller's idea that family ties and traditional religion won't help to solve our problems. The Communist's agenda includes destroying the traditional American family and replacing our values of privacy and independence with their value that society ought to raise our children. This is why Greens stress communal living, the village concept and giving up individuality for community. Communists are atheist. This is why destroying traditional religious beliefs is one of the Greens primary political goals.

It is interesting to look at the alternatives Rockefeller suggested 22 years ago and compare them to what Vice President Gore is promoting, what Hitler promoted and what has been popularized in our culture. Rockefeller suggested these alternatives to traditional religion:

- metaphysical 'religious consciousness'
- occult in general
- higher levels of consciousness
- sensitivity to the mystery of life
- transcendental philosophies
- Eastern religions
- mysticism
- extra sensory perception
- survival and nature

Rockefeller suggests this will curb Americans: *'overemphasis on science and behavioralism'*. If you're planning to use spiritual politics to shape America's environmental policies, it's a good idea to set Americans up to dismiss scientific facts and rely on Green ideology.

The Second American Revolution calls for radical changes to America's basic principles, ethics and values. Rockefeller explains that is the only solution to the problems we face. Rockefeller also quotes, *The Greening of America,* by Charles Reich regarding the revolution Reich predicted will take place in America in the 20th century and our political institutions:

> *"change the political structure only as its final act."*

That sounds an awful lot like John Drakeford's explanation of how Communists use scientific socialism to set the stage for violent overthrow of the political structure as the final step to dictatorship. He sites this from the *Communist Manifesto:*

> **"We openly declare that our ends can only be attained by the forcible overthrow of all existing social conditions."**

Is this part of the Communist agenda for the United States?

> **"Yes, we advocate a peaceful, electoral path to socialism. However, we have to be honest and say that we cannot predict, at this stage, whether a peaceful transition will be possible."**
>
> Gus Hall
National Chairman - CPUSA
Political Affairs, January 1989
(Bold Emphasis Added)

According to information related by Larry Abraham in Golitysn's book, *New Lies for Old,* Mikhail Gorbachev, in a 1989 speech to the United Nations suggested that the United States and the Soviet Union would work together as world police to protect the environment and stop international terrorism.

Golitsyn was a policy planner for the KGB before he defected to the West over 20 years ago. Golitsyn warned the West that part of the political strategy of the Soviets was to fake the fall of communism and the liberation of Eastern Europe. Golitsyn warned us over 15 years ago that this was the Communist plan, well before Gorbachev entered the picture.

If Americans agreed to world government and international police to enforce anti-terrorism and environmental laws on American soil, we would need some strong motivation to justify that level of submission. Beyond Green predictions of environmental doom, what might convince us we need help with terrorism? Maybe some major acts of terrorism in America. If the Communists planned 15 years in advance to fake the fall of Communism, it stands to reason they could have also planned to bomb the World Trade Center and the Oklahoma Federal Building to make terrorism an issue here.

According to retired Brigadier General, Benton K. Partin, of the United States Air Force, the collapse of the federal building in Oklahoma could not have been caused by a single car bomb. General Partin's opinion is based on 25 years of military experience in all phases of weapons development, from initial research to design and system testing.

> *"When I first saw the pictures of the truck bombs asymmetrical damage to the Federal Building in Oklahoma City, my immediate reaction was that the pattern of damage would have been technically impossible without supplementing demolition charges at some of the reinforced concrete column bases (a standard demolition technique)."*
> *Benton K. Partin*
> McAlvany Intelligence Advisor - May-June 1995

General Partin suggests, in the past when Communists have carried out terrorist activities, the wrong group of people have been conveniently set up to get the blame. Partin seriously questions why the federal building was destroyed before all the evidence could be carefully evaluated to see what other clues might be found.

General Partin indicates that according to his research on the Communist's plan to force the United States into socialism, the Oklahoma bombing is right in line with the strategy to foster violence and escalate terrorist activities. Partin indicates the Communist's objective is to push the American people to support disarming citizens.

What political issue area is likely to gain public support due to the Oklahoma bombing? Gun control, for one. The number nine rule for Communist revolution is:

> 'Cause the registration of all firearms on some pretext with a view of confiscation of them and leaving the population helpless.'

Every American wants terrorism stopped and prevented. Giving the President of the United States the power to declare any group or individual a terrorist threat is an extreme and dangerous step.

The Communist Rules for Revolution include preaching true democracy but seizing power as fast as possible. If the goal is to create a police state, enact gun control and render citizens helpless, then the call for high-tech surveillance equipment for wire taps of all militia groups and other citizen groups serves the Communist's plan.

Creating an unreasonable level of national hysteria about isolated incidents provides the excuse for some in positions of power to justify authorizing the government to take extreme action against American citizens. The incident at the Branch Dividian compound is a prime example of how things can get out of hand and turn from investigation to brutality.

Most Americans are law abiding citizens and cannot be blamed for the actions of a few. One bad apple doesn't spoil the barrel. The blanket indictment by the press and some politicians of all militias is completely irresponsible. This is like declaring all Americans who belong to XYZ auto club must be investigated because another member is accused of causing a traffic accident that killed hundreds of people.

What if this reactionary mentality was applied to other heart breaking tragedies? What about the incident involving Susan Smith and those two little boys that were drown? That was a gut-wrenching situation, but should it result in a government investigation of every divorced white female with two sons?

The situation regarding the militias is no different. Acts of violence are acts of violence. The alleged actions of some militia members should not result in the condemnation of all members based on the assumption these Americans are guilty of a crime. What happened to, 'innocent until proven guilty'?

It is critical that we keep our heads and work to eliminate terrorism without sacrificing the basic rights of innocent Americans. We do not know if these terrorist activities are coincidences or calculated political moves by the Communists. Caution is the watch word. As a nation we do not need to react, we need to respond to this situation intelligently. We also need to understand the Communists are actively pursuing their goals in the United States.

Gus Hall pointed out in his 1994 address to the Young Communist League, that he and his comrades have been:

> *"initiating, leading and participating in all great labor, political and progressive movements for reform and change...committed to socialism as the only viable...inevitable solution the inherent flaws, problems and crises that the capitalist system cannot solve. "*

Gus Hall
National Chairman - CPUSA
Political Affairs - June 1994

Whittaker Chambers, the former Soviet agent who defected in the late 1940's indicates in his book *Witness,* that the greatest mistake Americans make is assuming that the Communists think like we do. Chambers warns us we have nothing in common with Communists. He stresses Communists have irreconcilable viewpoints on:

- morality issues
- standards and judgments
- the fate and future of mankind

Chambers suggests that Communists will engage in espionage *'to the degree they are Communists'.* The deeper the faith in communism, the more they are willing to risk. It seems what Chambers wants us to understand is *Communists think differently than we do.* They have different moral and ethical values and will do whatever it takes to accomplish their objectives.

This relates to the way Hitler's mind worked. Reasonable people spent countless hours trying to understand, reason-with and make lasting agreements with Hitler.

Hitler had his own agenda. He would promise people anything, get them to believe what he needed them to believe and then do what he intended to do all along. Hitler did not worry about right or wrong. Hitler's purpose was to advance the Nazi cause. If making a phony agreement advanced his goals, he made a phony agreement. Efforts to form lasting alliances were faked. It kept his enemies off guard.

Chambers indicates Communists operate by the same morals and do not see lies or espionage as betraying anyone. They believe the salvation of mankind depends on world communism and that means the destruction of the capitalist system, *'which they believe to be historically bankrupt'*.

We should not blindly accept the Soviets no longer run a dictatorship, that the plan of world communism is void or that the Cold War is over.

A recent article featured in an August 7, 1995 issue of *U.S. News & World Report* suggests Chambers is correct that western values don't match Communist's values. According to the article, *Yeltsin's eyes and ears,* the former KGB secret police who rained fear are back in business with all their former power to abuse innocent people, including reestablishing their own prisons and wire tap privileges.

The KGB has been split into two different organs; the Presidential Security Service and the Federal Security Service. The Communists have not changed their values. It is a masquerade. They are pretending to have changed their values for a reason.

When We Least Expect It, Expect It

"the new Green vision places the environment at the center of public life, making it the context for both the formulation of economic policies and political decisions"

> Jeremy Rifkin
> Carol Grunewald Rifkin
> Voting Green - 1992

"the task of saving the earth's environment must and will become the central organizing principle of the post-Cold War world"

> Senator Al Gore
> Putting People First- 1992

"The only ultimate solution, of course, is the creation of a planned society in which the quest for profits has been abolished...."

> Gus Hall
> National Chairman, CPUSA
> Ecology 1972

"What we're talking about is creating new forms of life on the basis of new values"

> Mikhail Gorbachev
> From Red to Green - 1994

Rifkin: transform America based on his Green values
Gore: transform America based on his new principles
Hall: transform America based on his new values
Gorbachev: transform America based on his new values
Hitler: transform Germany based on his new values

"Our ideology is intolerant...and peremptorily demands ...the complete transformation of public life to its ideas"

> Adolf Hitler
> Psychopathic God

Like Hitler, these calls to completely transform our society are based on personal, spiritual, philosophical ideas. History can repeat itself, but only if we let it.

To further their goals, Greens recruit celebrities to promote environmental issues to advance their political ideas. This benefits the Greens in four ways:

- use the person to draw attention to their cause
- use opportunity to influence celebrity to go Green
- set celebrity up to appear Green in eyes of the public
- influences public to go Green based on emotion

Many Americans don't yet understand Green political goals, but every American needs to. Only then can we avoid becoming victims of Communist propaganda. Gorbachev's Green Cross International or GCI appears to be just another Green organization working on environmental issues. GCI and Gorbachev have specific plans to implement a Green world government. Gorbachev is hiding behind the environmental cause to impose his values on America.

Mikhail Gorbachev was asked to be the keynote speaker at the 1994 Environmental Media Association Awards. Some obviously questioned Gorbachev as an appropriate choice. This comment by Joseph Farah, appeared in the *Los Angeles Times*:

> "this is the same lifelong Leninist who presided over perhaps the most environmentally irresponsible nation in history."

Gus Hall, in his 1972 book *Ecology*, leads readers to believe Communists have better environmental ethics than Americans. Hall states:

> "One can judge a social system by it's history."

This is true. According to reports, the environment is in bad shape in Russia. Our environment is in better shape. Without our American way of life, citizens of the United States could not fund the 'bail-out' of the failed Russian economy. It appears we are funding our own demise.

Mikhail Gorbachev helped to organize GCI and serves as President of the organization. GCI Board of Trustees includes some of the same people involved in Green politics in America; Ted Turner, Robert Redford, Carl Sagan and Yoko Ono. The priorities of Green Cross International include:

- new paradigm for a global civilization or culture
- shift in basic values and how we view nature
- set of international environmental laws
- a world court to settle ecological conflicts
- local chapters to control international ecological threats

Gorbachev wants GCI to serve as the umbrella organization to handle global environmental issues. Gorbachev's vision includes using his celebrity status to promote these ideas and stimulate more public concern for the global environmental crisis. Global Green is the United States chapter of GCI. Gorbachev was personally involved in selecting Diane Meyer Simon to serve as President of Global Green.

Gorbachev and Meyer Simon met with leaders of major environmental organizations in November, 1993 in Washington D.C. The purpose of this meeting was to gain support for Green Cross International and Global Green. It was also to test the waters to see if the major environmental groups would accept GCI as the global environmental umbrella group and Gorbachev as their spokesperson.

The 1995 edition of the new international environmental magazine, *Grassroots* featured an interview with Meyer

Simon. She announced the results of that meeting with the major environmental groups. Meyer Simon stated:

> *"We expected some degree of resistance but instead heard a great willingness to join arms...they expressed a common need for someone to talk about values, whose words resonate with people in the streets as well as those in leadership."*

Gorbachev met with major environmental groups in 1993 and was selected to be the keynote speaker at the Environmental Media Association Awards in 1994. Is this a coincidence, or the result of a calculated political plan to move into America's environmental spotlight? Gorbachev's vision for GCI and Global Green is to create a 'new environmental consciousness' that includes changing all our values. Gorbachev made the following statement in the article, *From Red to Green, Audubon* magazine, Nov-Dec. 1994.

> *"We must change all our values ...What we are talking about is creating new forms of life on the **basis of new values**."*
> *Mikhail Gorbachev*
> (Bold Emphasis Added)

This may sound like a new idea, but it is not a 'Gorbachev original'.

> *"Socialism corrects the basic flaw of capitalism. It sets human society on a new path. The means of production, factories, mines and mills become the property of the people. They operate and produce only to fulfill human needs. They are not motivated by profits. **This is the foundation for a new set of priorities, for new values...What is involved is a 'conflict of values.'***
> *Gus Hall*
> 1972 - Ecology - Socialism and the Environment
> (Bold Emphasis Added)

Times haven't changed. The Communist strategy to take over our country in 1930, 1969 and 1972 all include the goal to gradually change American's values. It is the exact same message Gorbachev is using in 1995. Gus Hall, in a 1988 article for the *World Marxist Review,* indicated the Communists understood they needed to come up with some creative ways to get Americans to go along with their ideas. Hall also indicated that the Communists knew magnifying environmental doom would create the fear of human extinction and that fear could be used to persuade Americans to fight capitalism. He states:

> *"The fact is that **the bigger the stake the people have in the struggle for a more livable world, the better fighters they are in the fight to save humanity from extinction. The challenge is to formulate the tactics of unity in struggle that can be molded into an unbeatable fighting force** for human progress and human preservation".*
>
> Gus Hall
> National Chairman - CPUSA
> (Bold Emphasis Added)

Avoiding extinction was the issue selected by the Communist. Have environmental issues been twisted and exaggerated to intensify fear of a global environmental crisis to scare Americans into anti-capitalism? The next part of Hall's plan included formulating tactics to mold us to accept and fight for socialism.

Just 7 years later, Gorbachev's Global Green USA is creating a new television program called *Sacred Places.* It should be out later this year. This program will focus on the environment and feature prominent individuals who have experienced, a Green spiritual awakening. Green values for global environmental protection will be woven into the program. Meyer Simon is concentrating on:

> *"molding the message of international responsibility for an American audience."*

It looks like we're being set up to accept Green values on a global scale. The purpose of, *Sacred Places* is to mold our minds. Meyer Simon's job is to convince Americans to accept new values to avoid environmental disaster. This fits the plan outlined by Gus Hall. The Greens plan to cause a shift in our values, ethics and principles using the power of suggestion and entertainment to re-educate Americans to think correctly. Gorbachev makes his goal clear.

> *"A revolution has to take place in people's minds..."*
> *Mikhail Gorbachev*
> From Red to Green - Audubon - 1994

The Greens are planning to take advantage of our concern for the environment to literally brainwash the masses by ambushing unsuspecting American minds.

> *"The Gorbachev Foundation is run by Dr. James A.*
> *Garrison, a former executive of the Esalen Institute, a*
> *mind-control organization* *involved in conducting*
> *experimental psychological techniques in American school*
> *classrooms."*
> McAlvany Intelligence Advisor - 1995
> (Bold Emphasis Added)

If you plan to brainwash the American people, it's handy to have an expert on your team. Gorbachev's goal is to change our principles, values and ethics under the guise of environmental protection using mind control techniques. The Shevardnadze International Foreign Policy Association, headquartered in San Francisco is also run by Garrison.

Deliberately planning to use a program like 'Sacred Places' to brainwash Americans to change our morals and ethics by molding our opinions is beyond dishonest. This behind the scenes con job is a shameful violation of the public trust. It may not be illegal, but it is wrong.

President Clinton praised progressives in Hollywood, like Mr. Fleishman, for 'redefining' entertainment and using the behind the scenes approach, as a tool to:

> 'make the major cultural shifts our world is now experiencing to be as graceful and positive as possible.'

Is going behind our backs and using entertainment to mold our political opinions acceptable? Is it honest? Is this how we are being set up to accept major cultural shifts in America?

What about consumer protection? Americans cannot protect our minds without full disclosure. If the label says chicken, we don't expect to get fish. If a car is advertised, we don't expect to buy a bicycle. Americans who sit down to be entertained don't expect to be programmed. No different than expecting news professionals to present facts, professionals in the entertainment industry must be accountable for the products they offer.

The free flow of ideas is critical to the democratic process. This is not a free speech or censorship issue. This is about accountability. Redefining entertainment without disclosing the new rules to the American people is fraud. It is misrepresentation. The viewer expects an entertainment product, not a political soapbox product.

Does freedom of speech extend to ignoring America's national security? If we can say anything we want without regard to national security, why is Aldridge Ames, the spy, in jail? He was exercising his freedom of speech and sharing secrets with the Soviets. Is entertainment, specifically designed to change our values by using state of the art mind control techniques to foster revolution, without disclosing these goals, a censorship or a national security issue?

Redefining entertainment and using it for political gain is an issue that needs to be debated. Should politics and entertainment be mixed? Politicians are beginning to use entertainment to sell themselves to the American people. Political popularity, generated by which candidate gets on the most talk shows, will change evaluating a candidate. It will make it more and more a popularity contest instead of, an arms length, objective look at their political views.

Politics and entertainment ought to remain separate. A television program that focuses on political issues is different than using entertainment to popularize candidates or trick people into changing their values or forming a political opinion due to the power of suggestion. The entertainment industry, government officials and the American people need to examine this issue as it relates to consumer protection and America's national security.

The tobacco industry has to put warning labels on cigarette packages. Perhaps *Sacred Places* ought to carry the warning label; Hazardous to America. Viewer discretion advised. Contains brainwashing material designed to erase our culture.

Larry Abraham, indicates in the prologue for the 1984 book *New Lies for Old* that Gorbachev and others, who plan to create and impose world government, will use this approach:

> *"Perverting of the soul is far better accomplished by liberalism than it is by totalitarianism."*

Sold Out

Abraham correctly predicted how Mikhail Gorbachev and his cohorts would approach the subject of world government. Gorbachev is using the appeal of progressive ideas mixed with the fear of environmental disaster to convince us to change our values and submit to his ideas. Gorbachev is currently working on the Earth Charter. The Earth Charter looks like Gorbachev's 'shot' at quietly imposing world government. Beyond changing all our values, according to Gorbachev, the only way to protect our environment is:

> *"the development and **implementation** of an **Earth Charter**, a body of international ecological laws that would guide the actions of individuals, corporations and governments...the time has come for a code of ethical and moral principles that will govern the conduct of nations and people with respect to the environment."*
>
> Grassroots
> (Bold Emphasis Added)

The Earth Charter will contain a new set of environmental 'principles' designed to control the actions and behaviors of the people and nations of the world. Global Green along with the Earth Council has a three-step plan in place to promote, and then implement the Earth Charter in America. The Green plan is to get the Earth Charter passed in each country, then ratified as international law.

Global Green is working on a joint campaign designed to get Americans to support the Earth Charter. The United States is expected to support the Earth Charter so other countries will follow. Global Green plans to foster public support for the charter by using leaders in these sectors:

- Environmental
- Educators
- Philosophers
- Political leaders
- Religious
- Literary
- Performing arts
- American Indian
- Youth
- Non-Government Organizations

Some people are already pushing global government.

"David Rockefeller recently addressed the Business Council of the United Nations and warned that the 'window of opportunity' for installing the New World Order is very narrow, and that is because of opposition to it that is building (i.e. from U.S. conservatives and traditionalists) that if the opportunity is not realized quickly, it could be lost forever."

McAlvany Intelligence Advisor - March 1995

Gorbachev is working with Maurice Strong, former Secretary General of the United Nations, now Chairman of the Earth Council. Gorbachev and Strong are developing a draft of the Earth Charter to be completed by the end of 1995.

The final draft of the Earth Charter is to be ready in 1997. Gorbachev's Global Green plans on the United States being the first to sign the Earth Charter into law. Gorbachev's goal is to see the Earth Charter ratified by all nations and decreed 'global law' (a Green World Order), on January 1, 2000.

"When the Communist Party of the Soviet Union met for its 27th Congress in February 1986, it passed on a program of 'ideological and educational work' which provided guidelines for 'the struggle against bourgeois (Capitalists) ideology, to be valid toward the year 2000. The program said: The most acute struggle between the two world outlooks on the international scene reflects the opposition of the two world systems - socialism and capitalism."

Martin Ebon
The Soviet Propaganda Machine

Gorbachev was in power, in the Soviet Union, when the above plan was approved. The battle between socialism and capitalism has been taken to the international level. Mikhail Gorbachev is directly involved in the 'ideological struggle' between the two world systems. The question of capitalism or socialism is being presented as an environmental question by the Green movement. The Communist program to win their struggle against capitalism was to be completed towards the year 2000, the same year Gorbachev plans to have the Earth Charter ratified into international law.

The mass media was identified by the Communists as the key tool to convince people to accept socialism over capitalism. Gorbachev's GCI and Global Green are using mass media to reshape the values of the American people. The Earth Charter will be based on new Green ideas for how people of the world must live. Lenin and Hitler had new ideas. They also forced people to live by their rules.

Why is Gorbachev's GCI and Global Green targeting the United States to take the lead on the Earth Charter instead of Russia? If Gorbachev has a desire to protect the environment, he ought to be expected to prove the Earth Charter worked. Cleaning up the globe seems to be a big step, even for Mr. Gorbachev. Expecting the United States to agree to new values and global law with no track record, is arrogant. Is Gorbachev's goal, global environmental protection or, control of the globe? His goals include:

- a new civilization, a new governing paradigm
- new Green laws for citizens to live by
- International Environmental Laws
- form a World Court. Judge Gorbachev presiding?

The title of the *Grassroots* article is interesting:

> *"Green Cross International...Steering a course for global environmental reform with Mikhail Gorbachev at the helm."*

Mr. Porritt indicated the vision for the Green future went 'beyond world government'. The Earth Charter is the vehicle to gain legal control over the lives of the American people and establish Green Communism or the Green vision of 'compulsory Green living'. One washing machine per 20 people, rationed foods, curfews and Green Dictators.

*"The high office of the President has been used to foment a
plot to destroy America's freedom and before I leave office,
I must inform the citizens of their plight."*
                                            President John F. Kennedy

President Kennedy made the above statement when speaking
at Columbia University in 1963.

"Ten days later, John F. Kennedy was assassinated."
                                    McAlvany Intelligence Advisor

We will never know exactly what President Kennedy meant
when he warned us the office of the President would be used
against us. What we can learn from his warning is to pay
more attention to the actions of our government and the
actions of our Presidents. If the President of the United States
signs an International Treaty such as the Earth Charter, it
becomes the supreme law of our land. Americans will be
expected to comply with the values and laws laid down in the
Charter. If we do not comply, the laws would be enforced by
our government, from the top-down. If this occurs, the office
of the President will have been used to destroy America's
freedom.

A new American culture could be established with the stroke
of the President's pen. Communism would be instituted in
America as fast as it supposedly fell apart in Russia. The
American way of life, as we know it, could be erased in short
order. The Green flag would be flying instead of the Red one.
The long term goal of world communism would be achieved.

If Americans accept the Earth Charter, Mr. Krushchev will
have correctly predicted, *"The United States will eventually fly
the Communist Red Flag ... the American people will hoist it
themselves."*

H. Rowan Gaither, Jr., President of the Ford Foundation stated in 1953 that they intended:

"to use their grant-making powers to so alter life in the United States that we can be comfortably merged with the Soviet Union"

Funding for environmental groups comes primarily from the Environmental Grantmakers Association. The groups that funded Gorbachev's foundation are:

- Ford Foundation
- Pew Charitable Trusts
- Rockefeller Brothers Fund
- Rockefeller Family Fund

These same groups were among the top ten Environmental Grantmakers for 1990. This information was provided by the Environmental Data Research Institute, in the book, *Trashing the Economy*. These groups have and are playing a key role in the success of the Green environmental movement. If the Earth Charter is signed, life in the United States and Russia would be virtually guided by the same rules and the goal expressed by H. Rowan Gaither would be achieved.

The 'Communist Rules for Revolution' stress keeping citizen's minds off their government and on trivial things. Where is the American mind? Are we keeping close watch on the activities of our government?

Is this a coincidence, or have we been 'Set Up and Sold Out'?

Like The Man Who Winks In The Dark

The following statement was made by Gorbachev in a 1994 interview, in *Audubon* magazine, titled, *From Red to Green*.

> *"Now that we are rid of this syndrome of imposing the communist model on people, now that we've given them the chance to get rid of this dogma,*
>
> **I have to tell you Americans that you've been pushing your American way of life for decades. You thought it was perfection itself, the ultimate achievement of human thought** *...There has to be a different approach ... Americans have to be more modest in their desires. We have to stimulate human qualities in people rather than greed."*
>
> Mikhail Gorbachev
(Bold Emphasis Added)

Gorbachev's attitude about Americans and capitalism doesn't exactly sound like peaceful coexistence. What Gorbachev said in the first sentence is very important.

> *'Now that **we are rid of this syndrome of imposing the communist model on people,** now that we've given **them** the chance to get rid of this dogma,'*

Break it down. Who's we? Who's them? Who gave them a chance to do what?

Gorbachev's 'we' would be he, the Soviets and the CPUSA. 'Them' is us, the American people.

The Soviets have given Americans the chance to get over our fear of communism and of the Communists imposing their model on us by a take-over attempt. This is a critical point because the sentence reveals a Freudian slip. A Freudian slip occurs when someone accidentally reveals something they did not intend to reveal.

This statement was made by Gorbachev in a 1994 personal interview regarding the newly formed Green Cross International. It focused on his vision for GCI as a global environmental organization.

The 'we' in Gorbachev's statement can't be the environmental community because he has only begun to play a leadership role in the Green movement. It would not make sense for that group to give Americans the time to get over the conviction that Communists were a threat to our nation.

What did Gorbachev reveal when he stated Americans had been given the chance to get over their fear of Communism? What does it have to do with his involvement with GCI and the Green movement? The answer to that question is found in the following statement by a Soviet leader. Note: bourgeoisie means us, the capitalists.

> *"War to the hilt between communism and capitalism is inevitable. Today, of course, we are not strong enough to attack. Our time will come. To win, we shall need the element of surprise. The bourgeoisie will have to be put to sleep. So we shall begin by launching the most spectacular peace movement on record. There will be electrifying overtures and unheard of concessions. The capitalist countries, stupid and decadent, will rejoice to cooperate in their own destruction. They will leap at another chance to be friends. As soon as their guard is down, we will smash them with our clenched fist."*
>
> *Dimitri Manuilsky*
> Lenin School for Political Warfare -- 1930's

This explains Gorbachev's use of the terms 'we' and 'them.'

'...we've given them the chance to get rid of this dogma...'

We've been given time to forget Communism is a threat to us.

Have we have been set-up?

- Americans are not on the alert for communism
- Communists have made a spectacular bid for peace
- Communists have made unheard of concessions
- Americans have rejoiced for the new peaceful Russia
- Americans are accepting Green political ideas
- Americans are leaping at the chance to be friends
- America's guard is down

'As soon as their guard is down, we will smash them with our clenched fist'

Coincidence, or the execution of a calculated political effort?

The Green I.Q. Test

"A democracy can not be both ignorant and free."
Thomas Jefferson

Let's see if we've got this straight. Gorbachev, under the guise of environmental protection, is using entertainment to brainwash unsuspecting Americans. His goal is for us to change our values so we will support the United States being the first country to sign his Earth Charter. Then he can legally force his values on Americans. Take the Green I.Q. test.

- Our ex-arch enemy and Communist leader
- who has a terrible environmental record
- is working with environmental groups and
- using entertainment as a tool to brainwash Americans
- to get the U.S.A. to sign Earth Charter first
- to make 'compulsory Green living' mandatory
- to impose his values on Americans
- and make control possible, by making control legal

We fail the test, if we fail to understand, we are in the:

'war to the hilt between communism and capitalism'

The goal of the Communists remains the same. Golitsyn cautioned the West, in *New Lies For Old*, the Communist advance on America was in the final stages of implementation. The Communist goal was and is world domination and the overthrow of capitalism. This is a calculated political effort with national and international support. This is war on America.

Have we progressed to the point of being ignorant or is a Communist revolution still treason? Many members of the Green movement are revolutionaries who must face the consequences of their efforts to overthrow our government. Other than calling themselves Watermelons, Green on the outside, Red on the inside, can it be said in plain English?

> *"I am a Communist, a convinced Communist! For some that may be a fantasy. But to me it is my main goal."*
> Mikhail Gorbachev
> New York Times - 1989

If it looks like a Duck, walks like a Duck, quacks like a Duck, chances are, it's a Duck.

Like the man who winks in the dark, he knows what he's doing, but no one else does. The Greens know what they're doing. The American people have been left in the dark. This is not about environmental protection. The Green movement is about power and control. It is about setting-us-up to believe Socialism is an ecological imperative. The Greens are 'using our system to break down our system'. No American likes a them vs. us outlook, but the Greens created it. We must realize this is a war. If we do not stand up and be counted, we will be pressured into socialism, then forced into communism. One issue, one law, one company, one person at a time is the Green plan.

> *"Each year humanity takes a step towards Communism. Maybe not you, but in all events your grandson will surely be a Communist."*
>
> *Khrushchev*
> June - 1956

The Communists have been at this a long time. It doesn't matter what we call it; Green movement, Eco-Socialism, the Earth Charter or the New World Order. The Communists plan to take over America. The bottom line is, we're being had.

These revolutionaries, under the guise of environmental protection, intend to control the conduct of this nation. 'Compulsory Green living' will be forced on us if we do not take immediate responsibility for our future and respond to the Green threat to our freedom and national security.

The Gorbachev Foundation Directors includes these men who formerly held top security positions for the United States:

- Secretary of State George Shultz
- United States Senator Gary Hart
- United States Senator Alan Cranston

Is this a conflict of interest between the American people and the Soviet Union?

When Will We Say: Enough is Enough?

Americans have willingly given the Green movement their trust and hard earned cash. The question is, will Americans continue to support the Greens?

Lying to us, using our children, manipulating our political system, ridiculing our traditions and rewriting our history all add up to the Green goal to erase our culture and destroy the country we love. America is the target. We can take action and stop this or watch the Greens destroy our country. We need to understand we've all been used by the Communists to advance their goals, in one way or another.

A good example involves the use of the hyphen before the term American. The political purpose to use a hyphen before American is to change our culture by changing the way we identify with each other. That trendy little hyphen is forcing us to acknowledge differences instead of accepting and feeling our unity. During the research process, the first place the hyphen appeared attached to the word American was in Communist literature. Afro-American and Mexican-American were used.

America is the melting pot. That is our culture. People come here to become Americans and melt into this great culture. America is living proof of how all kinds of people can work together and achieve success. That is our connection to each other. The most important word in America is American. It stands alone. American is the term that defines who we are. There is no other culture, no other nation and no other people exactly like us. We are unique. We can be proud of who we are. We are all Americans first and our other heritage follows. If there was a war, would the Irish return to Ireland, the French to France or Africans to Africa? Obviously not, because this is now their country.

The Communists targeted these unsuspecting Americans to manipulate their issues and advance the Communist political agenda:

- Indians
- Puerto Ricans
- Asians
- Women
- Entertainers
- Children
- Religion
- Education
- Labor Unions
- Poor
- Blacks
- Whites
- Mexicans
- Gays
- Politicians
- Young adults
- Healthcare
- Jewish
- Senior citizens
- Homeless

The Greens targeted those involved in environmental efforts. January, 1989, *Political Affairs,* the journal of Marxist thought, featured an article: *The Environment: A Natural Terrain for Communists.* Author, Virginia Warner Brodine states:

> **"A specific Communist program will come from developing a Marxist understanding throughout the Party for the environmental crisis and from participation in environmental struggles** *which will help us to apply this understanding in local, national and international situations.* **This can advance the cause of all-people's unity and bring the most advanced environmentalists into the fight for socialism."**
>
> (Bold Emphasis Added)

Most Americans involved in the environmental movement are caring, honest Americans who can get off the Green bandwagon as fast as they got on. We need to slow down, step back and reassess the entire environmental situation. We need to question every piece of proposed environmental legislation and make distinctions about the political agenda of the Green movement. We must also consider and address the threat the CPUSA is to our national security.

> *"Yes, we advocate a peaceful, electoral path to socialism. However, we have to be honest and say that we* **cannot predict, at this stage, whether a peaceful transition will be possible.***"*

Gus Hall
Political Affairs - 1989
(Bold Emphasis Added)

Advocating *'a peaceful path to socialism'* is different than guaranteeing it. This statement indicates the Communists have considered and are prepared to use force and violence to implement socialism in America. The Greens are a serious threat to our personal safety and national security. Die Yuppie Scum, Visualize Industrial Collapse, and Subvert the Dominant Paradigm fit the implied idea, if we don't volunteer for communism, Green dictators will try and force it on us.

Albert Kahn, author of *High Treason*, indicates in 1948 the members of the CPUSA were charged with conspiracy because they:

- formed political party devoted to Marxist-Leninist ideas
- published and promoted principles of Marxism-Leninism
- set up schools to teach principles of Marxism-Leninism
- planned overthrow of Government with force and violence

Nothing has changed. The Communists have just gotten bolder. There is a fine line between free speech and treason. According to Julia Johnsen, author of, *Should The Communist Party Be Outlawed?* indicates that according to the Constitution, the founding fathers defined treason this way.

"Treason against the United States shall consist only in levying war against them or in adhering to their enemies, giving them aid and comfort.'

According to that definition the Greens ought to be considered traitors because they are:

- fighting against capitalism and government system
- supporting and aiding the enemy (Soviet Communists)
- referring to their cause as a war against America
- encouraging terrorist activities

The Greens are working with Gorbachev. Although the Soviets and Gorbachev have professed to no longer be enemies of the United States, one need only refer to the plan outlined by Dimitri Manuilsky in 1930 and what has occurred over the last 65 years. Communist's propaganda and disinformation are designed to catch Americans off guard.

Green Communists plan to use our system to break down our system. They plan to take advantage of our trust while they set us up for take-over by walking the fine line between free speech and treason.

Doesn't feel very good does it? Well, America:

> *"it ain't over, till it's over"*
> *Yogi Berra*

The first Americans rebelled against dictatorship and excessive government control. As Americans, we have an obligation to honor that tradition and to protect our individual liberty and freedom. We all have absolute freedom until we begin to infringe on the rights and freedoms of others. The Greens have crossed the line.

Americans do not agree on all things, all of the time. That is good. It shows we are independent thinkers. One thing we have in common is that we cherish our freedom and the opportunity to make all kinds of independent choices. From where we live to what we eat; rich, poor and in-between, no American wants to be dictated to.

This is not about environmental excellence. It's not about being a Democrat or a Republican. It is not about being a conservative or a liberal. This is about making a decision to save our country and choose our future.

When Patrick Henry said 'Give me liberty or give me death' he was not making a casual statement. The first Americans set the standard for what being an American meant. They had the will, the courage and the heartfelt determination to live free. It is our challenge to protect their legacy and once again show what Americans are made of. We have the will, the courage and the heartfelt determination to fight for America and the right to live free.

The future of a nation stems from a foundation of pride in the past and from that, hope for the future. If we continue to let the Greens butcher our national pride, our foundation slowly disintegrates and our culture becomes replaceable. Love of country and culture is what holds a nation together. We need to reclaim our patriotism and pride. We need to love and protect our country. It's where we live, where we work and what we pay taxes to support.

Americans set us free and Americans can keep us free.

Our forefathers and mothers risk it all to be free. They took heart, took a chance and beat the odds. They gave their lifetimes to give us our freedom. Rekindle that spirit. Our freedom is at risk and we don't have time to be timid.

"A ship is safe in the harbor, but that is not what ships are built for"

Shedd

Life is filled with risks. The time to act is now, before we wake up in a society we will not recognize. For too long, we have ranted and raved mainly at home. It's time to go public. We have the power and the opportunity to shape our future. Many Americans have become complacent. We depended on others because we did not realize there was a desperate need for our involvement. It's not that we didn't care, it's that we didn't know. Now we know and it's time to show we care.

The Weapons of Choice are Wit and Wisdom

The Green revolution will continue unless we realize it's up to each one of us to do whatever it takes to stop it. Wherever we live, whatever we do, we can find ways to help. The time has come to pick sides. The war is on. The weapons of choice are wit and wisdom. As the saying goes:

"We can not direct the wind, but we can adjust the Sails"

We can't pass freedom on to our children if we submit to Green Communism. How our children and grandchildren live in the years ahead depends on how we respond to the Greens today. The question every American must answer is: Am I willing to let the Greens push Green Communism down our collective American throat?

Don't forget what this Green thinks of us.

I have to tell you Americans that you've been pushing your American way of life for decades. You thought it was perfection itself, the ultimate achievement of human thought ...There has to be a different approach ... Americans have to be more modest in their desires. We have to stimulate human qualities in people rather than greed."

Mikhail Gorbachev
(Bold Emphasis Added)

What's on Gus Hall's wish list?

*"The end will not come when the commissars finally haul 60 million hopelessly diseased, capitalistic 'animals' off to liquidation centers or **when Communist Party Chief, Gus Hall, gets his wish to see the "last Congressman strangled to death with the guts of the last preacher"**...*

...The battle will be lost, not when freedom of speech is finally taken away, but when Americans become so 'adjusted' or 'conditioned' to 'getting along with the group' that when they finally see the threat, they say, I can't afford to be controversial."

John Stormer
None Dare Call It Treason
(Bold Emphasis Added)

Will the politically correct Green 'thought police' or independent Americans determine our future? If you don't agree with the Green vision for America, join the rest of us and read on.

It is time to call it treason. It is time to be controversial.

7

The Sleeping Giant

"The American people have a reserve of common sense and patriotism that will withstand the onslaught of the Communist propaganda campaign if it can be unmasked and reversed in time.

A defector from the Czech KGB described his organizations secret evaluation of Americans. Josef Frolik, testifying before the Senate Committee on the Judiciary on November 18, 1975, said, "The patriotism of the average American is extremely high...The KGB intelligence officer should not permit himself to be misled by the apparent indifference shown by the average American."

The American masses are referred to as 'the sleeping giant', who always requires a shock before he comes to his senses, but thereafter is merciless."

James Tyson
Target America
(Bold Emphasis Added)

We can jump-start a counter national movement today. We can start by Putting our flag up and our foot down.

Put Your Flag Up and Your Foot Down

Photo copy the list on the next two pages. Check the statements you believe will help to protect and rebuild America. Then sign it and send it to your Senators, Congressman and State Representatives.

Dear fellow citizen, I have checked the issues that are of greatest concern to me and my family. I request these issues be given your immediate attention, that you discuss them with House and Senate members and the following actions be taken to protect our nation.

___ I do not want the United States government to participate in or submit to world government. I want America to be our first priority and you to focus on internal affairs.

___ I do not want the United States government to sign the Earth Charter or any other International Treaties without full disclosure, a televised public debate and approval by the American people.

___ I want a full investigation into the activities of Mikhail Gorbachev, the Gorbachev Foundation and Global Green to ensure our national security. I want Gorbachev and members of his organizations stopped from further access to U.S. military bases or other sensitive information that could compromise our national defense. The investigation ought to include seizure and review of all records that may contain information pertinent to national security.

___ I want Gus Hall and other Communist revolutionaries who have alluded to the violent overthrow of our government to be charged with treason and prosecuted to the full extent of the law as a matter of national security.

___ I want you to protect our country, our system of government and our constitutional rights. I want to be notified of any legislation designed to change our basic rights as Americans. The National Biological Survey and Congressman Dellums, Living Jobs for All bill are the kind of legislation I want to know about.

___ I request a full government investigation into the subversive activities of the Green movement.

___ I want to know the true status of the environment. I request to know the facts as documented by our leading scientists instead of more Green propaganda.

___ I support limiting the number of bills introduced each session. I want good laws, not more laws.

___ I request an investigation into the objectives of the Environmental Grantmakers Association with full disclosure to the American people.

___ I request reconsideration of downsizing our military by 75%. I want a strong military defense.

___ I expect full disclosure of any proposed international legislation that will cause any change in how our government and society functions, violates our rights or threatens our national security. The Biodiversity Treaty and the Earth Charter are immediate concerns.

___ I want the United States to stop all immigration so our nation can adjust to the large influx of immigrants as an issue of national security. The Greens have suggested importing votes, to out-vote the American people.

___ I support a stronger border defense and an effort to locate and deport illegal aliens. The Greens advocate reducing border control and eliminating borders internationally.

Thank You. I will be monitoring your progress.

Signed:_____

Next...Put Your Flag Up!

- Get it on your house, your car and at the office. Send a message. If Americans put their flags up, it would send a loud and clear message to the Greens and to our political leaders that American patriotism is not dead.

- Buy a flag for a friend, parent or neighbor. Help them put it up. Explain this is a fast and effective way for Americans to let political leaders know we will not accept being Sold Out to Green Communism.

When political leaders on the local, regional and national level learn why Americans across the nation have put their flags up, they will understand these things:

- we the people, are paying attention
- we intend to choose our future

- Our flag symbolizes freedom. Put it up and leave it up. Let it serve as a constant reminder of the dedication it took to create this nation and how fortunate we are to live in the greatest country in the world.

- Teach the Pledge of Allegiance to your children. Recite it with them. Explain what liberty and justice means.

   I pledge allegiance to the flag of the United States of America and to the Republic for which it stands, one nation, under God, indivisible with liberty and justice for all.

No Time to Reinvent the Wheel

The Green assault on our nation is too serious. We can't start from scratch and win. We must be creative.

Americans can speak up and be heard in Washington D.C. in a matter of weeks. How? Work together and nationalize this issue. We can send a powerful and immediate message to our political leaders.

Major industries, small businesses and individuals across America are under fire from the Greens. They are in a battle for survival. Each is trying to stop the Greens from passing laws that will make it impossible for them to stay in business or exercise their constitutional rights. We can help ourselves by helping them.

Regardless of our politics, our occupation or our income, we must understand the Green issue transcends all conventional lines of disagreement. We can't take care of the environment or anything else under the present circumstances. We have to stop the Greens first.

We must look at this as the war it is. When we enlist to defend America, we are all on the same side. We can't worry about matters of less importance we could disagree on. Our common objective must be to defeat our enemy. Our objective is to stop the Green Communists. This is a tug of war. It will take the combined strength of all Americans, pulling together, to win. It is essential Americans understand individual participation is the key to success.

To be heard in Washington D.C., we need to create a loud political voice. Getting a political voice is not difficult, but it takes cooperation. It's like trying to be heard in a capacity crowd at the Los Angeles Coliseum. If a few people stand up and yell something, they get no respect. If the crowd stands up and yells the same thing, at the same time, what they say, will be heard. The same goes for getting the attention of political leaders. If Americans add their voice to those already in the fight to protect our rights and national security, then we, the general public, can speak and be heard.

Put the Greens on Hold

We know the Green Communists have infiltrated our government system and environmental organizations. They are using environmental issues to justify making control possible by making control legal.

Green politicians and every environmental organization must be subject to public scrutiny as a matter of national security. We can't allow these organizations to continue to influence decisions regarding the future of our nation.

We do not know to what extent the Communists have infiltrated our government or environmental groups. We can not trust Green groups to operate on the honor system.

We don't have to put environmental groups out of business to put the Greens ability to influence political decisions on-hold. The Greens have a loud voice in Washington D.C. and across the nation due to the number of voters attached to their groups. American citizens are the source of the Greens political power. Remove number of voters attached to the Green groups and we put their ability to influence our future on-hold. If you contribute to environmental groups, resign and request the return of your annual dues. Don't buy anything that gives the Greens more money. Don't buy posters, stickers, Christmas cards, cups, food, clothing, stuffed toys, or anything else.

Hitler Youth, Never Again. How to Protect Our Children

- Petition the school board to end Earth Day celebrations in local, or statewide schools. Check the regulations to make sure your petition is legal and meets all the requirements before you get the signatures. Include in the petition, a request that the earth flag not be flown at school. It is not appropriate to display this revolutionary political symbol on school grounds. Request that environmental studies be discontinued until the Green abuse of our children and use of our schools as Green recruiting and training centers for young activists is addressed to the public's satisfaction.

- Petition the school board or the State Board of Education to have students say the Pledge of Allegiance again, in all schools, at the beginning of each day.

- Petition the school board to disallow any further teaching re-written American history, unless it is approved by the majority of the American people. Teachers do not have the right to teach anything they desire. These are America's children. We pay the teachers' salaries. Say NO and mean it.

- Take your child out of environmental clubs, organizations, Green politics and Green social activities. Help your child understand what happened to the Hitler Youth is the reason. Go to the library and check out books about the Hitler Youth and the Nazi movement. Show your child what can happen when children get involved in politics. Explain why you won't let that happen to them. Help them recognize the difference between environmental protection and Green propaganda.

- Don't let your child watch *Captain Planet* or other cartoons with environmental themes unless you have time to explain the message. Read children's environmental books with your children. Point out what you agree and disagree with.

- Watch all movies with environmental themes with you're children. Point out what's right or wrong with the message. Explain movies are make-believe, not real-life. Make it a family thing. See who can spot the Green message first. Green messages are easy to hear once you know what political 'programming' to listen for.

- Look for Sunflowers, with your children. Help them see the Sunflower is just a beautiful flower. If they are old enough to understand, explain what it means politically. Explain to friends and family what the flower represents so they understand the significance of the Sunflower.

- Write to product manufacturers, explain to them what the Sunflower represents.

- Word of mouth is one of the most effective forms of communication. Get this information to business peers.

Other Activities

Every American has different talents and interests. Following are just a few ideas of what Americans can do.

- Join groups and organizations working to protect constitutional rights or start your own.

- Get involved in politics, local, regional and national.

- Celebrate Columbus Day

- Celebrate Constitution Week

- Celebrate the Fourth of July, make it a real celebration.

- Teach your children more about the Declaration of Independence. Explain what this document means and what their life would be like without it. Make a copy of it from a reference book at the library or a copy of the document can be obtained by sending $1.00 to cover postage and handling to, Historical Documents Co., 8 N. Preston Street, Philadelphia, PA. 19104. Request the Declaration of Independence.

- Honor our veterans who fought for the freedom we enjoy. Get veterans involved in Fourth of July activities.

Think American, Act American

It's time to stand up for ourselves. Stay with what works. If the Greens want to try Communism, they have the option of going to Russia. Do your part. Don't rely on anyone else to do this for you.

- Stop using hyphens to identify ethnic origin. Don't participate in social trends that divide American citizens.

- Spread the word. Print some **Think American, Act American** or **Put Your Flag Up and Your Foot Down** bumper stickers to sell or give away.

- Vote. Don't let the Greens decide your future.

- Request corporations stop funding Green groups. Ask them to donate that money to charity.

- Use your imagination.

Our forefathers chose their destiny and in the heart of every American that spirit burns. The will to be free is part of who we are. It's our turn to do whatever it takes to reclaim our country and preserve our American legacy. This is our gift and our duty to all future Americans. With a past like ours, we could never explain failure. Think American, Act American and remember:

"Choice, not chance determines destiny"

Green References

This resource list is provided as a service for readers who are interested in learning more about the Green Movement and Communism.

Greening America

Ecology	Hall	1972
The Second American Revolution	Rockefeller	1973
The Greens and Politics of Tranformation	Resenbrink	1992
From Red to Green	Bahro	1984
The Green Revolution	Sale	1993
Building the Green Movement	Bahro	1986
Biosphere Politics	Rifkin	1991
Green Political Theory	Goodin	1992
Communes and the Green Vision	Pepper	1991
Eco-Socialism	Pepper	1991
Ecology and Socialism	Ryle	1988
Earth in the Balance	Gore	1992
Radical Ecology	Merchant	1992
Getting There - Steps to a Green Society	Wall	1990
Seeing Green -Politics of Ecology	Porritt	1984
Save the Earth	Porritt	1991
Green Politics -The Global Promise	Spretnak	1986
	Capra	
The Green Alternatives	Toklar	1987
The Greening of America	Reich	1970
Green Lifestyle Handbook	Rivkin	1990
GAIA Atlas of Green Economics	Ekins	1992
Home -Bioregional Reader	NSP	1990
The Way -An Ecological World View	Goldsmith	1993
Toward a Transpersonal Ecology	Fox	1990
Sixteen Weeks with European Greens	Feinstein	1992
The Little Green Book	Lobell	1981
Voting Green	Rifkin	1992
	Grunewald	
Blueprint for a Green Economy	Pierce	1989
	Markandya	
	Barbier	

Eco-Spirituality

Goddess Mythology in Ecological Politics	Biehl	1989
Spiritual Dimension of Green Politics	Spretnak	1986
Greenspirit -Ecological Spirituality	LaChance	1991
How Deep is Deep Ecology	Bradford	1989
GAIA	Lovelock	1979
Deep Ecology and Anarchism	Bookchin and Others	1993
Spiritual Politics	McLaughlin Davidson	1994
The Green Bible	Scharper Cunningham	1993
Green Egg	Church of All Worlds	1993

Little Green Army

The Kids Guide to Social Action	Lewis	1991
Changing Our World Handbook Young Activists	Fleisher	1993
Captain Eco and the Fate of the Earth	Porritt	1991
Save the Earth -Created by Kids	Hirsh	1992
Earth Book for Kids	Schwartz	1990
The Kids Environmental Book	Pedersen	1991
Kid Heroes of the Environment	EarthWorks	1991
Wild, Wild Wolves	Milton	1992
Save the Earth -Action Handbook for Kids	Miles	1991
Dear World	Temple	1993
For the Love of Our Earth	Hallinan	1992
Hands Around the World	Milford	1992
Student Environmental Action Guide	EarthWorks	1991
Teaching Kids to Love the Earth	Herman Passineau	1991
This Planet is Mine	Metzger Whittaker	1991
Going Green	Elkingoon Hailes Hill Makower	1990
Rethinking Columbus	Rethinking Schools	1991
Green Teacher Education for Planet Earth #34	Jun-Sept	1993
Radical Teacher Socialist & Feminist Journal #43	Fall	1993

Additional References

Educating for the New World Order	Eakman	1991
Environmental Agenda for the Future	Island Press	1985
Unsettling of American Culture & Agriculture	Berry	1977
One World or None	Harris	1993
Biosphere Politics	Rifkin	1991
The Unfinished Agenda	Barney	1977
You Can Change America	EarthWorks	1993
Putting Power in Its Place	Plane	1992
Climate in Crisis	Bates	1989
The Way Ahead	Shapiro	1992
The Indian Way Communicate with Mother Earth	McLain	1990
Millennium -Winners & Losers in World Order	Attali	1991
Entropy -A New World Order	Rifkin	1980
Entropy -Revised Edition	Rifkin	1989
Earth	Ehrlich	1987
Earthwatch	Savan	1991
Seeds of Change	Ausubel	1994
Earth in the Balance	Gore	1992
1992 Earth Journal	Buzzworm	1992
The Turning Point	Capra	1982
Call to Action	Erickson	1990
Vote for the Earth	EarthWorks	1992
Psychopathic God	Waite	1977
Living Richly in an Age of Limits	Devall	1993
Last Refuge	Robbins	1994
The Rainforest Book	Lewis	1990
The End of Work	Rifkin	1995
Environmental Literacy	Dashefsky	1993
Avoiding Social and Eco Disaster	Bahro	1994
New Options for America	Satin	1991
Agenda 21 Earth Summit Strategy	Sitarz	1993
Planet Hood	Ferencz	1988
The Rediscovery of North America	Lopez	1992
Negotiating Survival	Gardner	1992
The Closing Circle	Commoner	1972
Voluntary Simplicity	Elgin	1981
Save the Animals	Newkirk	1990
Direct Action and Liberal Democracy	Carter	1973
Balancing on the Brink of Survival	Kohm	1991
Real Choices New Voices	Amy	1993
State of the Ark	Durrell	1986

Free Things for Teachers	Osborn	1990
Macrocosm USA	Brockway	1992
Working with Earth, Economy & Environment	Kraft	1993
	Mcleod	
	Wells	
Putting People First	Clinton	1992
	Gore	
The Animal Rights Handbook	L P Press	1990
It's a Matter of Survival	Gordon	1990
	Suzuki	
Media and the Environment	LaMay	1991
	Dennis	
Moving Towards a New Society	Gowan	1976
	Lakey	
	Moyers	
	Taylor	
Forward Motion Socialist Magazine		1989
Green Man A magazine for Pagan men #2		1993

Bibliography

Books

Bates, Albert K., *Climate in Crisis*, The Book Publishing Company, Summertown, TN., 1990

Brockway, Sandi, *Macrocosm USA* (includes insert), Macrocosm U.S.A. Inc., Cambria, CA, 1992

Clinton, Bill and Gore, Al, *Putting People First*, Times Books, New York, 1992

Communist Party U.S.A., *The United States in Crisis*, New Outlook Publishers, New York, 1969

Cuddy, Dennis, *Now is the Dawning of the New Age, New World Order*, Hearthstone Publishing, Ltd. Oklahoma City, 1991

De Roussy de Sales, Raoul, *My New Order*, Reynal & Hitchcock, New York, 1941

Drakeford, John W., *Red Blueprint for the World*,Wm. B. Eerdmans Publishing Company, Grand Rapids, MI, 1962

Durrell, Lee, *State of the Ark*, Gaia Books Limited, Bodley Head Ltd, London, 1986

Eakman, B.K.,*Educating for the New World Order*, Halcyon House, Portland, OR, 1991

Earth Journal 1993, Editors, Buzzworm Magazine, Buzzworm Books,Boulder, CO, 1992

Ebon, Martin, *The Soviet Propaganda Machine*, McGraw-Hill Book Company, San Francisco, 1987

Ehrlich, Anne H. and Paul R., *Earth*, Franklin Watts Inc., New York, 1987

Golitsyn, Anatoliy, *New Lies For Old*, Clarion House, Atlanta, GA, 1984

Gore, Albert, *Earth in the Balance*, Houghton-Mifflin Company, New York, 1992

Hall, Gus, *Ecology*, International Publishers, New York, 1972

Heck, Alfons, *A Child of Hitler*, Renaissance House, Frederick, CO. 1985

Hitler, Adolf, *My Secret Book*, translated by Salvator Attanasio, Grove Press Inc., New York, 1961

Hitler, Adolf, Speech 1933, *The Rise and Fall of the Third Reich*, Chapter 8, Education in the Third Reich,1959

Johnsen, Julia E., *Should The Communist Party Be Outlawed?*, The H.W. Wilson Company, New York, 1949

Koenigsberg, Richard A., Hitler's Ideology, Library of Social Science, New York

Marx Karl, *Communist Manifesto*, Regnery Comany, Chicago, 1954

Marx, Karl,*Critique of the Gotha Programme*, 1885, repr. Karl Marx, Selected
    Works, Vol.1, 1942
Miles, Betty, *Save the Earth, An Action Handbook for Kids*, Alfred A. Knopf,
    Inc., New York, 1974, 1991
Milord, Susan, *Hands Around the World*, Williamson Publishing, Charlotte,
    VT. 1992
Milton, Joyce, *Wild, Wild Wolves*, Random House, Inc., New York, 1992
Pearson, Michael, *The Sealed Train*, Putnam, New York, 1975
Porritt, Jonathon, *Save the Earth*, Turner Publishing Inc., Atlanta, GA, 1991
Porritt, Jonathon, *Captain Eco and the Fate of the Earth*, Dorling Kindersley,
    New York, London, 1991
Rensenbrink, John, *The Greens and the Politics of Transformation*, R.& E.
    Miles, CA, 1992
Rifkin, Jeremy, *Entropy*, Bantam Books, New York, 1980
Rifkin, Jeremy, *Entropy*, Revised Edition, Bantam Books, New York, 1989
Rifkin, Jeremy, Carol Grunewald Rifkin, *Voting Green*, Doubleday, 1992
Rifkin, Jeremy, *Biosphere Politics*, Harper, San Francisco, 1991
Rockefeller, John D., *The Second American Revolution*, Harper and Row,
    New York, 1973
Stormer, John A., *None Dare Call It Treason*, The Liberty Bell Press,
    Florissant, MO., 1964
Turner, Henry Ashby, Hitler, *Memoirs of a Confidant*, Yale University
    Press, New Haven, 1985
Tyson, James L., *Target America*, Regnery Gateway, Chicago, IL 1981
Waite, Robert G.L.,*Psychopathic God*, Basic Books, Inc. New York, 1977
Williams, Albert Rhys, *Journey Into Revolution*, Quadrangle Books,
    Chicago, 1969

Articles, Newspapers, Magazines and Newsletters

Brodine, Virginia Warner, 'The Environment: A Natural Terrain for
    Communists', Political Affairs, January, 1989
Cohn, Bob and Turque, Bill, 'Clinton rescues the Mexican economy', Time
    magazine, February 13, 1995.
Corliss, Richard, 'Princess of the Spirit', Time magazine, June 9,1995
Crawford, Peter, *Common Future*, Premier Issue, No. 1, Prout Research
    Institute, 1995
Doder, Dusko, *Experiment That Failed, The Bolshevik Revolution*, National
    Geographic, Vol. 182, No. 4, October, 1992

Democratic Socialists Brochures, Democratic Socialists of America, New York

Earth First Journal, *Eco-Depth Guage*, March, 1991

Earth First, slogan, The Macmillan Dictionary of Political Quotations, Lewis Eigen and Jonathan Siegel, Macmillan Publishing Company, New York, 1993

Ecologist, Vol. 21, No.6, Nov.- Dec. 1991

Ecology, Anarchism and Green Politics, Youth Greens, Minneapolis, MN, Left Green Network, Burlington, VT. September, 1990

EcoSocialist Review, Chicago, Democratic Socialists of America, Summer 1990, Summer 1991, Spring 1994

Earth Times, Vol. VII, Number 4, June, 1994, Earth Times

Elliott, Michael,'*Why the Mexican Crisis Matters*', Time magazine, February 13, 1995.

EnviroScan, September, 1994, Biodiversity, Rik Scarce, Eco-Warriors

Evans, Harold, The Sunday Times, 1971, Political Quotations, Daniel Baker, Editor, Gale Research Inc., Detroit, London, 1990

Grassroots,'*Green Cross International*' and '*A Clear and Simple Message*',Volume 2, Issue 1, Grassroots Publishing, Ltd., Blaine, WA, 1995

Greens - *Green Party U.S.A. Program*, Prompt Press, Green Committees of Correspondence, Kansas City, MO. Camden, NJ, 1992

Hall, Gus,'*The World We Preserve Must Be Livable*', World Marxist Review, May, 1988

Hall, Gus, '*A Mass Party In The Making*', Political Affairs, June 25, 1994

Hall, Gus, '*The Caricature of Communism*', Political Affairs, January, 1989

Hershey, A. & H., *Communists Rules for Revolution*, Maxine Salade

Herzen, Alexander, Russian Journalist

In CONTEXT, '*Redefining Entertainment*', No. 24, Fall 1989

McAlvany Intelligence Advisor, Don McAlvany, March, 1995, May, June 1995, Phoenix, AZ

Marquart, Kathleen, Putting People First, From the Trenches, February, 1994, September 29, 1994, November 7, 1994

Medford Mail Tribune, *Gaylord Nelson, Earth Day speech*, March 10, 1995

Montaigne, Fen, *From Red to Green*, Audubon magazine, Nov.Dec. 1994

Parade Magazine, *Best News for Friends of the Spotted Owl*, January 1,1995

Progressive, The Progressive Inc., Madison, WI, February, 1995

Rensenbrink, John, *A Green Strategy for the 90s*, E, The Environmental magazine, September-October, 1990

San Francisco Examiner, Richard Powelson, *Religious leaders see green, Agree to take up environmentalism*, June 16, 1991

San Joaquin County Citizens Land Alliance, Tracy, CA. Feb., June 1995

Sierra, the magazine of the Sierra Club, Sierra Club Bulletin, September,
    October 1995
Thatcher, Margaret, IMPRIMIS, March, 1995, Volume 24, No.3
Fedarko, Kevin, *From Russia With Venom*, Time magazine, July 11, 1994
Trilogy, Trilogy Publishing Inc., Winter 1991, Number 34, Lexington, KY
Utne Reader, *Voting Green*, Carol Gruenwald Rifkin, Sept. Oct. 1992,
    LENS Publishing Co. Inc., Minneapolis, MN
World Conservation Strategy, IUCN, International Union for Conservation
    of Nature and Natural Resources, UNEP, United Nations
    Environmental Programmme, WWF, World Wildlife Fund, in
    collaboration with FAO, Food and Agriculture Organizations of the
    United Nations and UNESCO, United Nations Educational Scientific
    and Cultural Organizations, Steps in a Strategy, 1980

Audio, Video Recordings

Elicker, Roy, Counsel, National Wildlife Federation, Pacific Northwest
    Resources Center, *'Public Lands Grazing'* Panel, Land, Air, Water
    Conference (LAW), University of Oregon, 1991
Liverman, Marc, Audubon Society Conservation Director, *Innovations in
    Endangered Species Protection Panel*, Land, Air, Water Conference
    (LAW), University of Oregon, 1991
Stahl, Andy, Sierra Club Legal Defense Club, Research Analyst, 'Allbrook
    Panel: *Old Growth's Last Stand'*, Western Public Interest Law
    Conference, University of Oregon, 1988

Index

About the Author

Author, Holly Swanson founded and directs the Citizens
Information Network, an organization dedicated to citizen
awareness and political action. Swanson is a former public
relations professional turned citizen activist. Initial
investigation into the environmental movement triggered
concerns about the undisclosed political agenda of the
Greens. Set Up & Sold Out is the result of six years of
extensive research into both sides of the environmental
debate. Swanson believes Americans have a right to full
disclosure.

Disclaimer

This book is designed to provide information regarding the subject matter presented. It is sold with the understanding that the publisher and author are not the sole authority on the information covered. You are urged to read all the available material, learn as much as possible about the Green Party, Green environmental movement, Communist Party USA and Communism to reach your own conclusions about the topics covered. For additional information, see references. Every effort has been made to make this book as complete and accurate as possible. However, there may be mistakes both typographical and in content. Therefore, this text should be used only as a general source of information on the subjects presented. The purpose of this book is to stimulate political disussion about the subjects presented. The author and CIN shall have neither liability nor responsibility to any person or entity with respect to any loss or damage caused, directly or indirectly by the information contained in this book.

Order Form

Please send me ___ copies of, **Set Up and Sold Out** at $14.95 each plus shipping.

Name:_____

Address:_____

City:_____State_____Zip:_____

Telephone: Area code (   )_____

Telephone orders: 503-830-1445
Fax orders: 503-830-1448

Payment: ☐ **Visa**   ☐ **Mastercard**   ☐ **Check**

Credit Card number_____

Name on Card_____

Expiration Date_____

Postal orders: CIN, P.O. Box 2645, White City, OR 97503

Shipping: Check one:

☐ Regular Mail   ☐ UPS Ground
☐ Priority Mail   ☐ Federal Express

Make checks payable to: CIN

Thank You.